SECRETS OF ANCIENT EGYPT

SECRETS OF ANCIENT EGYPT

from the editors of

ARCHAEOLOGY
M A G A Z I N E

HATHERLEIGH PRESS
New York

Secrets of Ancient Egypt
A Hatherleigh Press Book

The articles in this compilation were previously published in ARCHAEOLOGY magazine with the following exceptions: "Weird Animals" (pp. 47–48), "How Big is the Elephant" (pp. 51–52), "Holy Abydos" (pp. 53–56), "Selling the Past" (pp. 184–186), "Last Shot for Schultz" (p. 186), and "Shaking up the Land of the Pharaohs" (pp. 187–190) were published on Archaeology Online (www.archaeology.org); "Enduring Achievements" (pp. 1–4), "KV5, A long-neglected tomb" (p. 125), "The Valley of the Golden Mummies" (p. 126), and "Rediscovering Alexandria" (pp. 143–145) are ©Mark Rose, 2003.

Hatherleigh Press
5-22 46th Avenue
Long Island City, NY 11101
1-800-528-2550

www.hatherleighpress.com

Secrets of Ancient Egypt / from the editors of Archaeology magazine.
        p. cm.
Includes bibliographical references and index.
  ISBN 1-57826-159-7 (hardcover : alk. paper)
  1. Egypt--Antiquities. I. Archaeology.
  DT60.S42 2003
  932--dc22

                            2003026660

ISBN 1-57826-159-7

All Hatherleigh Press titles are available for special promotions and premiums. For more information, please contact the manager of our Special Sales department.

Project Credits

ARCHAEOLOGY Staff
Publisher: Phyllis Pollak Katz
Editor-In-Chief: Peter A. Young
Executive Editor: Mark Rose

Hatherleigh Press Staff
President & CEO: Andrew Flach
Publisher: Kevin Moran
Editorial Director: Lori Baird
Art Director & Production Manager: Tai Blanche
Manager, PR: Meredith Cosgrove
Associate Editor: Myrsini Stephanides
Cover Design: Tai Blanche
Interior Design: Corin Hirsch & Regina Starace
Indexer: Jessica Stasinos, Pegasus Indexing

10 9 8 7 6 5 4 3 2 1
Printed in Canada on acid-free paper

ABOUT THE ARCHAEOLOGICAL INSTITUTE OF AMERICA

The Archaeological Institute of America (AIA), publisher of Archaeology Magazine, is North America's oldest and largest organization devoted to the world of archaeology. The Institute is a nonprofit group founded in 1879 and chartered by the United States Congress in 1906. Today, the AIA has nearly 10,000 members belonging to more than 100 local societies in the United States, Canada, and overseas. The organization is unique because it counts among its members professional archaeologists, students, and many others from all walks of life. This diverse group is united by a shared passion for archaeology and its role in furthering human knowledge.

Contents

Part II:
EGYPTIAN ORIGINS

Part III:
MARVELS OF GIZA

Part IV:
FARTHER AFIELD—OTHER SITES & FINDS

Part V:
REDISCOVERING EGYPT

ACKNOWLEDGMENTS

The editors of ARCHAEOLOGY have benefited over the years from the willingness of many outstanding scholars to make their discoveries known in our pages and on our web site. Through our authors' generosity, our readers have learned of discoveries at many important sites in Egypt, including the Giza Plateau (Zahi Hawass and Mark Lehner, W.B. Hafford), Hierakonpolis (Renée Friedman and colleagues), Abydos (David O'Connor, William Kelly Simpson, Stephen Harvey, Josef Wegner, and colleagues), the Valley of the Kings (Donald Ryan), Nubian pyramids (Bob Brier), Alexander's elusive tomb (Robert Bianchi), and Sikait, the Emerald City (Steven Sidebotham and colleagues); mummies (Bob Brier, Frank Holt, and Joyce Filer); survival of ancient traditions (Shelley Wachsman); and the landmark Schultz antiquities case (Alexi Baker and Marisa Macari). We have also benefited over the years from valuable advice offered by Aidan Dodson and Salima Ikram. We hereby acknowledge our debt to all of our authors and advisors on ancient Egypt, and thank especially for their help and friendship over the years Zahi Hawass, director general of the Supreme Council for Antiquities, and Bob Brier of C.W. Post Campus of Long Island University.

ENDURING
ACHIEVEMENTS
ENDURING FASCINATION

by MARK ROSE

Who has not heard of the pyramids of Egypt? Whose mind has not swelled at reading the descriptions or hearing the recital of these prodigies of human power? Their indestructible mass, the admiration of ages, and despair of time....

Charles Sonnini, 1799

Centuries have past since Charles Sonnini spent three years exploring Egypt at the behest of Louis XVI of France, but from the Sphinx and Great Pyramids of Giza to the royal tombs in the Valley of the Kings, this ancient civilization continues to fascinate us. In creating *Secrets of Ancient Egypt,* we have brought together informative, and entertaining, articles on Egypt from ARCHAEOLOGY and ARCHAEOLOGY Online. Some detail recent discoveries, present new interpretations, and explore what really are unsolved mysteries about the people who lived along the Nile so long ago. Others address such issues as how to protect the precious remains of this ancient culture in the face of increasing development and growing tourism, and how to combat looting and the illicit antiquities trade.

Mummies and ancient Egypt are virtually synonymous. In this volume, you'll find the earliest Egyptian mummies, buried more than 5,500 years old, and the most recent one, a modern mummy made to investigate ancient methods. And you'll meet three long-neglected mummies, one now being properly cared for in a museum, one relegated to a curiosity shop, and one—newly returned to Egypt—that may well be the mortal remains of Ramesses I.

Join us, too, as we investigate the origins of this remarkable civilization at Hierakonpolis, the hometown of the earliest pharaohs, and Abydos, the most sacred site in ancient Egypt. At Giza, in addition to the Pyramids and Sphinx, you'll read about the discovery of the tombs belonging to the workers who built those great monuments, a descent into the deep shaft-like Osiris tomb, and a young Egyptologist's recent, strange encounter with pioneer American archaeologist George Reisner and the Nazis while excavating an ancient tomb. In the Valley of the Kings, you'll explore little-known tombs and try to unravel the mystery of who was buried in Tomb 55. Farther afield, we take you to the

EGYPTIAN DYNASTIES AND CHRONOLOGY

The exact dates for particular pharaohs are open to interpretation. In ARCHAEOLOGY, we have followed the preferences of those scholars authoring individual articles, but the outline of dynasties and their dates below (adapted from A. Dodson's *Monarchs of the Nile*) is a convenient overview of the historical framework of ancient Egypt.

ARCHAIC PERIOD

Dynasty 1   3050–2813 B.C.
Unification of Egypt completed under King Narmer

Dynasty 2   2813–2663 B.C.

OLD KINGDOM

Dynasty 3   2662–2597 B.C.
First pyramid builders

Dynasty 4   2597–2471 B.C.
Khufu, Khafre, and Menkaure; construction of Giza pyramids and Sphinx

Dynasty 5   2471–2355 B.C.

Dynasty 6   2355–2195 B.C.

FIRST INTERMEDIATE PERIOD

Dynasties 7/8 2195–2160 B.C.
Collapse of central government

Dynasties 9/10 2160–2040 B.C.
Dynasty 11a   2160–2066 B.C.
Rival dynasties from Herakleopolis (9/10) and Thebes (11)

"Emerald City" in the Eastern Desert and to Nubia's pyramids far to the south.

As you will find here, the story of the scholars who accompanied Napoleon's campaign in Egypt is one of intellectual triumph salvaged from military catastrophe. Earlier travelers had written about their journeys and investigations along the Nile, but the works of Napoleon's savants—the monumental *Description d'Égypte* and Dominique Vivant Denon's *Voyages in Upper and Lower Egypt*—were in a different league altogether. The enthusiasm for things Egyptian that these volumes fueled has never subsided. Certainly in the nineteenth century, as you'll read, it accounts for the raising of obelisks in Paris, London, and New York.

Pioneering Egyptian scholars included individuals such as Rifaa al-Tahtawi, who in 1835 headed an attempt to establish an antiquities department and museum, and Ahmad Kamal (1851–1923), who, in addition to composing official reports in French for the Antiquities Service, wrote and translated works into Arabic for his countrymen and taught Egyptology to Egyptian college classes. Read how their tradition is being maintained today as Zahi Hawass of the Supreme Council for Antiquities revolutionizes archaeology within Egypt and pursues those who traffic in stolen Egyptian artifacts at home and abroad.

MIDDLE KINGDOM

Dynasty 11b   2066–1994 B.C.

Dynasty 12   1994–1781 B.C.
Prosperity and expansion

Dynasty 13   1781–1650 B.C.
Gradual decline

SECOND INTERMEDIATE PERIOD

Dynasty 15   1650–1535 B.C.
Hyksos invaders from Palestine rule northern Egypt

Dynasty 16   1650–1590 B.C.
Egyptian rulers in the south, based in Thebes

Dynasty 17   1585–1549 B.C.
Theban dynasty kings push back the Hyksos

NEW KINGDOM

Dynasty 18   1549–1298 B.C.
Dynasty of Ahmose, including Tuthmose III, Hatshepsut, Amenhotep III, Akhenaten, Nefertiti, and Tutankhamun

Dynasty 19   1298–1187 B.C.
Dynasty of Ramesses I, including Seti and Ramesses II

Dynasty 20   1187–1064 B.C.
Later Ramesside pharaohs

THIRD INTERMEDIATE PERIOD

Dynasty 21   1064–940 B.C.
Theban rulers

Dynasty 22   948–743 B.C.
Dynasty 23   867–724 B.C.
Overlapping northern, Libyan (22) and Theban (23) dynasties

Dynasty 23   743–715 B.C.

Dynasty 24   731–717 B.C.

Dynasty 25   752–656 B.C.
Nubian dynasty

The explorer and naturalist Charles Sonnini recorded many Egyptian antiquities during his investigtions in the region on behalf of Louis XVI of France, including obelisk and Pompey's column in Alexandria.

Long before Charles Sonnini described the Pyramids as "the admiration of ages, and despair of time," the works of the ancient Egyptians were already a source of wonder. The Greek historian Herodotus marveled at the monuments along the Nile. Of the Egyptians themselves, he wrote simply that "they have existed ever since men existed upon the earth." This ARCHAEOLOGY collection attests—twenty-five centuries later—both the enduring achievements of the ancient Egyptians and our enduring fascination with them. ▲

MARK ROSE is the *executive editor of* ARCHAEOLOGY *magazine*

SAITE PERIOD

Dynasty 26   664–525 B.C.
Initially under Assyrian domination, Egypt over throws foreign yoke

LATE PERIOD

Dynasty 27   525–405 B.C.
Persian conquest of Egypt

Dynasty 28   404–399 B.C.
Dynasties 28–30 oppose Persians

Dynasty 29   399–380 B.C.

Dynasty 30   380–342 B.C.

Dynasty 31   342–332 B.C.
Persian return

HELLENISTIC PERIOD

Dynasty of Macedonia
332–310 B.C.
Alexander the Great to death of Alexander IV

Dynasty of Ptolemy
310–30 B.C.
Independent rule of Egypt ends with death of Cleopatra VII in 30 B.C., Roman rule begins.

PART I:

MUMMIES

A THOROUGHLY MODERN MUMMY

Experimental archaeology—step by gruesome step, the Egyptian way

by BOB BRIER

For 3,000 years the ancient Egyptians mummified their dead, but no embalmer ever wrote down how he did it. Egypt was a nation of accountants who recorded almost everything—battles, offerings to temples, long lines of kings—but not a single papyrus exists telling how a human cadaver was prepared for the journey to the afterlife. For centuries mummification remained a closely guarded secret, that is, until Herodotus, the Greek historian and traveler, visited Egypt around 450 B.C. Herodotus described mummification in great detail:

As much of the brain as possible is extracted through the nostrils with an iron hook, and what the hook cannot reach is dissolved with drugs. Next the flank is slit open with a sharp Ethiopian stone and the entire contents of the abdomen removed. The cavity is then thoroughly cleansed and washed out, first with palm wine and again with a solution of pounded spices. Then it is filled with pure crushed myrrh, cassia, and all other aromatic substances, except frankincense.

The incision is sewn up and then the body is placed in natron, covered for 70 days, never longer. When this period, which may not be longer, is over, the body is washed and then wrapped from head to feet in linen which has been cut into strips and smeared on the underside with gum, which is commonly used by the Egyptians as glue. In this condition the body is returned to the family....

Modern research has confirmed much of Herodotus' account. X-ray images have shown that, for top-of-the-line mummifications, the brain was indeed removed via the nasal passages. It is also well established that the internal organs were removed. Chemical analyses of materials found within the bodies have shown that myrrh and other spices were used in the cleansing process.

Based on Herodotus' account and Egyptologists' research, the basics of mummification had been pieced together by the 1920s and scholars felt that little more was to be learned. In 1992, while writing a book on mummification, I began to realize just how wrong they were. There was a lot that we didn't know. Did the embalmers drain the blood? How do you remove a brain through the nose? What kind of tools did the embalmers use? How was natron used? What surgical procedures were performed? I realized that the only way to answer such questions was to actually mummify a human cadaver.

It would take nearly a year just to assemble the materials we needed. The ancient Egyptians used both bronze and copper knives. Michael Silva, a New York silversmith with a passion for archaeology, would

manufacture ours, using a ratio of 88 percent copper and 12 percent tin, the same as found in ancient examples. He would also fashion a long coat hanger-like instrument that we could use to remove the brain through the nose. Herodotus said the embalmers used "a sharp Ethiopian stone" for the body incision. This meant obsidian, volcanic glass. My sister-in-law introduced me to archaeology graduate student James Eighmey at Arizona State University who could flake obsidian (a very difficult task), and he provided an assortment of blades, both fancy and crude.

The natron was the most difficult material to obtain. Natron is a mixture of sodium carbonate, sodium bicarbonate, sodium chloride, and some minor impurities—basically baking soda and table salt. The ancient Egyptians obtained their natron in an area they called "the salt fields" about 60 miles north of modern Cairo. Today it is called Wadi Natrun. It is an amazing place. Several small lakes, colored red by algae and brine shrimp, are rimmed by thick, white natron crusts. Natron, present in the soil, goes into solution when the water table rises each year. When the water table falls, the natron is deposited on the shores. Armed with a shovel and empty cement sacks, I went to gather my natron. I collected 400 pounds, breaking it up into small chunks which I would pulverize later. This was enough, I estimated, to comfortably cover one cadaver. I also picked up frankincense and myrrh at Cairo's spice market, imported, as in ancient times, from the Sudan, Yemen, and Somalia. Without doubt, one of the strangest ingredients we needed was palm wine, which according to Herodotus was used to wash out the abdominal cavity. Only one wine store in Cairo could get it for us, importing it from Nigeria. The label had a pyramid on it, which we took as a good omen, but the label also said "Shake well for full nutritional value."

Back in the United States, other preparations had to be made. Several caches of embalmers' equipment—including linens, wooden ankh symbols, an embalmer's board, and jars used to store natron—have been found by Egyptologists. Herbert Winlock, a curator in the Metropolitan Museum of Art's Egyptian department in the 1920s, had discovered the most complete embalmer's cache on the west bank of Luxor. Using the Met's records of the find, we set to work to copy the natron storage jars. Soon Evan Rosenthal, a graduate student and master potter at the C.W. Post Campus of Long Island University, was making replicas of the ancient jars at the rate of two a day. He was so good at it that I asked him to make the four canopic jars in which the mummy's internal organs would be stored.

As resurrectionists, Egyptians believed the body would literally get up and go into the next world, but to keep the mummy from decaying, they had to remove the internal organs. Because the body had to be complete in the afterlife, the internal organs were saved in four canopic jars. The word "canopic" derives from early Egyptologists, who linked the human-headed jars to Canopus, a Greek ship captain, according to Homer, deified after his death and worshiped in the form of a jar. Prior to the New Kingdom (before 1570 B.C.), jars had lids in the shape of human heads, representing the Four Sons of Horus (the falcon god), who watched over the internal organs. Later, three of the four human heads were replaced with animal heads: those of a jackal, an ape, and a falcon.

The ancient Egyptians were often buried with small magical statues called *ushabtiu*, ancient Egyptian for "answerers." If you were called upon in the next world to do work, the statues would answer for you and do the required task. They were often painted with magical spells to ensure that they would indeed do the job. A wealthy Egyptian could be buried with 365 *ushabtiu*, one for each day of the year. For a few weeks, C.W. Post looked like an ancient Egyptian funeral workshop, with the ceramic department cranking them out and my hieroglyph class painting them with spells.

Finally, we had all the materials except a proper embalmer's table. With the help of Tom Wood, a retired physics professor from the University of Pennsylvania and master carpenter, we made a replica of the board Winlock had found at Luxor in the 1920s. Using only hand tools, we pegged it together, but questions about the board that earlier Egyptologists had raised quickly

> AS RESURRECTIONISTS, EGYPTIANS BELIEVED THE BODY WOULD LITERALLY GET UP AND GO INTO THE NEXT WORLD.

resurfaced. At nearly six feet wide, it seemed far broader than necessary. Wood was scarce in Egypt, so there must have been a reason for the extravagant size. And what was the purpose of what looked like four railroad ties spaced across the width of the board? These questions would answer themselves once we began.

For the cadaver we used a body donor, someone who had left his body to science. We screened possible donors for health hazards, and eventually selected an elderly man who had died of a stroke.

I now had everything I needed, as well as a tremendous support team, of which the most important member was Ronn Wade, director of Maryland's State Anatomy Board and co-director of the project. His long interest in mummification began as a kid when he mummified a rat for a science project. Ronn is not only an anatomist, he is also a licensed mortician. His knowledge of anatomy and surgical skills would prove essential when the going got tough.

We would perform our mummification at the University of Maryland's School of Medicine in Baltimore. Would it work? We certainly had our doubts. The ancient embalmers were professionals at mummification with millennia of experience, while we were trying it for the first time. As Ronn and I discussed the impending surgical procedures, we agreed that the removal of the brain would be the most difficult. We were right.

Egyptology journals occasionally contain articles theorizing how the brain was removed through the nose. They describe a cadaver lying on its back while a long hooked tool is inserted into the nose and pushed through the cribiform plate (a thin,

honeycombed bone behind the eyes) and into the cranium. A small piece of the brain adheres to the end of the tool and can be pulled out. The process is repeated until the entire brain is removed. That was the theory, but no modern researcher had ever actually done it. One week before we were to begin, Ronn and I tested this process on two heads obtained from body-donors, but could not get the brains out—they weren't viscous enough to stick to the tool. We finally hypothesized that if we used the tool much like a kitchen whisk inside the cranium, the brain would liquefy and then, if we inverted the cadaver, would run out through the nose. We would try this method on the donated body waiting to be mummified. We inserted a long bronze instrument, shaped like a miniature harpoon, inside the nasal passage and hammered it through the cribiform plate into the cranium with a wooden block. Then we inserted the coat hanger-shaped instrument into the cranium and rotated it for ten minutes on each side, breaking down the brain enough so it would run out when the cadaver was inverted. It worked. Using the coat-hanger tool, we then forced thin strips of linen into the cranium via the nasal passages and used them as swabs. With repeated swabbing they eventually came out clean. It was now time for the removal of the internal organs.

The first step was the abdominal incision. Herodotus wrote that a "sharp Ethiopian stone" was used. I had always thought that this must have been for ritualistic purposes (perhaps harkening back to Archaic times when only stone knives were available). The Egyptians had bronze knives, which I thought would have been more effective surgical instruments, but, we quickly discovered that bronze knives were too dull for such a use. So when the time came for the abdominal incision, I made it with an obsidian flake.

Egyptian incisions were almost always on the left side of a mummy's abdomen, and, in preparation for this project, I had taken careful notice of the length of these incisions on existing mummies. They were surprisingly small, only about three and one-half inches long. Embalmers wanted to minimize damage so that when the body was resurrected it would look natural. That is also why the brain was removed via the nasal passages rather than opening the cranium itself.

Working through such a small abdominal incision created two problems. Only one hand fits inside, which makes internal cutting difficult. It is also impossible to see what you are doing, which raises a question about the anatomical knowledge of ancient Egyptian embalmers. It is often asserted that because they practiced mummification, the Egyptians were the most knowledgeable about anatomy in the ancient world. Not so. Working through such a small incision, embalmers weren't able to see the organs as they dissected them. Until the Greek occupation of Egypt (beginning in 332 B.C. with Alexander the Great) and the establishment of a medical school in Alexandria (during the Ptolemaic period, 332–30 B.C.), dissection of cadavers for the purpose of study was prohibited in Egypt. Indeed, even when a mummification

took place, the man who made the abdominal incision—"the slitter"—was ritually pelted with stones "for he had defiled a human body." Additionally, there is linguistic evidence that the Egyptians did not know their anatomy. For instance, there is no word for "kidney" in the ancient Egyptian language and it is possible many embalmers were unaware that human kidneys existed or simply did not know their function. Hidden behind the peritoneum, a membrane in the abdominal cavity, and not easily reached through a small abdominal incision, the kidneys were often left inside mummies.

The hieroglyphs that normally come at the end of words to clarify their meanings (determinatives) suggest that much of Egyptian anatomical knowledge was based on animals, not on humans. Often the hieroglyphs in the words for both internal and external organs, the heart for example, depict non-human organs. So, when we began to remove the internal organs in our mummy, I had the feeling that although ancient embalmers were far more experienced at what they did than were we, Ronn and I certainly knew more about anatomy.

As we proceeded, a natural order for removing the organs emerged. The small intestine came out first and along with it the pancreas, followed by the spleen. Then we removed the kidneys. As we removed the bladder and stomach, I began thinking about the liver, which can weigh several pounds and requires two hands to hold. Could we

THE HEART WAS THE ONLY ORGAN INTENTIONALLY LEFT IN PLACE BY THE EGYPTIANS.

Bob Brier treats the extracted organs with natron to preserve them. After desiccation, the organs are placed in four canopic jars.

Pat Remler

remove it intact through such a small abdominal incision? We tried manipulating it from the outside, moving it to the opening, then trying to squeeze it through. The liver is composed of lobes and our idea was to push it out one lobe at a time. It didn't work. In the end, we lengthened the incision another half inch, and it popped out, much like a newborn. The lungs were next.

We cut through the diaphragm, which separates the abdominal and thoracic cavities. Just as in an ancient mummification, we removed the lungs but left the heart. The heart was the only organ intentionally left in place by the Egyptians. They believed that you thought with your heart and therefore would need it so you could recite magical spells when you were resurrected in the next world. Indeed, there is little evidence that Egyptians understood the function of the brain, which explains why it was the only organ they did not preserve at the time of mummification.

With the removal of the lungs, our surgical procedures were complete. We had established which tools were most likely used by the ancient embalmers, how the brain was removed, and the probable order in which the organs were taken out, but we were still far from finished. The body now had to be dehydrated in natron; just how it was done in antiquity has been the subject of considerable debate.

At the end of the 1932 Boris Karloff

Working-Class Stiffs

The earliest evidence for mummification in Egypt has been found in a cemetery of working-class inhabitants at Hierakonpolis, the largest site of the Pre- and Protodynastic period (3800–3100 B.C.), 390 miles south of Cairo. One plundered and two intact burials, all of women and dating between 3600 and 3500 B.C., show clear evidence that the forearms, hands, and base of the head were padded with linen bundles and then wrapped in resin-soaked linen bandages. Although the bodies weren't fully wrapped like later mummies, they are 500 years earlier than the next known example of mummification, a wrapped arm from the tomb of the 1st Dynasty king Den (ca. 2980 B.C.) found wearing four bracelets (and now in the Cairo Museum).

Why the head and hands were padded and wrapped is not certain. Perhaps the intent was to keep the body intact, especially the hands and mouth which would be needed for eating food in the afterlife. Renée Friedman, Heagy Research Curator at the British Museum and director of the Hierakonpolis Expedition, who directs the working-class cemetery excavations, notes that the jaw and hand bones tend to separate from the rest of the skeleton as a body decomposes or if a grave is disturbed. "This is not any kind of ad-hoc treatment," she says. "This is very carefully thought out, and you have the finest linen against the body, which gets progressively coarser as it goes out."

Examination of one woman's remains revealed that her throat had been slit. The position of the cut marks on the first and second neck vertebrae suggests the head had been tilted back at an unnatural angle, indicating that the cutting took place after death and a certain amount of desiccation. In all, seven bodies, both men and women, have lacerations to the throat, resulting in decapitation in two cases. There may be a link between this and the myth of the god Osiris, who was killed and dismembered by his brother Set, but was later reassembled and mummified in order to be resurrected as Lord of the Underworld. The earliest of Egypt's funerary texts, the Pyramid Texts, includes an obscure passage that reads, "put your head back on your body, gather up your bones," which may refer to this ritual act. "Perhaps they're laying the bodies out to dry," says Friedman, "then ritually decapitating, re-assembling, and wrapping them up."

Of an estimated 2,000 burials in the cemetery, 170 have been investigated. Other finds include the oldest preserved beard (well trimmed); a unique sheepskin toupee used to cover a man's bald spot; and, in a woman's burial (3500 B.C.), the oldest proven use of the plant henna to dye gray hair a dark reddish brown and the earliest evidence of hair weaving, in which locks of human hair were knotted onto the natural hair to produce an elaborate beehive-like hairstyle.

For more on the excavations at the site, see www.hierakonpolis.org and www.archaeology.org/interactive/hierakonpolis/index/html.

—MARK ROSE

movie, *The Mummy*, when the villain is preparing to mummify the heroine, an embalmer is shown stirring a large vat of natron. This scene was based upon the best available archaeological information of the time. Egyptologists Warren Dawson and Alfred Lucas of England had just published separate papers suggesting that the ancient Egyptian embalmers soaked their cadavers in solutions of natron and then dehydrated them. The theory that a solution of natron was used originates in a mistranslation of Herodotus. When describing how the natron was used, he employed a Greek verb that means to preserve like fish. Fish of course can be either salted or pickled in brine. One of the earliest works on mummies, Englishman Thomas Pettigrew's 1834 *History of Egyptian Mummies*, relied on a translation that used the word "steep," and later scholars assumed the Egyptians soaked their mummies in a natron solution.

There are several compelling arguments against natron having been used in solution. First, it may have seemed counterintuitive to the ancient embalmers to soak the bodies in a liquid when the ultimate goal was to dehydrate them. Second, the Egyptians mummified millions of bodies over the centuries, so there would have been thousands of huge vats if this method was used, but none has ever been found. Third, Herodotus notes that the body cavity was packed with crushed spices and then placed in the natron. If it were in a solution, the spices would have washed out. All this suggests that the Egyptians used their natron dry.

From studying ancient mummies, we knew that the embalmers often placed small packets of natron inside the mummy to absorb internal body fluids. These packets were formed by cutting a square of linen, placing the natron in the center, and then gathering and tying the four corners together. One of the hieroglyphs in the combination that forms the word "natron," may even depict an embalmer's packet. The first four hieroglyphs are purely phonetic and indicate how the word was pronounced, something like hesmen. The last sign (actually two combined), the determinative, helps clarify the meaning of the word. On top is a banner or flag, the sign for "god" which suggests the religious use of natron. At bottom is

a small pouch, a natron packet. We filled the abdominal and thoracic cavities with 29 packets. Then we were ready to put the body on the embalmer's board and cover it with natron to dehydrate it from the outside.

When we placed the body on the embalmer's board, we discovered the function of the planks running across it. When the heart stops beating, the only factor affecting the location of body fluids is gravity, so the fluids come to rest at the lower portions of the body. Since the natron is the primary desiccant, one wants it as close to the body fluids as possible, and this is the function of the planks—they held a considerable amount of natron in place beneath the body, near most of the fluids. Without the planks, the natron would slide out from under the body. We covered the board with natron to the height of the planks, set the body on top it, and then poured more natron over the cadaver until it was completely covered. Here we discovered why the board was so wide: to reach a height sufficient to cover the body a rather wide base was needed. We also determined that more than 400 pounds of natron, which we had, were required.

The internal organs were placed in pottery dishes, covered with natron, and put at the corners of the board to dehydrate along with the body. The conditions in our mummification room were controlled to roughly approximate a tomb in the Valley of the Kings, with the humidity just below 30 percent and the temperature around 105 degrees Fahrenheit. The big question was how long to leave the body in this environment before removing it for wrapping.

No one knew for certain how long the

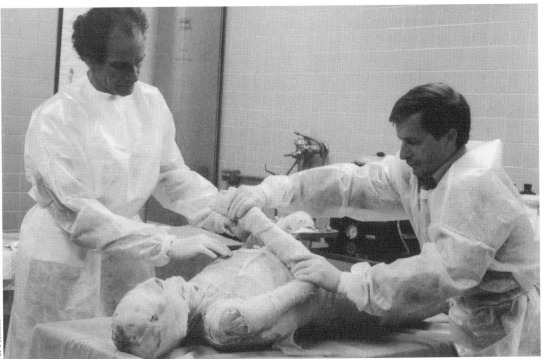

Pat Remler

Egyptologist Bob Brier and anatomist Ronn Wade wrap the mummy in white linen.

body remained in natron. Ancient texts mention different periods. Herodotus wrote "They conceal the body for 70 days, embalmed in natron; no longer time is permitted for embalming." Diodorus, a later writer, says "they carefully prepare the entire body for more than 30 days…." Other references indicate that Diodorus is closer to the mark than Herodotus. The Bible says that Joseph's father, Jacob, died in Egypt and notes that 70 days was the period of mourning, and that 40 of those days were for embalming. Some of those 40 days would have been taken up with preparations, so the body would have been in natron for something less that 40 days. The Rhind papyrus, one of the few ancient Egyptian texts that

discusses mummification, indicates that the body was "at rest for 30 days in the Place of Cleansing." In an ancient Egyptian short story, a man named Neneferkaptah is mummified; we are told there were 35 days for wrapping and he was in his coffin on day 70. All of these clues suggested to us that 70 days was the period for the entire process, from death to burial, and that the body remained in natron for approximately 35 of those days, the amount of time we left our cadaver in natron.

Ronn and I wondered why a mummy looks like it does, shriveled and dark colored. Was it the result of thousands of years in a tomb or buried in the sand, or was it because of the mummification process itself?

We would soon be the first people in 2,000 years to see what one looked like right after it was removed from natron.

When we entered the room after 35 days of waiting, there was a strong odor, but not of putrefaction. The smell was probably from the cedar, palm, and lotus oils used in the mummification. Around the body the natron had formed hard clumps stained dark brown from the body fluids they had absorbed. In some places the natron had congealed so firmly that a metal bar had to be used to break it up so it could be shoveled away. The natron beneath the body had not clumped, but was moist—the consistency of wet sand.

As the natron was removed and the hands, feet, and head emerged, we were struck by how similar they were to those of an ancient mummy—dark brown, with the hands and feet rigid, fingers and toes incapable of being flexed. The head still retained the hair and though desiccated, the facial features were essentially unchanged. The process was responsible for all this, not the millennia in a tomb; mummies are brown probably because as the tissue and blood dehydrates, various elements, like iron, become more concentrated.

We then removed the natron packets with which we had filled the abdominal and thoracic cavities. They had nearly doubled in weight with the absorption of fluids. When the mummification began, the body weighed approximately 180 pounds, now it weighed about 77 pounds. There was still a bit of moisture in the larger muscles—the quadriceps of the thighs and the gluteus maximus of the backside; these areas were still soft to the touch. There was no doubt that if we replaced the wet natron beneath the planks with dry natron and replaced the mummy in the "tomb" (the climate-controlled mummification room) it would dehydrate quickly. We also had the option of wrapping the mummy and placing it in the tomb without natron. We chose this second option because we would learn more. The official 70 days of mummification were over, but undoubtedly there were times when ancient embalmers wrapped bodies while they were still a bit moist; we would see what happened in these cases.

We did a preliminary wrapping and placed the mummy in its tomb on the blocks of the embalmer's board, but with no natron, where it remained for more than four months. When we entered the tomb for the second time, once again there was no smell of putrefaction. The moisture remaining in the body had not caused it to decay. The body had lost an additional 28 pounds, and now almost all the moisture was gone. We took tissue samples from the organs we had removed and also from different parts of the body so we could later determine the efficacy of our dehydration method. It was now time for the final wrapping, and our big surprise.

Using pure white linen we wrapped the individual fingers and toes and then the

> OUR INABILITY TO CROSS THE ARMS MAY HAVE BEEN OUR MOST IMPORTANT FINDING.

limbs and torso. We intended to cross the arms over the chest, in a manner similar to mummies of the pharaohs of the New Kingdom, but were shocked to find it was impossible. The fully dehydrated body was too inflexible, the arms could not be bent without breaking them. Rather than damage the mummy, we placed the arms at the sides with the hands over the pubis and completed the wrapping. Our inability to cross the arms may have been our most important finding. We had assumed that the goal of placing the body in natron was total dehydration. This, we now see, is probably wrong. When the body is totally dehydrated it can't be positioned for wrapping. The goal of the embalmers was to remove as much fluid as necessary to prevent decay, but to leave just enough so the arms and other parts could be placed as desired. After 35 days in the natron, we could have positioned the arms.

It has been five years since we began our experiment, and up to the present our mummy has been kept at room temperature at the State Anatomy Board in Maryland. Periodically we check the body for signs of decay and so far have detected none.

Our mummy may help to answer a question that has been puzzling researchers, namely, why has it been so difficult to reproduce long sequences of DNA from ancient Egyptian mummies? Has the DNA degraded over the thousands of years? Or is its absence the result of the mummification process itself? Tissue samples are frequently requested by colleagues for their studies on various aspects of tissue preservation; currently, laboratories around the world are attempting to reproduce the DNA from our mummy. If they are successful, we will know it is the thousands of years and not the process that makes DNA replication so difficult. DNA studies in mummies may also hold the answers to many Egyptological questions—we may be able to establish the origins of the Egyptians, and we may also be able to identify unknown royal mummies by comparing their DNA to that of mummies who are positively identified.

Since the mummy project, both Ronn and I have tried to resume normal lives. Ronn still directs Maryland's State Anatomy Board. I am back to teaching Egyptology at the C. W. Post Campus of Long Island University, and am currently conducting research on the mummies of the frozen Inka sacrifices, three children, recently found on Mount Llullaillaco in Argentina. A major part of our task regarding the mummy Ronn and I made now lies in bringing information about our work to the attention of the public. When we give lectures, one of the most frequently asked questions is: "Did the body donor know he would be mummified?" No, he didn't. Body donors don't know to which scientific project their bodies are going. So our mummy will be very surprised when he wakes up in the next world. ▲

Under Wraps: Rosalie David In Conversation

For nearly three decades, Rosalie David has directed the mummy research project at the Manchester Museum at Britain's Manchester University, home of one of Europe's finest Egyptian antiquities collections and one of the oldest research institutions in Egyptology. ARCHAEOLOGY spoke to David about her work with the Manchester Mummy Research Project and her latest book *Conversations With Mummies*, published in 2000 by William Morrow.

Manchester has one of the oldest programs in Egyptology. Could you tell us something about the program you inherited and your role in shaping it over the past 30 years?

RD: *The Manchester Egyptian collection was started in the 1890s with objects from the excavations of William M. Flinders Petrie. When I came to Manchester in 1972, the museum had not had an Egyptologist on the staff for about 25 years. One of the first things I did was to establish the Manchester Egyptian Mummy Project in order to investigate the 24 human and 34 animal mummies in the collection using scientific techniques. We have developed this over the past 30 years, pioneering the radiographing of mummies under near ideal conditions in the hospital and the medical school. Before our project, mummies were x-rayed with portable equipment in museum galleries or at archaeological sites. We have also examined the mummies with endoscopes, a virtually non-destructive technique, to investigate and take tissue samples from them. When Margaret Murray brought together a team of medics and scientists to investigate two mummies in the Manchester collection in 1908, it was a real watershed in mummy research. It placed such studies on a scientific and academic basis, instead of the frivolous "unrollings" of mummies performed in front of society audiences in the early nineteenth century.*

Among Manchester's 24 mummies you have some interesting subjects. Tell us about a few of them.

RD: *Yes, we have Asru, who was a Chantress of Amun in the Temple of Amun at Karnak around 900 B.C. She has been extensively examined, and we have found that she suffered from a range of diseases including sand pneumoconiosis, a hydatid cyst in the lung, strongyloides and schistosomiasis (both parasitic diseases), and arthritis. The Two Brothers, who were unwrapped by Margaret Murray, are interesting both in terms of their diseases—parasitic diseases, arthritis, pleurisy, sand pneumoconiosis— and also because anatomically they are so different that, genetically, they could not have been full siblings. They may be half-brothers or one may have been adopted—we plan DNA tests to find out the truth, if possible. Natsef-Amun, Keeper of the Sacred Bulls of Amun, belongs to Leeds City Museum. He was autopsied in 1825, and studied again by us in 1992. When he died, his tongue was so swollen that it could not be pushed back into his mouth, probably the result of an insect bite.*

Speaking of disease, what do you consider the most interesting pathology found in the mummies to date?

RD: *Perhaps the most interesting pathology we have found was in mummy No. 1770, which we autopsied in 1975. We found evidence of Guinea worm infestation—radiography revealed the calcified remains of a male Guinea worm in her abdominal wall. Her lower legs had been amputated probably about two weeks before death, possibly because they were ulcerated as the result of trying unsuccessfully to extract the female Guinea worms which sometimes try to break out and emerge through the skin on the legs.*

We have been led to believe that DNA is rarely preserved in mummies because of the passage of time and embalming methods. Has Manchester had much luck in recovering genetic material from mummies?

RD: *There are considerable difficulties in identifying DNA in mummies. However, we have had success in Manchester with several mummies, including Natsef-Amun. Currently, we are attempting to identify parasite DNA in some of the mummies.*

Could you tell us something about the mummy tissue bank you are developing?

RD: *A few years ago, we decided to establish at Manchester the International Egyptian Mummy Tissue Bank, so that there would be a resource of material that would be available for research undertaken by ourselves and others, particularly in relation to the study of disease patterns. We approached 8,000 institutions worldwide (outside Egypt) to ask if they possessed mummies and if they would be interested in contributing samples to the bank. The bank is now developing, and currently there are several research projects that are using tissue samples.*

Did ancient Egyptians suffer the same diseases common in Egypt today?

RD: *The ancient Egyptians suffered many of the same diseases as those commonly found in Egypt today. In particular, they suffered from a variety of parasitic diseases. We are currently studying one of these—schistosomiasis or Bilharzia—over a 5,000 year period, in co-operation with the Egyptian Ministry of Health. They have a long-term program to assess the incidence, diagnostic methods, and treatment of this disease in Egypt today, and have*

data on 100,000 cases. Our Manchester team is building up a picture of the pattern of the disease in ancient Egypt, using the tissue bank samples and immunological tests specially developed in Manchester as a diagnostic tool to identify the presence of the disease in mummies. Ultimately, we will compare the patterns and development of the disease over 5,000 years, and try to determine if the genetic make-up of the causative parasite has changed over that time span. This may help to inform preventative treatment methods being developed for use in modern patients.

What does the future hold for the Mummy Project?

RD: *The Mummy Project has, I believe, added a new dimension to the study of ancient Egypt. Whereas art, archaeology, and literature provide us with only a limited and often propogandistic view of the society, these biomedical studies really tell us what people's lives were like. In the future, we hope to continue to study the patterns and evolution of more diseases from ancient to modern times, and to develope our work on immunological techniques and DNA identification, with particular emphasis on research into viral, bacterial, and parasite DNA. At Manchester, we have a very favorable set of circumstances for this work: a university museum with a fine Egyptology collection, and the availability of expertise in science and medicine in the university departments and the teaching hospitals. At the university, we provide an M.Sc. degree course in biomedical and forensic studies in Egyptology—the only one in the world—and currently, we also have nine Ph.D. students working in this area. With these programs, we hope to train a new generation of scientists to take these exciting studies forward into the twenty-first century.*

MYSTERY MUMMY

Unraveling the Remains of Ankh-hap the Egyptian Mummy

by Frank L. Holt

It's been 5,000 years since the dawn of Egyptian civilization, yet the history of this great culture of antiquity remains surprisingly elusive. While many of the deeds of the elite were chronicled in hieroglyphic texts, the more mundane aspects of daily life, of diet and disease, of work and worship, too often remain unknown. To help overcome this knowledge gap, historians and scientists are developing new techniques to explore an old and unusual source of important evidence—ancient mummies.

Earlier in this century x-rays were used to investigate the condition of still-wrapped mummies; this procedure is still widely used and has been applied in important studies of the British Museum collection, the royal mummies in Cairo, and the Manchester Museum Mummy Project in England. More recently, however, the sophisticated images made possible by CAT-scans (three dimensional computerized tomography) have proven to be even more valuable for the nondestructive examination of mummies. Though more costly and time-consuming to produce than conventional x-rays, CAT-scans generate a wide array of data on soft, as well as hard, tissues; and the ability to view a wrapped body layer by layer, in vertical or horizontal cross sections, allows specialists to analyze a specimen thoroughly and safely. Pioneering CAT-scan projects in Boston, Minneapolis, Indianapolis, and elsewhere have alerted historians to the potential of further studies. The additional information that can be gleaned from other scientific methods, such as carbon dating and spectroanalysis, as well as whatever procedures may become available tomorrow, make this an exciting and innovative time for the study of ancient peoples.

These techniques are available none too soon. Egyptian mummies, and their counterparts from other cultures, represent a precious legacy that has been nearly lost through modern indifference. Few of the millions of ancient Egyptian mummies have survived the depredations of man and nature, and too many lie ignored and unstudied in the stairwells and storerooms of museums around the world. In private collections, too, mummies are often consigned to oblivion. Occasionally, the press reports a mummy found in a pawnshop or abandoned in someone's attic; these accounts match somewhat older stories of mummies being "stripped" for entertainment, ground up for "medicines," and even burned for fuel. It is impossible to reckon the number of mummies destroyed, or of those left simply to decay.

It is thus imperative that every existing mummy, no matter how humble its ancient status or how modest its present appearance, be soberly and scientifically examined with the latest nondestructive technology. This must be the responsibility of every museum that has a mummy in its care, and of every scholar who has the scientific means available to assist in this task.

Such sentiment led a small group of concerned scholars from the University of Houston (UH) and the Houston Museum of Natural Science (HMNS) to establish the Houston Mummy Research Program (HMRP) on June 19, 1987. The focus of this program has been a poorly preserved, enigmatic mummy in the HMNS collection, a mummy whose history and human remains are a mirror, reflecting the tortured path of mummy studies from sideshow to science.

When our work began we knew little about the mummy or the wooden coffin in which it lay. We were aware that the HMNS had acquired these artifacts in 1970 as part of a permanent loan from a disbanded collection at Texas A&M University. Kept in storage for the next 15 years, mummy and coffin were officially registered at the HMNS on June 26, 1985. The museum's accession records for that year note the poor, brittle condition of the two-piece coffin. The body was in worse shape: The exposed, broken skull was held in place by a wooden dowel, and "assorted bones and wrapping debris" were littered about the floor of the coffin. A wasp's nest was visible in the cranium. According to a display label that accompanied the assemblage from Texas A&M, the mummy was that of "Anh-hr-h3cpj" (at the time hieroglyphs were transliterated using an alphanumeric system), allegedly a tax collector from approximately 2000 B.C. To substantiate and add to this scant information, and to improve the museum's display of these important artifacts, an interdisciplinary research program was established.

Our first step was to undertake a thorough CAT-scan of the mummy. In the summer of 1987, using the facilities of the Enhanced Oil Recovery Lab on the UH campus, nearly 600 separate CAT-scan "slices" were taken of the mummy: 60 from chest to back, 100 from right side to left, and 403 from foot to head. These images, taken at four-millimeter intervals, produced a three-dimensional cube of complex data. Display of the data was made possible by the Cullen Image Processing Lab, part of the UH Allied Geophysical Lab, using software developed specifically for this purpose. In addition to black-and-white images, color codes can be selected to differentiate materials of different density. The program allows us to distinguish between soft tissue, cloth, bone, and hardened resins.

Of immediate concern to us was the unexpected condition of the body "exposed" beneath the bandages. The CAT-scan revealed that the mummy had wooden poles inside it—not just the dowel visible at the neck, but as many as six wooden poles carefully aligned down the torso, arms, and legs. Also rather startling was the general condition of the upper body, where the spinal column was clearly severed with no evidence of intact skeletal structure between mid-torso and neck. From the first glimpse under the CAT-scan, we confronted a rather mysterious-looking body.

Broadening our investigation, we invited experts to render a new translation of the text on the coffin and to examine the coffin decoration. The hieroglyphics revealed that "Anh-hr-h3cpj" was no tax collector at all but rather a man of no known occupation named Ankh-hap (meaning "the Apis lives"), whose mother was Maat-Djohuty and whose father's name is unclear, perhaps Padi, Pya, or Pamaa. The text calls upon the gods to provide the dead man with "bread, beer, flesh and fowl, milk, wine, incense, oil, alabaster, cloth" and, for good measure, "everything good and pure which is sweet and pleasant to the deceased." The coffin is in the shape of a man with painted black wig and beard; the latter is broken and largely missing. The figure wears a painted floral collar along with representations of such common Egyptian deities as Horus, Isis, Nephthys, and Anubis.

Rebecca Storey, a noted physical anthropologist on the UH faculty, examined the CAT-scan data, as well as the body itself. Using the CAT-scan, Storey was able to study the body's internal structure and compare her findings with the results of her examination of the body's exposed features, particularly the skull. The skeleton proved more or less complete from the lower thoracic vertebrae to the feet, though it lacked

> FROM THE FIRST GLIMPSE UNDER THE CAT-SCAN, WE CONFRONTED A RATHER MYSTERIOUS-LOOKING BODY.

part of the pelvis and some toes. Torso and arms were quite incomplete, except for some pieces of ribs, scapula, one humerus, and the right ulna and radius, although generally not in their correct anatomical positions. Though the mummy has two fake hands made of bundled cloth, parts of both real hands were actually found. Some of the bones from the right hand, however, were located in the area of the left hand, and left hand bones were found on the exposed left foot. Clearly, the body had been disturbed in the past—and showed rather clumsy efforts to restore the pieces to their proper positions and to fabricate unnecessary substitutes out of cloth packing.

The facial region and mandible were missing from the exposed skull; yet fragments of facial bone and a broken tooth were found in the debris lying on the floor of the coffin. Some of these pieces could be fitted into place, suggesting that the body was buried intact. Fortunately, the base of the skull was intact; the brain had been removed through the nasal passage, using hooks, in typical Egyptian fashion. The skull still contained the hardened resins from this embalming process (showing, incidentally, that the head was originally tilted slightly); there are traces as well of the wasp's nest from much more recent times. It is unfortunate that the mandible was missing; it might have told us much more about the deceased. One upper jaw fragment, found on the coffin floor, holds a broken incisor and a molar.

Storey concluded that the body is that of a mature male, age 31–51, but most likely in his late 30s or early 40s. The CAT-scan images of the femur and tibia could be measured and indicate an overall stature of about 5'4". Finally, it could be deduced from the examination of exposed remains that the deceased had survived a case of childhood anemia, perhaps associated with disease. There were signs of moderate arthritic degeneration of a cervical vertebra, but no indication of serious arthritis elsewhere.

After the body's examination we turned our attention to the problem of the wooden poles inside it. We found, for example, that several mummies in the British Museum exhibit similar features. We corresponded, too, with Rosalie David, director of the Manchester Museum Mummy Project. Her experience with Manchester mummy no. 1770, unwrapped in 1975, suggested the reburial of a plundered, stick-braced mummy in much the same condition as our own at the HMNS. To find out whether the two cases were indeed rare examples of stick-braced reburials, we needed more data on the sticks themselves. We had already turned to the UH Biology Department for help in searching for possible remains of parasites (we found none); we returned there for an expert opinion on the type of wood found inside the HMNS mummy. A microscopic analysis was made of a small shaving taken from the exposed pole at the mummy's neck. This examination revealed that the wood was from a conifer indigenous to a temperate climate; the presence of resin canals narrowed the range to pine, spruce, larch, or Douglas fir.

Although we knew that wooden poles had been found in other mummies, including some with similar signs of "dismemberment" and disarray, we were concerned that the coniferous wood from the HMNS mummy might be quite modern, and even local. To investigate the true relationship between the coffin, mummy, and sticks, we decided to submit a sample of each for carbon dating. Because of lab costs, we found the prospect of doing this work rather daunting. Fortunately, we were able to secure the voluntary services of the Radio-Carbon Lab of the Balcones Research Center at the University of Texas at Austin.

First, we carbon-dated a small sample of undecorated wood that had broken off from a corner of the coffin. The result was an age of 3,000 years B.P. (before the present) ±80 years, which would place the cutting of the tree from which the boards were made sometime in the late second or early first millennium B.C. According to experts, the design and decoration of the coffin suggested that it was made around the seventh century B.C. or later. Art and science, then, would place the burial in the first millennium B.C., probably in the Late Period of Egyptian history.

Next, we dated a fragment of cloth wrapping that formed an odd assemblage found amid those "assorted bones and wrapping debris" lying on the coffin floor. This separately wrapped, resined package contained a right rib attached (anatomically incorrectly) to the left scapula. Like the displaced hands, these bones belonged to the mummy but were somehow removed from the body and later rewrapped and returned to the coffin. Such an assemblage suggested that the mummy had indeed been disturbed and then restored and reburied in either ancient or modern times. This carbon date was decidedly old and offered more evidence for a possible reburial in antiquity: 1632 years B.P. ±130 years, or sometime in the first cen-

turies A.D. when Egypt was ruled by Rome.

Finally, a wood shaving from the large pole protruding from the mummy's neck was analyzed. The result was 250 years B.P. ±70 years (ca. A.D. 1700), showing us that at least one of the sticks bracing the body was quite modern. Since the CAT-scan revealed a clear uniformity in size and shape among the main wooden braces, it can be concluded that all of the sticks are similarly modern. From our three tests, then, we obtained three very different ages. Carbon dates are not precise under the best of circumstances; they merely suggest a range of probable ages. We concluded that the coffin dates to the first millennium B.C., the mummy wrapping to the first half of the first millennium A.D., and the wooden poles in the mummy to more modern times.

Taken together, these first phases of the HMRP produced a fascinating mystery. We had learned much about the coffin, and about the age, sex, height, and general health of the dead man in that coffin. But we had also been surprised at what the CAT-scans revealed about the incomplete and disarranged body of the deceased. The various carbon dates then suggested a further puzzle: Was the mummy really that of Ankh-hap, or was a horribly mutilated Egyptian of the Roman period haphazardly embalmed and buried in a recycled coffin from an earlier millennium? Or, had Ankh-hap's tomb been robbed and his body profaned in the Roman period, but then piously repaired and reburied as best the locals could? Or, alas, was this a case of entirely modern mischief and mishandling, whereby a stray coffin and mummy were mismatched and sold on the antiquities market, only to be further

Corpse in the Curiosity Shop

Nonesuch House of antiques in Wiscasset, Maine, is a white-clapboard temple to the packrat gods. An eight-foot replica Statue of Liberty, a life-size concrete Venus on the half shell, and a bright red London phone booth line the strip of dirt between the sidewalk and the shop. Come closer, though, and you may be shot: A sign in a front window offers a view down the barrel of a revolver and asks, "Is there life after death? Trespass here and find out." But for the gun, the sign might be inviting the casual shopper to seek an answer from someone more qualified to know, an ancient mummy that has for the past several years been the shop's principal curiosity.

Bought in Egypt in the 1920s, the mummy was first displayed at Benson's Wild Animal Farm, a zoo and training center for exotic circus animals in Hudson, New Hampshire. In 1945 it was sold to local shoe salesman and African big-game hunter Ira Morse, who displayed it in a museum he owned in the village of Warren. There it lay alongside a stuffed lion, a tea service made of ostrich eggs, and a lock of hair from a participant in China's Boxer Rebellion (not to mention a second mummy).

Morse died in 1960, his son Philip in 1991, after which the museum was dissolved, its contents sold at auction. The mummy was bought for $4,950 by Massachusetts antiques dealer David Preble. Shortly thereafter Preble sold it for an undisclosed sum to Terry Lewis, the ex-merchant marine and self-described recluse who owns Nonesuch House.

Lewis put the mummy on display in a glass case inside the front door. Atop the case he put a collection jar for an animal shelter, a copy of the tell-all Joan Crawford biography Mommie Dearest, *and a sign advertising the mummy as an Egyptian princess. "She's the first woman I've met who could stand me for more than two years," boasts Lewis.*

Then, in 1996, a visitor to the shop called the Maine attorney general's office to inquire if posses-
sion of a mummy was legal. The state contacted the Customs Service, which alerted the Egyptian Embassy, which demanded that the mummy be returned. The Customs Service sent an agent to investigate, "a young punk," in Lewis' words, "trophy hunting and f--ing everybody up." A media miniblitz ensued, with CBS quoting Zahi Hawass, the director of the Giza pyramids, saying, "If this man keeps this mummy, I hope there is a curse on him." Lewis was steadfast. "If the Egyptian government tries to take it back without adequate compensation," he warned, "I'm going to take the mummy to the Bath Bridge at noon, hire a helicopter, light some flares, and over she goes"—into the frigid waters of the Kennebec River.

In the end, two Egyptologists examined the mummy and determined that Lewis' "royal princess" was neither royal nor a princess. In fact it was a man, probably a temple functionary who had died between 600 and 300 B.C. Lewis was crushed, but, not being royal, the mummy was not a national treasure, and the scholars recommended that Egypt drop its claim. Lewis relabeled it imaginatively, "Mummy of Temple priest…found 1922 by Howard Carter…during King Tut dig."

Thanks to the publicity, Lewis has a sheaf of letters from both the shocked and the sympathetic, calling him everything from a grave robber to a true man of principle. A Brazilian businessman reportedly offered him $30,000 for the mummy, and the Museum of Death in Sand Diego suggested a trade, the ancient corpse for two classic Harley-Davidsons. Even in his current home, the temple functionary is probably better off than his old New Hampshire compatriot. According to the auctioneers who liquidated the Morse Museum, the second mummy left in a car with New Jersey license plates, and when last heard of was beckoning the curious to its tent as a freak at county fairs.

—Andrew L. Slayman

damaged and rebuilt by incompetent curiosity-seekers?

To address these problems, especially in light of the recent age of the sticks among the ancient bones, it was necessary to investigate more closely the modern history of the Ankh-hap artifacts. Searching archival records and old newspaper accounts, we found a bewildering array of modern "facts": the mummy was "dug up in 1873," "found in the Valley of the Kings in 1891, "the body of a Tax Collector for Ramses II 4,000 years ago," "exhibited in a traveling show in Texas," "bought from a Museum by a famed veterinarian," "dismissed as a fake by Texas A&M students," "revered as an icon by A&M cadets," "x-rayed by the vet," "lost on several occasions," "found neglected in a men's restroom," and so on. Following this elusive trail, interviewing people from New York to Texas, we relived much of the history of modern Egyptomania. We "witnessed" the way in which Egypt's antiquities became the playthings of curiosity-seekers in the nineteenth century, when large numbers of mummies and other artifacts were exported—usually without documentation—to avid collectors in Europe and America. We experienced, too, the sad sequel, when many of these precious objects were discarded, damaged, or destroyed. It is all too common today to read about the rediscovery of such mummies; in a recent case, a mummy's head was found in a hatbox hidden away in someone's attic. The man who rests in Ankh-hap's coffin has suffered many of these misfortunes.

Among the scraps of information available to us were six pieces of newspaper and an old mailing label crammed in the bottom of the coffin. These papers had been used to stuff around the body, apparently as packing material. What intrigued us most was the consistent nature of these scraps. The newspapers (one *Los Angeles Examiner*, the rest from the *Rochester Herald*) all were dated between March 25, 1914, and May 29, 1914; the label, addressed to George English of Ward's Scientific Est., Rochester, New York, was dated May 12, 1914. We found that Ward's, a company still headquartered in Rochester, did indeed employ Mr. English as a geologist/mineralogist from 1913 to 1921. The company was a leading supplier of scientific equipment and specimens, from fossils and minerals to anatomical models and human remains. A search is under way, in the company's many old catalogs, for possible references to the HMNS mummy. Meanwhile, 1914 is the earliest fixed date for the modern history of these artifacts; earlier reference's are more difficult to substantiate.

According to a number of Texas newspaper accounts spanning the decades from the 1930s to the 1970s, the mummy and coffin were acquired early in the twentieth century by Mark Francis, "Father of the Texas Cattle Industry" and dean of the School of Veterinary Medicine at Texas A&M. In one version of the tale, Francis got the mummy from a traveling show that went broke in College Station; another suggests that he bought out the collection of a defunct museum in Wichita Falls. The latter story was published while Francis was still alive and might therefore carry more weight. But what then of the Ward's connection through Rochester? At the moment it seems most likely that Francis acquired the mummy via

Mystery Mummy • 27

Ward's. Correspondence of 1921 shows that Francis did indeed buy sundry materials (such as mastodon bones) from Ward's Scientific. It is quite possible that Ward's sold to him the stock of the Wichita Falls museum, including the mummy, at some point between 1914 and 1921. There are alternative possibilities—Francis simply used the packing papers from a 1914 Ward's shipment to stuff around his Wichita Falls mummy, or the Wichita Falls museum itself had gotten the mummy from Ward's—but these are less plausible on present evidence. We hope to discover precisely when (1873? 1891?) and where in Egypt the mummy and coffin were unearthed, and whether they were found together or paired subsequently.

The first real attempt to study the objects was made in 1921, when Francis's colleague Professor O.M. Ball secured a rough translation of the coffin inscription. By a letter dated May 16, 1921, a Dr. Lutz of the University of Pennsylvania deciphered the text and produced from it the famous name "Anh-hr-h3cpj," which freshmen in the A&M Corps of Cadets were later required to recite in answer to the question: Who is the oldest man on campus? Newspapers report that Francis kept the mummy in his classroom for many years, where it served as a comical prop and general curiosity. According to local historian John Adams of College Station, Francis may have x-rayed the mummy to prove its authenticity. There

Protected and Nourished Forever

Ankh-hap's six-foot-long wooden coffin is covered with a thin coating of painted plaster. The lid shows a male figure wearing a large wig; his beard is now missing. Below the wig is a broad, floral collar ending in the heads of the falcon-god Horus. Between the collar and the inscription is the kneeling figure of the sky-goddess Nut, with outstretched wings meant to protect the deceased. In her hands she holds feathers of Maat, symbols of truth. Depicted to the sides of the inscription are the four Sons of Horus, minor gods associated with the embalmed internal organs of the deceased, below which are the goddesses Isis and Nepththys with their hands raised in an attitude of mourning. Two images of a recumbent jackal in a shrine represent the god Anubis, patron of embalming and the necropolis. They are drawn upside-down on the foot of the coffin lid, but are actually right-side-up when viewed from the head. Along the sides of the lid are additional scenes showing Isis and Nepththys embracing the symbol of Osiris, the king of the underworld, Anubis as a jackal-headed man

making offerings, 11 protecting genies with knives, and the god Aker, a reclining lion who guarded the entrance to the underworld. On the foot of the coffin is a symbol of the sun, which passed each night into the underworld and was reborn each morning. The inscription is written in cursive hieroglyphs, and contains a magical spell intended to provide eternal funerary offerings for Ankh-hap. Both the sacred images and text were placed on the coffin to insure that the deceased would be protected and nourished in the afterlife.

Surviving in the wrappings of the mummy itself are decorated plaques of cartonnage, a material similar to papier-mâché. These include fragments of a broad, floral collar, a winged figure of the goddess Nut and an "apron" over the legs of the mummy. All of these appear to be contemporary with the coffin and may have been painted by the artist who decorated the coffin.

—FRANK L. HOLT

is some debate as to whether Francis unwrapped the mummy. We have not been able to locate the veterinarian's x-rays; they could prove if the body was already stick-braced when Francis examined it or if this was done subsequently. It is interesting that a 1931 account mentions the "toe" bones lying loose on top of the mummy; these are probably the finger bones that we found improperly "replaced" on the foot.

After the death of Francis in 1936, the "Aggie" mummy grew in local fame while being displayed in A&M's museum. The strong bias in favor of an elitist past soon transformed the enigmatic Anh-hr-h3cpj into a government official, a tax collector, and, eventually, a tax collector for Ramesses II (this was long before the recent international exhibition centered upon this pharaoh's long and illustrious reign). The tomb of the "Aggie" mummy was, of course, assumed to have been in the Valley of the Kings, where Tutankhamun and other rulers of the period were buried.

But even this exalted and exaggerated pedigree could not spare Anh-hr-h3cpj from the fate of so many mummies in the modern world. After World War II, the A&M museum was closed and the collections of Francis and Ball were scattered to new homes. Old museum archives show that much care was devoted to the process of de-accessioning the artifacts, but somehow the mummy suffered nonetheless. There are news reports of the mummy being lost, and of university officials finding the body and coffin sitting unprotected in an old rest-room. The mummy's jaw (a vital source of anthropological data) was lost or stolen in

this dismal period; it appears intact in newspaper photographs taken as recently as 1939. Insects built their nests in the broken skull, and the cloth wrappings began to fall apart. Finally, in 1970, what remained of Texas A&M's "oldest man on campus" was permanently loaned to the HMNS.

We have explored the ancient history of the coffin, the more recent (but still quite ancient) history of the mummy, and the very modern history of both. It is interesting, and ironic, that this scholarly endeavor actually re-enacts the very process that it studies. According to ancient Egyptian legend, the god-king Osiris was attacked and dismembered by his jealous brother Seth. In time, Isis was able to recover the far-flung remains of her brother Osiris and restore him to life. This deeply religious myth became the model for mummification in Egypt, whereby even mortals could be assured a comfortable eternity, like Osiris, through the embalmer's restorative art. It was through mummification that Egypt's dead could be revived, body and soul, in a ritual that made each an Osiris.

Like its ancient god-king, Egypt itself has suffered at the hands of its jealous brothers. Its riches have been uprooted; its antiquities have been scattered recklessly around the world. As a result, we are finding that an ancient life we admire and wish to reconstruct cannot easily be revived. The Houston Mummy Research Program has played the part of Isis in saving an important body of evidence—evidence that must be gathered one piece at a time, evidence that might help restore the living history of the ancient Egyptian people. ▲

CASE OF THE DUMMY MUMMY

Psst!...
Hey buddy, wanna buy a falcon?

by BOB BRIER

For generations, vendors on Luxor's west bank, near the Valley of the Kings, have offered fake antiquities to tourists, who are warned by guides to bargain vigorously. It is all harmless fun. When the price of a carved pharaoh's head blackened with shoe polish drops from $200 to $20, everyone is happy. The traveler has his souvenir along with a good story to tell, and the seller has still made a huge profit. Forging Egyptian objects was also an ancient practice, a multi-million dollar industry in its time.

My first experience with ancient fakes came 20 years ago during a seminar that I was teaching on mummies. At the time, animal mummies were plentiful and could be legally taken out of Egypt. My classes would unwrap and perform an autopsy on a fish or bird mummy. Only once did we work on a cat, but it was too painful for cat lovers in the

Pat Remler

Bob Brier holds what appears to be a mummified falcon, but is it?

class. My students would form an archaeological team, one serving as photographer, another as artist. One would take the mummy to be x-rayed, another would analyze the linen wrappings, and yet another would conserve the bones.

One year, we unwrapped a falcon, or so we thought from its shape. A beak had been formed on the outside with a bit of resin, and a falcon's eyes had been painted on the wrappings. The x-ray, however, revealed a jumble of bones. When the class unwrapped the mummy, it became clear that something was very wrong. The head was missing and there were not enough bones to make up a complete skeleton. The mummy was simply a random bunch of bones wrapped to look like a falcon.

I didn't think much more about this

experience until two years ago, when I was filming a documentary for The Learning Channel. I wanted to x-ray a few mummies and show what was inside. Yale's Peabody Museum kindly loaned me a cat and an ibis. I contributed a friend's falcon mummy. The ibis came out beautifully, with its long beak clearly defined and all the bones perfectly in place. Then came the falcon's turn. I had selected a beautiful one, with markings carefully painted on elaborate wrappings. The x-ray, however, showed no bones within—only rolls of cloth. We nicknamed it the "dummy mummy."

Animal mummification was a big business in ancient Egypt, and it seems as though a large portion of it was fraudulent. Ancient Egyptians mummified all kinds of creatures, from bulls to birds, and for different reasons. Some were pets, preserved to keep their masters company in the next world, but most were raised to be sacrificed as offerings to the gods.

When someone wished a favor from a god, he or she might leave an offering of a bronze statue, food, or an animal mummy in the god's temple. Cats were associated with Bast, a feline goddess. Cat mummies were still so numerous at the end of the nineteenth century that shiploads of them were sent to England to be ground into fertilizer. Cat cemeteries were located at Bubastis, the city of Bast in the Delta, and at other towns up and down the Nile.

More extensive than the cat cemeteries were the ibis and falcon galleries at Saqqara—miles of tunnels containing mummified birds. Carved into the walls of tunnels were thousands of niches, each with a mummified bird. When space in the walls ran out, the mummies were placed in ceramic pots and stacked floor to ceiling. The ibis was sacred to the god Toth, who was often depicted as a human with the head of an ibis. Toth was associated with the moon. The falcon was sacred to the god Horus, associated with the sun.

Along the route to the galleries were stalls where pilgrims could purchase mummified birds, many of which had been raised for that purpose. After a pilgrim selected one, it was placed in a ceramic pot and sealed. Priests of the gallery would place it in a niche and, for a small fee, say a prayer for the pilgrim.

A collection of the writings of Hor, a priest in charge of the ibis galleries around 200 B.C., explains that hundreds of people were involved in the animal mummification business at Saqqara. One of the more important jobs was that of the "doorkeeper," whom Hor says supervised the birds and their young, and was probably responsible for raising the ibises.

Unlike ibises, falcons cannot be raised in captivity, so there was no way that the supply of birds could meet the demand. Dummy mummies, like the one I x-rayed for television, were thus created out of fancy bundles of rags and sold to unsuspecting pilgrims. My colleagues Salima Ikram, who has studied animal mummies at the Egyptian Museum in Cairo, and Sue D'Auria, an assistant curator at the Huntington Museum of Art in West Virginia, confirmed our experience—many falcon mummies they have examined also proved to be ancient fakes.

Like the guides on the west bank of Luxor, Hor wanted to ensure that the pilgrims were not cheated. In one memo he wrote, "There must be one god in one vessel," or a bird in every sacrificial pot. ▲

Falcons and Rats or Shrews, Oh My!

Ever consider preserving your beloved pet for the afterlife? The ancient Egyptians did, as evidenced by the recent discovery of an animal cemetery at Abydos, 350 miles south of Cairo. Antiquities inspector Yahya al-Masri and his team unearthed the remains of 25 falcons and 8 small mammals—either rats or shrews—that had been mummified in the fourth century B.C. The falcons had been placed in 6 large pottery jars, the mammals in tiny individual limestone coffins, several covered in gold leaf and embossed with images of the animals.

Mummification of animals, either beloved pets or those that had been sacrificed to the gods, is well known from ancient Egypt. Crocodiles and cats, associated with the deities Sobek and Bastet, were among the most popular. Several farms where animals were raised, mummified, and later sold as offerings have been found in Egypt, the most recent being a crocodile farm excavated by an Italian team at the site of Narmuthis in the Faiyum.

An animal cemetery containing dogs and ibises was excavated at Abydos in the nineteenth century but remains largely unpublished. "Historically, animal cemeteries never attracted the scholarly interest of their human counterparts," says Salima Ikram of the American University in Cairo. "The new-found cemetery is sure to enhance our understanding of Ptolemaic cult practices."

—ANGELA M.H. SCHUSTER

IDENTIFYING A PHARAOH

A royal body may be that of Ramesses I, but can we ever be sure?

by MARK ROSE

The dark brown-black body of a man who may have ruled Egypt more than 3,000 years ago lies before me on a padded cushion in the conservation laboratory at Emory University's Michael C. Carlos Museum. Seeing it there—stripped of linen wrappings, arms crossed over chest, lids nearly closed over empty eye sockets, dried lips pulled back from teeth—I am amazed at the body's extraordinary preservation and feel an intense curiosity about its identity. Tempering these feelings is the knowledge that, whether or not they are a pharaoh's remains, they are from a person who died and was buried millennia ago only to be sold by tomb robbers in the nineteenth century and exhibited in a Niagara Falls museum alongside a two-headed calf and barrels in which daredevils braved the falls. A sad fate, but that will change because many scholars are now convinced that it is indeed a royal mummy, and Egypt is poised to reclaim it later this year [2003].

Long-neglected, the mummy came to the public's attention two years ago, after the Niagara Falls museum closed its doors and its Egyptian collection was acquired by Atlanta's Emory University ("New Life for the Dead," ARCHAEOLOGY September /October 2001). The media noted the mummy's crossed-arms pose and a resemblance between its face in profile and those of the mummies of the 19th Dynasty pharaoh Seti I and his son Ramesses II. Could the Niagara Falls mummy be that of Seti's father, Ramesses I, which has never been found? If it were, said Carlos Museum curator Peter Lacovara, it would be returned to Egypt.

Looking at the royal mummies in the Cairo Museum, this past December, I could see that the one in Atlanta would not seem out of place among them, but I did ask three Egyptologists who have seen it firsthand if they believe it could be a pharaoh's. "The mummification techniques used are certainly consistent with a 19th Dynasty mummy," says ARCHAEOLOGY contributing editor Bob Brier. "In addition, this is top-of-the-line mummification, a wealthy person who got what he paid for. Furthermore, the position of the arms is consistent with a royal mummy. So there are real reasons to entertain the idea that we have a royal 19th Dynasty mummy." In Egypt, I spoke with Salima Ikram, a mummy specialist at the American University in Cairo. "I went there completely suspicious," she says, recalling her own trip to Atlanta. "The method of mummification is what I was looking at, and what it looked like to me was more late 18th, as in tail end of 18th, to 19th Dynasty. Obviously

it is royal because of its arm position." The high position of the Atlanta mummy's arms is, she says, unlike the lower crossed-arm pose found centuries later on some 26th Dynasty mummies.

"I first met this particular mummy something like ten years ago, when I went to Niagara," says Aidan Dodson of Bristol University, speaking to me in his Cairo hotel suite with a view of the Giza pyramids. "I walked into the room and looked at it and said, 'Oh my god, it looks like a New Kingdom pharaoh's mummy.'" Like Brier and Ikram, Dodson places great weight on the position of the mummy's arms. "There are," he says, "no mummies of the New Kingdom of which I'm aware with both arms fully crossed like that of anybody other than a pharaoh."

Given that the mummy may well be that of a pharaoh and that it bears a resemblance to Seti I and his descendants, it would seem a simple matter to compare their DNA to see if they matched. Knowing that the retrieval and analysis of DNA from Egyptian mummies has proved problematic in the past, Emory University geneticist Douglas Wallace began by first trying to extract it from the other mummies acquired from Niagara Falls, which are later and definitely nonroyal. He reportedly had some success, but before he sampled the possible royal one, Zahi Hawass, head of Egypt's Supreme Council of Archaeology, made it clear that comparative samples from the pharaohs in the Cairo Museum would not be forthcoming. "In Egypt," Hawass told me, "DNA testing is not permitted. From what I understand, it is not always accurate and it cannot always be done with complete success when dealing with

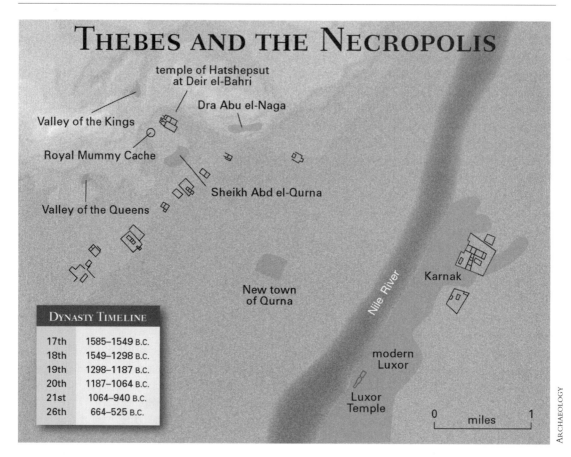

THEBES AND THE NECROPOLIS

temple of Hatshepsut
at Deir el-Bahri

Dra Abu el-Naga

Valley of the Kings

Royal Mummy Cache

Sheikh Abd el-Qurna

Valley of the Queens

New town
of Qurna

Nile River

Karnak

modern
Luxor

Luxor
Temple

Dynasty Timeline	
17th	1585–1549 B.C.
18th	1549–1298 B.C.
19th	1298–1187 B.C.
20th	1187–1064 B.C.
21st	1064–940 B.C.
26th	664–525 B.C.

0   miles   1

ARCHAEOLOGY

mummies. Until we know for sure that it is accurate, we will not use it in our research." Brier echoes Hawass' cautious approach: "We just haven't been able to get that much information out of ancient Egyptian mummies. We are perhaps a couple of years off from being able to do that, so I don't think DNA is going to help right now." With DNA ruled out, any chance of identifying the mummy lies in tracing its history and making a close examination of it—inside and out—using both "eyeball" observation and high-tech scientific techniques.

Thebes was the heart of Egypt during the New Kingdom, with the temples of Karnak and Luxor on the Nile's east bank and the necropolis on the west, including the Valley of the Kings and the Valley of the Queens. In the later nineteenth century, the area was already a tourist destination. "Luxor is a large village, inhabited by a mixed population of Copts and Arabs, and doing a smart trade in antiquities," wrote English novelist Amelia Edwards in *A Thousand Miles Up the Nile*, an account of her journey through Egypt in 1874 and 1875. "As workmen, the Copts are perhaps the more artistic. As salesmen, the Arabs are perhaps the less dishonest. Both sell more forgeries than genuine antiquities." Pitted against the looters, the forgers, and the wealthy foreign travelers who bought most anything was Auguste Mariette, a French Egyptologist who had been appointed head of the nascent Antiquities Service and given exclusive excavation rights by the Egyptian viceroy, Said Pasha, in 1858. After his death in 1881, Mariette was succeeded by countryman Gaston Maspero.

At the center of the Luxor antiquities trade was Mustapha Aga Ayat. The consular agent for Britain, Belgium, and Russia, he took advantage of his diplomatic immunity to act as a middleman for tomb robbers and tourists. Quebec City physician James Douglas described him in his *Photographic Views Taken in Egypt and Nubia* (1860): "Mustapha himself may be considered one of the institutions of Thebes. He is now about fifty years of age, is dark in complexion, of Bedouin extraction, speaks tolerably good English, is greedy, grasping and unscrupulous, yet among the Arabs, sustains a high character for hospitality and openhandedness." What is crucial about Douglas' account is a passage that begins by describing Mustapha fleecing "an English Gentleman" who paid him in advance for any jewelry that might be found on two mummies. The mummies were unwrapped and no gold or jewels were discovered. Then Douglas comments: "The first Mummy unwrapped was certainly a very good one, and its double cases [nesting coffins] were very good. During my last visit, I obtained a finer one, in double cases, for Mr. Barnett, of Niagara Museum, for seven pounds." There is only one high quality mummy from the Niagara collection, so this passage must refer to the supposed royal

mummy now in Atlanta. It appears that in the winter of 1858–1859 or 1859–1860—the date of his visit is uncertain—James Douglas bought a pharaoh for £7.

If Mustapha sold the mummy, where did he get it? Again, Douglas' account helps, stating that Mustapha dealt with "a couple of Arabs who resided in the tombs at Sheik Abd el Goorneh." There is little doubt that this is a reference to the notorious Rassul brothers, of whom Edwards wrote in *Harpers*, "They live together, with their wives and families, in a terrace of rock-cut tombs...their ostensible calling being that of guides and donkey-masters, their private profession that of tomb-breakers and mummy-snatchers."

The Rassuls are best known for their plundering of the royal mummy cache at Deir el-Bahri. "There were whispers about this time of a tomb that had been discovered on the western side, a wonderful tomb rich in all kinds of treasures," wrote Edwards of her stay in Luxor in 1874. The "whispers" were of finds from Deir el-Bahri, but authorities didn't break the case until 1881. "On arriving at Luxor, I caused to be arrested one Ahmed Abd-er-Rasoul, an Arab guide and dealer, to whom a mass of concurrent testimony pointed as the possessor of the secret," Maspero wrote to Edwards. Ahmed and his brother Hussein were questioned by the provincial governor, the soles of their feet being beaten with sticks—the same torture undergone by tomb robbers interrogated three millennia before. Amazingly, they maintained their silence, even after being imprisoned for two months. But Mohammed, the eldest of the brothers, later confessed and led Émile Brugsch, Maspero's

Gaston Maspero (reclining) and Emile Brugsch (center) of the Egyptian Antiquities Service visit the cache site with tomb robber Mohammed Abd er-Rassul (left, in white).

assistant, to the Deir el-Bahri tomb. Brugsch was astounded by what he saw, "reaching the turn in the passage, a cluster of mummy cases came into view in such number as to stagger me." In the tomb, originally carved for a 21st Dynasty high priest of Amun and his family, were forty mummies and coffins, including royals from the 17th through 20th Dynasties, New Kingdom nobles, and members of the 21st Dynasty priest-king Pinudjem I's family.

From the testimony of ancient judicial proceedings recorded on papyrus and the evidence of the tombs themselves—artifacts in disarray and sealings broken—we know that the burials were often violated in antiquity, sometimes soon after interment. At the end of the 20th Dynasty, during a period of weakened rule, impoverishment, and upheaval, matters became critical, and the priests and officials of the royal necropolis began to dismantle it. Continuing through the 21st Dynasty, the tombs were opened and the dead stripped of their treasure—for which the living had a need—then rewrapped, placed in recycled coffins, and cached in a few places for safekeeping.

The necropolis workers left a record of their efforts: graffiti on tomb walls noting the removals of pharaohs and labels or dockets on the new bandages and coffins identifying the deceased. From these, we know that by Pinudjem I's death in 1026 B.C., the remains of Ramesses I and Ramesses II had been removed from their tombs and placed in Seti I's. Around 958 B.C., the three pharaohs were moved to Queen Ahmose-Inhapi's tomb before being placed in the cache at Deir el-Bahri in about 918 B.C. But although the lid and fragments of the bottom of Ramesses I's coffin were found there, his mummy was not.

Could the Rassul brothers have found the cache before 1860 and through Mustapha sold the mummy of Ramesses I to James Douglas when he visited Luxor? Ahmed claimed he had found it while searching for a lost goat in 1875, but the real discovery date is unknown. "My own feeling has always been that pushing the discovery back into the 1860s is stretching it a bit," says Eton College Egyptologist Nicholas Reeves, but he notes that the late A.F. Shore of Liverpool University suggested to him that a papyrus Book of the Dead in the British Museum was probably acquired by the future Edward VII when he visited Mustapha at Luxor while touring Egypt in 1869. The papyrus was written for Nodjmet,

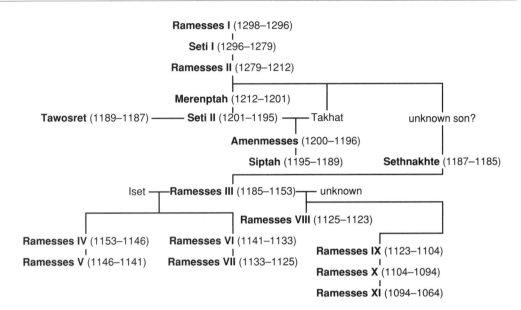

Ramesses I (1298–1296)

Seti I (1296–1279)

Ramesses II (1279–1212)

Merenptah (1212–1201)

Tawosret (1189–1187) ——— **Seti II** (1201–1195) ——— Takhat   unknown son?

Amenmesses (1200–1196)

Siptah (1195–1189)   **Sethnakhte** (1187–1185)

Iset ——**Ramesses III** (1185–1153)—— unknown

Ramesses VIII (1125–1123)

Ramesses IV (1153–1146)   **Ramesses VI** (1141–1133)   **Ramesses IX** (1123–1104)

Ramesses V (1146–1141)   **Ramesses VII** (1133–1125)   **Ramesses X** (1104–1094)

Ramesses XI (1094–1064)

a noblewomen whose mummy, coffin, and grave goods were found in the cache. So it seems likely that it came from the cache and that the Rassuls had found it by at least 1869. This is consistent with Maspero's suspicion, which he mentioned to Edwards in an 1881 letter: "Having noted how Egyptian antiquities of every description were constantly finding their way to Europe, I came ten years ago to the conclusion that the Arabs had discovered a royal tomb."

For Peter Lacovara, closing the gap between the discovery of the cache, around 1869, and the purchase of the Niagara Falls mummy, around 1859, to only a decade helps make an identification of the mummy as Ramesses I more plausible. "If it is Ramesses I," he tells me over coffee at the Carlos Museum, "then perhaps the Rassuls unwrapped it and found no jewelry because the 21st Dynasty priests had already stripped the royal mummies. They didn't then bother

to unwrap the others which is why they survived intact until the cache was seized by the Antiquities Service in 1881." Brier, however, is skeptical that the Rassuls could have kept the cache secret for a decade. "It's a hell of a long time for it to be festering," agrees Dodson.

If a historical link between the Atlanta mummy and Ramesses I can't be proved, other candidates must be considered. Many royal mummies were recovered from two major caches, the one at Deir el-Bahri and another in the tomb of Amenhotep II. "The kings you've got missing," says Dodson, "are Ramesses I, Amenmesses, then you've got Ramesses VII, VIII, X, and XI." He then proceeds to narrow the field. The tombs of Ramesses X and XI in the Valley of the Kings were never finished, he notes. They were probably buried in the Delta, where the Ramesside pharaohs had established their capital, and their mummies are unlikely to have survived the wetter conditions there.

Courtesy Mark Rose

Seti I

Amenmesses, he continues, was a usurper and may not have been given a burial at all. "Which brings you to Ramesses I and VII. I think that's where the debate is, and Ramesses V, but we don't even know where he was buried, he only reigned for a few months." Ramesses VIII, he says, probably did not have an elaborate mummification and burial. "So it is vaguely possibly Ramesses VIII, but Ramesses I or V always struck me as the most likely."

The two pharaohs were separated by the better part of two centuries, Ramesses I at the start of the 19th Dynasty and Ramesses VII in the middle of the 20th, so a close examination of the mummy might yield clues as to which one it might be. "It looked to me late 18th or earlier 19th and not 20th because of certain things," says Ikram. "In the 20th you start getting painted-on eyebrows and sometimes a black line just giving you a hairline over the forehead, and this one didn't

have those features. Also in the later Ramessides you do start getting the eyeballs stuffed [with linen] or with a dried-up little onion bulb under the lid so you have a feeling that there is something going on and it's not just blank space. Again, this mummy didn't have this." Although it was rewrapped to some extent during the 21st Dynasty, and later stripped by tomb robbers, Ikram finds some evidence from the remaining scraps of original linen on the mummy. The wrapping around the neck, she says, is "absolutely" like that on Seti I. And on the stomach, "first you have very fine linen closest to the body then slightly cruder linen on top, so even the positioning of the linen and the fineness of the linen match with what I have seen with Seti I." The embalming incision is a less certain indicator. Its position is not wrong for an early 26th Dynasty date, according to Ikram, but "I think it is more New Kingdom.... It is actually at a slight angle, which is post–Thutmosis III, which makes it more late 18th, early 19th, even more precisely."

So, from its exterior, the mummy would appear to be earlier, closer to the time of Ramesses I, rather than later. But what about inside? Here, x-ray images and CAT scans made at Emory come into play. The amount of resin, which fills half of the skull, suggests to Ikram early 19th Dynasty rather than later 20th. Another clue comes from the images showing rolls of linen inside the mummy's chest. Resin-soaked linen is found in the body cavities from Seti I through Seti II. The only exception is Merenptah, who was found to be filled with a white mixture typical of the 21st Dynasty and probably inserted when his mummy was rewrapped then. The later Ramesside mummies Siptah and Ramesses IV were packed with dried lichen, and Ramesses V with sawdust. "You seem to get from the middle of the 20th Dynasty some rather unusual packing, probably as precursor to full stuffing of the body, which you get in the 21st Dynasty," says Dodson. "So if Mr. Niagara hasn't got major stuffing in the abdomen that would lead me back in the direction of Ramesses I."

With the mummy's own evidence seeming to favor Ramesses I over Ramesses VII, Ikram introduces a dark horse candidate for the Atlanta mummy—Horemheb, the last pharaoh of the 18th Dynasty. "Everyone has been rattling on about Ramesses I," she says, "and I would just like to throw into the broth [that] Horemheb's mummy is missing." But Nicholas Reeves has suggested that the bones found in his sarcophagus and elsewhere in his tomb in the Valley of the Kings in 1908 might include the pharaoh's remains. Funeral garlands in the tomb indicate to him it was used as a mummy cache in the 21st Dynasty. "Look at the tomb of Ramesses II's children," Ikram counters. "Yes, there are lots of bones in it and they're all maybe 26th Dynasty. I think Horemheb's tomb having some bones doesn't necessarily mean they're Horemheb's." The Atlanta mummy would fit what one would expect for Horemheb in terms of its mummification, says Ikram. Since the bones from his tomb have not been studied and may no longer exist, it is impossible to determine if they were late 18th Dynasty or from intrusive burials of the 26th Dynasty as are found elsewhere in the Valley of the Kings. He can't be excluded from consideration as the mummy in Atlanta.

Of course, the Atlanta mummy needn't

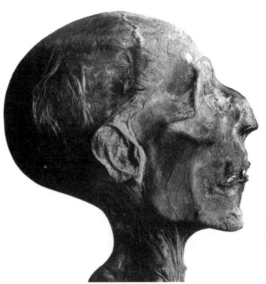

Ramesses II

Courtesy Mark Rose

have come from the Deir el-Bahri cache. Several royal burials were discovered in the middle and late 1850s, close to the mummy's purchase date. In 1857, Mariette's workmen found the burial of Kamose, the pharaoh who founded the New Kingdom, which had apparently been removed from his original tomb, been rewrapped, and reinterred in an isolated grave at Dra Abu el-Naga. Two years later, they found another isolated royal coffin there, that of Queen Ahhotep, mother of Ahmose I. There were also other caches. A tomb found at Sheikh Abd el-Qurna in 1857 had been used by the 21st Dynasty priests to cache a number of 18th and 19th Dynasty princesses, and a collection of papyrus scrolls bought in 1855 were said to have been found in a tomb full of mummies, another possible cache.

"The idea of gathering up mummies from plundered tombs and putting them somewhere safe is not unusual," says Dodson, commenting on the implications if the Atlanta mummy were actually Ramesses VII. "And bear in mind that he's got a very shallow tomb in an extremely exposed spot. So, if the priests were going to start evacuating royal tombs his was probably evacuated first. It may have been he was first out before they fully organized caching and he was simply put in a little tomb somewhere in the Theban hills, and he was tripped over there in the 1860s or 1850s. He just happened to be a mummy which was found and happened to be sold." The same scenario, an isolated tomb and chance discovery, could also apply to Horemheb.

One other avenue of investigation remains open—the resemblance between the Atlanta mummy, Seti I, Ramesses II, and Ramesses V. Does it really mean anything? Bob Brier is skeptical: "We all know people who look like brothers but are not related. With mummies, this is a little complicated because they are all desiccated, which makes them look a bit alike. Add to this that bandaging distorts the cartilage of the nose in similar ways and makes noses seem similar." These problems notwithstanding, both Egyptologists and the media have speculated about the resemblances, some claiming the Atlanta mummy looks just like Seti I, others maintaining it is closest to Ramesses V. I presented the images to Adelphi University forensic anthropologist Anagnostis Agelarakis, and asked him if it was possible to determine familial relationships based on them. The slightly different angles, depths of field, lighting, and shading of the images compromises their value, says Agelarakis. "Any evaluations based on the images will have serious scientific flaws." So, simply looking

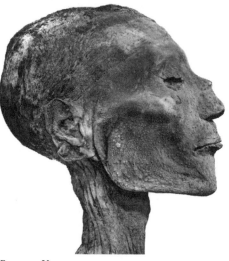

Ramesses V

at the profiles and guessing who is most closely related gets us nowhere.

To go a bit deeper, Emory called in James Harris, who took a side view x-ray image of the mummy's head. Harris, a former University of Michigan orthodontics professor, has x-rayed the royal mummies in Cairo. His images have the advantage of having been taken from the identical orientation. Those familiar with his work say that the closest match he found for the Atlanta mummy was Seti I, the son of Ramesses I. There may be, however, difficulties with this sort of analysis. We have, for example, the mummy of Ramesses VI, the father of Ramesses VII, but much of his skull is missing. So for one candidate, the closest supposed relative can't be compared. In a larger sense, there is the question, how closely does the shape or morphology of our skull reflect our genetic heritage? What if the Atlanta mummy is Horemheb, who was entirely unrelated to the Ramesside pharaohs, and he just happens to look more like Seti I than any of the others?

"We no longer believe the skull is an exact reflection of an individual's genetic makeup," says Agelarakis. "The head of a living human undergoes many changes during life that are dependent not only on the genetic data of the individual, but also on a plethora of other conditions. Hence, an evaluation based exclusively on morphology may not provide a great level of accuracy." He also sees a problem with comparing a few skulls without knowing more about the general population from which they come. As it is, he notes that while the three related mummies—Seti I, Ramesses II, and Ramesses V—all have a slightly sloping forehead, the Atlanta mummy has a more bulging forehead. Furthermore, the Atlanta mummy seems to have more prominent jaw muscle attachments, which can be related to age, diet, and tooth loss.

There is another problem with determining relationships based on photographs or x-ray images of the pharaohs' heads. "We've not got the bodies of any of the mothers," says Dodson. For Agelarakis, not having the women is like "working in a 50 percent vacuum." He concludes that, based on skull shape alone, it is difficult to provide scientifically substantiated data supporting genetic similarity or difference between the Atlanta mummy and any of the others. To do this

sort of evaluation, he says, one would need photographic and x-ray images of the front, back, top, and sides of the skull. That work has not been done, so yet another line of evidence about the mummy's identity is inconclusive.

The Atlanta mummy was displayed at the Carlos Museum, before returning to Egypt in the fall of 2003. For more than 140 years, the mummy was neglected and unrecognized. "Nobody was prepared to believe—it seemed too incredible—there could be a royal mummy in a freak show in Niagara Falls," says Dodson. Who is it? The mummification techniques and pose point to it being a pharaoh of the late 18th or 19th Dynasties, but the historical evidence is equivocal, and none of the three possible candidates—Horemheb, Ramesses I, and Ramesses VII—can be entirely eliminated. The Atlanta mummy's estimated age at time of death, more than 45 years, doesn't help since all three came to power later in life. Perhaps an identification will be made one day. DNA analysis might do the job, eliminating Horemheb as a candidate. Carbon dating would be able to separate Ramesses VII from the other two. New evidence might also come from the Deir el-Bahri cache site, or a comprehensive comparative study of the royal mummies. But that is for the future. For now, it is enough that the mummy has gone home. ▲

PART II:

EGYPTIAN ORIGINS

CITY OF THE HAWK

From ancient breweries to the earliest mummies, excavations at Hierakonpolis are rewriting the origins of Egyptian civilization.

by RENÉE FRIEDMAN

In early 1897, the antiquities markets of Luxor were awash with objects of Predynastic date (4000–3100 B.C.). It was suspected that the source of these artifacts was Hierakonpolis, 60 miles to the south. British archaeologist James Quibell rushed to the site to investigate and within a week discovered a gold-headed cult statue of a falcon god. His colleague Frederick Green soon joined him and together they found a finely carved gray stone palette depicting a king named Narmer, on which our understanding of the rise of Egyptian civilization would be based for the next hundred years.

The Greek name Hierakonpolis (*hierakon* means "of the hawk") comes from the falcon-headed god Horus of the city Nekhen, the site's ancient Egyptian name. Pharaohs were considered the earthly incarnation of this all-seeing celestial bird, who was the patron deity of kingship. And the first pharaoh? On either side of the palette, Narmer is shown engaged in battle and its aftermath wearing the traditional crowns of the two culturally and politically distinct regions of Egypt: the white crown of the Nile Valley and the red crown of the Delta. The palette was thought to celebrate the unification of the two lands after a bloody battle won by Narmer, who marched forth from his capital of Hierakonpolis at about 3100 B.C. and, with his victory over the Delta people, inaugurated Egypt's 1st Dynasty.

Today, Hierakonpolis is a sandy, desolate landscape with mounds and craters left by farmers who mine its organic-rich middens to fertilize their fields. It is difficult to envision the site in Narmer's time, or even 500 years before that, when it was a vibrant, bustling city—perhaps the largest in all of Egypt—stretching for almost three miles along the edge of the Nile floodplain. From ongoing excavations here, begun some 30 years ago by the late Michael Hoffman of the University of South Carolina, we now know that the rise of Egypt did not happen suddenly with Narmer's victory, but was a gradual, if not necessarily peaceful, process and that unification was only the end point of social and technological developments that began at least five centuries before Narmer was born.

Egypt would be barren without the Nile and its annual flood, but the life-giving river was not always predictable. One of every five inundations would be too high, destroying settlements on the edge of the floodplain, or too low, resulting in famine. Such disasters were known to the Egyptians as "chaos." In the face of such possibilities, control of the food supply must have been a key step in the concentration of power in a small number of hands and, ultimately, in pharaonic rule. Among the discoveries was an industrial facility with huge ceramic vats showing that the brewing of beer was already a big business at Hierakonpolis by 3500 B.C. The eight vats found so far could churn out more than 300 gallons of beer a day, and only a small part of this precinct has been explored. From the same time period, more than thirteen kilns have now been tentatively identified throughout the site, some having produced rough domestic cooking wares, others fine red polished and black-topped vessels that are among the finest pottery Egypt ever produced. These discoveries show that the basic economic infrastructure that later supported pharaonic civilization—large-scale production and specialization—was already developing at this early date.

Dominating the Predynastic town was an impressive ceremonial center, one of Egypt's earliest temple complexes, with a 130-foot-long oval courtyard in front of a monumental shrine. The shrine's facade was marked by four immense wooden pillars, possibly cedar logs imported from Lebanon. It is a prototype of temple facades characteristic of Egypt for millennia after. During excavation of this sacred precinct in 1985, I joined the Hierakonpolis team, cataloging sherds from hundreds of fine vessels manufactured specifically for use in temple rites in which wild and dangerous animals—crocodile, hippopotamus, gazelle, and barbary sheep—were sacrificed as symbols of the natural chaos the temple was built to control. The temple proclaimed the authority of the king, but this was not the only way the established social order expressed itself, as our work in the site's cemeteries has shown.

Weird Animals from the Elite Cemetery

Last season [2002] the remains from the unique animal burials found at the elite cemetery (designated HK6), were restudied in preparation for a detailed report on their contents. The burial of animals alone or with humans is known from other Predynastic cemeteries, but it is not especially common. At other sites the buried animals include dogs, sheep, and goats, but no other site has the range of exotic animals of Hierakonpolis. Among the many questions this material presents is: Were these animals—baboons, wild cats, and even elephants—pets or part of a royal zoo? Were they captured in an attempt to domesticate them? To answer some of these questions a detailed examination was carried out. The fauna was systematically identified, inventoried, and measured. Observations were made on the pathologies of the specimens and the minimum number of individuals represented by the remains was calculated. These new analyses added important information to what was previously known about the fauna from the elite cemetery.

For example, Tomb 12, excavated in 1982, had been described as a semi-intact burial of four baboons. In fact, during re-analysis we found the remains of at least seven! In addition, a well-preserved skeleton of a very young hippopotamus and a young cat were found in the same tomb, but these had not been mentioned in the earlier faunal reports. In these reports, the baboons were described as hamadryas baboons, which in the past may have lived in the Red Sea mountains. The anubis baboon is another species that may have occurred in Egypt during Predynastic times and, taking its modern distribution and habitat requirements into account, it may have lived in the Nile Valley of Upper Egypt. It was therefore not surprising that the specimens from Tomb 12, and two skulls found near Tomb 2 are actually anubis baboons, a species that may have been easier to obtain than the hamadryas. Although it is not possible to distinguish the two

species from the long bones, the skull and mandibles have a few morphological characteristics, that allowed us to make this precise identification.

Some of the baboons showed severe fractures (in one instance a lower jaw) that could only have healed in a protected environment. The most common pathologies observed among the baboons are fractures on the hand and foot bones that must have resulted from capture or from the conditions in captivity. It appears that at least four of the seven baboons suffered from a fractured hindfoot and at least five had a fractured forefoot. The healed nature of these fractures indicates that the animals must have lived at least four to six weeks in captivity after the trauma occurred and probably longer.

This season, the faunal analysis of the animal bones excavated at the temple complex (HK29A) took up most of our time but we unpacked the baboons from the elite cemetery once again to do some more analyses. This time we were mostly interested in the information their teeth could give us. Teeth wear down as an animal gets older and this causes different enamel patterns on the biting surface depending on age. The study of tooth wear patterns allowed us to determine that all baboons were between 8 and 12 years old when they died. In modern times, baboons often live up to 30 years of age in captivity.

The week before we left for Hierakonpolis, a specialist in primates, Gildas Merceron, visited the Africa Museum in Belgium, where we work, to do research on our collection of primate skulls. He is also studying baboon teeth to gather more information on their diet. From the analysis of microscopic traces on their teeth he can tell what they ate just before they died because hard particles in different types of food produce distinct types of traces. This kind of research is called microwear analysis. Merceron agreed to take a look at the baboon teeth from Hierakonpolis for us as we are very interested in what these animals may have been fed. This may provide clues as to how they came to be buried in this elite cemetery. In reality he does not study the teeth themselves but replicas of them. This meant that we "simply" had to bring back molds of each tooth for him. Merceron provided us with detailed instructions and we quickly gathered up the equipment required and a little bit extra just in case is wasn't as easy as it sounded. In fact, it didn't sound easy at all!

Before the molds could be made, the teeth had to be cleaned. This was done with cotton wool and alcohol. Other cleaning instruments, like toothbrushes, were strictly forbidden, as these would produce new marks on the teeth. Once dry, dental alginate, a molding agent, more commonly known among the Hierakonpolis staff as "blue goo" because of its bright blue color, was applied to each tooth, one at a time. After a few minutes the alginate was dry and could easily be removed without damaging the teeth. They were then carefully wrapped in foil and labeled. Time consuming, but not as difficult as initially imagined; despite our director's agitation that the puddle of blue goo would damage this fragile archaeological evidence, the teeth emerged clean and unscathed. The molds popped off with ease when dry. It was so easy, for every tooth two molds were made this way. The molds are now on their way to the microwear analyst and we are all very anxious to hear what kind of traces he will find!

—VEERLE LINSEELE

Of the hundreds of known Predynastic sites, Hierakonpolis is one of the few at which distinct cemeteries for the different segments of society have been found. On the southern edge of town was the burial ground for the working class, while the elite were interred in the large *wadi* or dry valley that runs through the center of the site. We began digging in the working-class cemetery in 1996 and have so far uncovered the remains of more than 400 individuals interred here from about 3600 to 3400 B.C., with very few, if any, grave goods. The pit-like graves were dug into hot, dry sand that has preserved mats and baskets as well as hair, bone, body tissue, and foods.

As at other Predynastic cemeteries in Upper Egypt, the body was usually placed on a mat in a crouched position on the left side facing toward the west and the setting sun. Covered with a linen shroud, the corpse was protected by more mats. More than ten different mats had been laid over one intact burial. We have been able to distinguish two basic types that came in two standard sizes, suggesting that a specialized mat-making industry was already in existence at this time. One type was for everyday use, but the other was apparently produced especially for the grave, as it is too flimsy for daily use and none shows signs of wear.

Study of the bones shows that these people were generally healthy and well-nourished, but died around 25 to 35 years of age. The examination has also revealed cut marks on the front of the upper neck vertebrae of 13 men and women. The high location of the lacerations suggests the cuts were not the cause of death—there are easier ways to kill someone. In some cases the cut marks indicate decapitation, but curiously, where the burial is intact, the head is always found in place on the body. It would appear that this treatment is part of a funerary ritual of dismemberment followed by the reassembling of the body. We also have three examples of what may be another part of this ritual—the removal of internal organs that were wrapped in resin-soaked textiles and then returned to the body.

Deciphering The Narmer Palette

The most striking aspect of the Narmer Palette is the king's head gear—this is the first document on which a king is shown wearing both the red and white crowns. On one side he wears the white crown of Upper Egypt in the regal stance of smiting an enemy, who is identified by hieroglyphs as possibly coming from the domain of the "Harpoon," a place in the Nile Delta. This act takes place in the presence of the falcon god Horus, who presents the king with the people and land of the papyrus plant as captives, symbolized by a man held by a hook through his nose and papyrus reeds on his back. Below, the sprawled dead of still unidentified cities or realms underscore the king's triumph. The meaning is clear: The king has defeated the Delta enemy and Horus, the patron god of Narmer's kingship, takes them prisoner. The king's name, written with a catfish (nar) and a chisel (mer), appears at the top in a panel that represents the gates of the royal palace, or serekh. On either side of his name, the cow goddess Bat offers her personal protection.

Narmer's smiting stance, destined to be an icon of royal power for the next 3,500 years, and the presence of a servant bearing sandals and a ewer with which to wash the king's feet have suggested to some that the action depicted is ritualistic rather than historic. But the recent discovery of a similar scene—with the king as a catfish smiting an enemy out of whose head sprout papyrus reeds—on a carved bone tag used to date an oil shipment suggests that this

was a real event that occurred in a certain year. Whether this event is the decisive battle that wiped out the final pocket of resistance, a minor skirmish, a battle beyond Egypt's borders (a fortress of Narmer has recently been found in Gaza), or a ceremonial occasion remains unknown.

On the other side, Narmer, now wearing the red crown of Lower Egypt, marches in a victory procession to view decapitated prisoners. Accompanying him are his sandal bearer and his vizier or eldest son, who wears an animal skin and carries some as yet unidentified piece of regalia. Before them are carried four standards on high poles that may represent the royal ancestors or portray certain aspects of kingship. The identity of the enemy laid out in two rows is also debated. Whoever they are, they have been dealt with harshly: their arms are trussed, and between their feet lay their severed heads upon which have been placed their severed genitals in a display meant to humiliate completely and strike fear. Below, the serpentine necks of two captive lions frame the dish in which cosmetics were ground. These animals symbolize unity and portray the control and balance of the powerful, but opposing, forces vested in the king. The lowest register indicates that when necessary the king, as a raging bull, can trample town walls and gore inhabitants to maintain order, cosmic or otherwise.

—Renée Friedman

Altogether, these practices indicate the beginning of that hallmark of Egyptian civilization—mummification. Ours was an unexpected discovery in a working-class cemetery from about 3500 B.C., because the next evidence of mummification we have is five centuries later and from a king's tomb. Despite the early date, one can link such practices with the myth of the god Osiris, who was

killed and dismembered by his brother Seth, reassembled by his wife Isis, and then wrapped and mummified by the embalming god Anubis before attaining the afterlife as king of the underworld. For later periods, when there are texts to guide us, we know that in death all Egyptians became Osiris, and the mummification of the body was viewed as a reenactment of the events in Osiris' death. Here at Hierakonpolis we may have the very first manifestations of this belief.

Rich burials at Hierakonpolis contemporary with the working-class cemetery were explored from 1997 to 2000 by the late Barbara Adams of the University College London. The contrast between the two could not be more stark. The wealth of the elites is evident in the objects still to be found within their plundered graves—flint figurines, beautiful pottery, and funerary masks. Made of fired clay, these expressive masks with cut out eyes and mouth, finely modeled ears and nose, are curved to fit over the human head and attached by means of a thong passed through holes behind the ears. As Egypt's earliest funerary masks, they stand at the beginning of a tradition whose origins had long been a matter of conjecture.

The size and complexity of the graves also distinguishes the two cemeteries. One elite tomb was surrounded by a rectangular wooden post enclosure at least 30 feet wide and probably 65 feet long, while stout timbers along the edge of the grave itself suggest a substantial superstructure over it. This is the earliest example of above-ground funerary architecture in Egypt and it is clearly the forerunner of complexes constructed in stone centuries later, as at the Step Pyramid at Saqqara.

During her excavation of this funerary complex, Adams observed animal bones on the surface nearby. Investigating there last year, we found a large grave with a posthole at each corner suggesting it, too, had a superstructure above it. This was not, however, a tomb constructed for more of Hierakonpolis' great ones, but for an elephant. On the tomb floor we found the creature's massive pelvis,

A Protective Presence

One of the most intriguing burials found in the workers' cemetery at Hierakonpolis is that of a woman 40 to 50 years of age at the time of her death. When we cleared the sand away from the four complete pots by her head, we knew the burial would be an interesting one, but just how important we could never have guessed. Our first surprise was to find a stone palette in the shape of a bird nestled between her elbows and knees. Only three such palettes had been found previously in this cemetery and this one was the most elaborate, but our attention was riveted to the basket against which it rested. It was filled with remarkable objects, most of which we had never before encountered. Just beneath its lid was a string of stone pendants including one carved with the face of a bearded man. Then there was a set of tools made from animal bone, an ivory hair comb, chunks of galena (lead-ore or kohl) and ocher to be ground as cosmetics on the palette with polished stones, fine flint bladelets, a hook-shaped object of shell believed to be a forehead pendant, and rounded stones of unknown purpose. A leather bag contained resin and small clay cones resting within a mixture of plant remains, seeds, and chips of what may be imported cedar and juniper making up an aromatic incense mixture or potpourri.

The care and effort taken with this particular burial indicate the deceased was a very important woman, also evidenced by her special Mohawk hairstyle. While some of the objects in the basket are known from other sites, their purpose and function has long been a matter of speculation. If the collection has any coherence at all, it may represent a magic or medical kit. This woman may have been a witch doctor or wise woman, a suggestion supported by the number of children that were interred around her burial, indicating she was considered a strong protective presence even after her death. —RENÉE FRIEDMAN

tail, and foreleg still in place, proving the beast had been laid on its left side and covered both above and below with what must have been a vast quantity of fine fabric. A thick layer of blackened elephant skin and a substance that looked like bone but felt like soap, later identified as blubber, confirms that the elephant had gone to its grave fully fleshed. No expense was spared: this elephant was buried with grave goods including decorated and imported pottery, red ocher and green malachite cosmetics, a stone macehead, alabaster jars, a slate palette, an amethyst bead, and an ivory bracelet.

Study of the bones revealed the tomb owner to be a male African elephant 10 or 11 years old, the age at which males are expelled from the maternal herd and go off to live with other young bulls. Young and inexperi-enced, they can be captured and trained. Other burials in the same cemetery provide evidence for a royal menagerie, with smaller animals like baboons and even a wild cat captured and kept to accompany their owners to the next life. The effort and expense involved in the burial of this elephant, however, suggests that this mighty beast was not simply a trophy or an exotic pet, but a very special animal, perhaps the spiritual manifestation of the strength and power of a ruler—what later Egyptians called the *ka*.

In ancient Egypt, everyone had a *ka*, a creative life force that came into existence in the womb as a spiritual double of the person that lived on after the body died. The *ka* of the king was a special entity and *ka* statues, the focus of lavish funerary offerings, were sometimes buried with kings in special shrines.

How Big is the Elephant?

My first task upon returning to Hierakonpolis was to unwrap a sea of foil wrapped parcels containing the elephant bones. Although the bones are large, all the sediments were sieved and no bone was missed. Every parcel and every bag was inspected, the bones numbered and then sorted by type: head bones, teeth, toes, etc. This task completed, it was then time to take stock and inventory the finds. Despite the severe disturbance of the burial that had strewn matching bones all over the area, almost the entire animal was present. Of course some parts are more informative than others. Teeth are especially important.

There is a lot that we can learn from the dentition: it tells us what species we are dealing with and how old the animal was at the time of its death. Elephant molars look very different from the tooth types with which we are more familiar. Each molar is composed of a number of plates (lamellae) that are formed inside the jaw. These plates are firmly held together with cementum once the tooth becomes functional. From the shape of the teeth it is clear that our elephant is an African elephant and not an Indian elephant, which at that time still occurred in the Levant. The grinding surfaces of the molars in use show lozenge-shaped enamel ridges that are typical of the African species. In the Asiatic elephant the lamellae are closer together and almost parallel to each other.

The dentition also allows us to establish the age of the elephant. Adult elephants have a series of six molars on each side of the jaw, upper and lower. Peculiar to elephant dentition, however, is that throughout life there is continuous movement of the teeth. A molar that is formed at the posterior end of the jaw gradually moves forward toward the anterior end of the jaw where small fragments break off during use and are lost. The forward movement of a given molar results from the pressure exerted by newly formed lamellae behind the tooth. This continuous movement and replacement of teeth is a phenomenon that can be used to age the elephant. The number of plates and the size of the teeth tell us what molar we are dealing with and this in turn indicates how old the animal was based on tooth replacement studies on modern elephants of known age.

The number of plates and the size of the molars from the HK6 elephant reveals an animal that had its third molar in use. The fourth molar was almost completely erupted and about half of the plates were already worn. There is of course a certain individual variation in the eruption dates of the various teeth, but the fourth molar is generally considered to be fully in use in animals of 10–11 years old. At that age young elephants are still associated with their mothers, but they start being socially independent and soon reach puberty. Female teenagers of the same age still live in the maternal herd with their mother, grandmother, aunts, younger brothers, and sisters, but the male sub-adults are expelled from the herd and live in herds of young bulls.

The combination of the data on age and sex allows us to formulate a hypothesis on why this particular elephant was captured. Maybe the animal was an unexperienced young male that had walked off too far from the maternal herd with which it was still loosely associated, or maybe the animal had recently been expelled from the group and was on its own looking for a bulls' herd to join. In either case, the people who captured this individual must have been well aware of elephant behavior and group structure. At this age, an elephant can still be trained and this must have been necessary to bring it from its place of capture to Hierakonpolis.

An elephant of this age is already pretty tall and heavy with a shoulder height of approximately 2.50 meters (8.2 feet) and a weight of about 1,000 kilograms (2,200 pounds). Such an animal would have needed about 50 kilograms (110 pounds) of fodder per day. Elephants can feed on a wide variety of forage but tend to concentrate on grasses, herbs, and—in the dry season—on woody plants. However, in order to find out what our elephant was eating, we must enter the microscopic world of our archaeo-botanist Ahmed Gamal Fahmy where the evidence is small in size but the information it contains is almost as big as an elephant.

—Wim Van Neer

Although the *ka* was shown in human form later on, an animal form seems likely in the Predynastic period. We know the earliest kings all had animal names and derived their spiritual might from the power of the animal whose name they bore. King Scorpion and King Catfish (Narmer) are the best-known examples, but there were earlier kings who wrote their names with signs including bulls, elephants, and other powerful creatures. If the elephant is the *ka* or animal manifestation of an early ruler, this may help to explain discovery elsewhere in the elite cemetery of remains of a wild bull or aurochs buried on a funerary bed with grave goods. With time it may be possible to reconstruct from animal burials at Hierakonpolis a dynasty of early kings stretching father back into prehistory than ever imagined.

Taken together, the evidence of industrial production, temples, masks, mummies, and funerary architecture as early as 3500 B.C. is placing Hierakonpolis at the forefront of traditions and practices that would come to typify Egyptian culture centuries later. These discoveries may have knocked Narmer and his palette off their historical pedestal, but they confirm the central role the city played in the long development of Egyptian civilization. It is little wonder that for millennia the deified early kings of Hierakonpolis, called the Souls of Nekhen, were honored guests at the coronations and funerals of all pharaohs. ▲

HOLY ABYDOS

New investigations at ancient Egypt's premier pilgrimage site

by STEPHEN P. HARVEY

Modern visitors to the beautifully decorated temples at Abydos reenact the pilgrimage to this sacred place once made by many ancient Egyptians to fulfill their religious obligations—in much the same way that Jerusalem has attracted worshipers of many faiths for the past two millennia. For more than 3,000 years, Abydos was revered as a holy center where pharaohs and commoners participated in festivals and processions in honor of the gods, especially Osiris, ruler of the Egyptian underworld. Those who could afford it memorialized their visit to Abydos, building a permanent monument in stone or brick to house a carved stone stela depicting themselves and their families. This was their way of ensuring permanent participation in the sacred rituals of the town.

During most periods of ancient Egyptian history, people settled in the fertile plain around the temples and cemeteries, and made Abydos a bustling place. A large portion of the population must have been involved in supporting pilgrimage and worship. Similarly, villagers who live today among the ruins of Abydos hope for plentiful tourism to supplement their income from farming and small businesses. The forebears of today's souvenir sellers might have been vendors of votive offerings, amulets, and carved stelae upon which visitors could have their name and prayers for a good afterlife carved. Others would have made a living as accountants, priests, farmers, brewers, bakers, and craftsmen supporting the daily functioning of the enormous temple complexes erected to celebrate the relationships between rulers and the gods. The stone temples, which are today the attraction for tourists, were in ancient times largely hidden from view by enormous brick enclosure walls. Temple complexes in ancient Egypt would have been surrounded by great expanses of storerooms, workshops, offices, houses, gardens, and granaries dedicated to the functioning of the cults of gods and kings. The campus of a modern university provides a good idea of the diversity of activities which went on in an ancient Egyptian temple, which extended far beyond the sacred rituals carried out in the temple's innermost recesses. Temples stood at the center of local economies as well, and we know that the temple of Seti I at Abydos received revenue from far-off ventures such as mineral rights in Nubia, water rights on the Nile, and holdings of farmland throughout Egypt far beyond Abydos itself.

Ancient pilgrims sailing west from the Nile along manmade canals would have taken in views of a large ancient city built up around the fortress-like brick enclosures of numerous royal temple complexes built along the desert's edge. The sandy expanse of desert beyond these temples would have been dotted with brick memorial structures and tombs of those who chose to be buried here, as well as by royal stone shrines and chapels built as waystations along major processional routes. Reminders of the beginnings of Egyptian history 5,000 years ago would have still been as visible 3,000 years ago as they are today. These include the brick enclosure known as Shunet es-Zebib (a later Arabic name meaning the "Storehouse of Raisins"), as well as the reddish mounds concealing the tombs of Egypt's first kings.

Explorers and archaeologists working at Abydos since the early nineteenth century have largely focused on the stone remains left behind by the ancient pilgrims, particularly the impressive buildings inscribed and decorated by kings and the high elite. Despite the wealth of objects in museums worldwide that derive from Abydos, it is really only in the past 35 years that we have begun to understand the setting and context of most of this material, largely through excavation since 1967 carried out by the University of Pennsylvania-Yale University-Institute of Fine Arts, New York University Expedition to Abydos (co-directors David O'Connor and William Kelly Simpson) working closely in cooperation of the Supreme Council of Antiquities of Egypt. The Abydos Expedition has done much to place earlier discoveries in perspective, and has added volumes of new data on ancient activity at Abydos through exciting discoveries which in many cases rival those of Flinders Petrie's generation.

Each season of excavation since 1986 has seen important results that are of interest in isolation, but combined together enable a re-evaluation of one of Egypt's most important ancient centers. Clarifying the relationship between temple, town, and cemetery is a thread which connects much of the work done at Abydos in the past three decades. In a basic way, this means looking at the fugitive brick and organic remains of towns and cemeteries, and turning our attention to deriving information from careful excavation of badly destroyed ancient buildings which were often neglected by earlier archaeologists and explorers. Careful attention to traces of domestic activity, most often preserved in the architecture and trash of fallen-down brick and mud houses, is significantly fleshing out our picture of life in this ancient place.

In recent years at Abydos, re-excavation of sites that were identified and partially studied a century ago has repaid the effort. Modern approaches, techniques, and questions, as well as a more deliberate and meticulous approach, has revealed new detail about long-known parts of Abydos, and has revealed that far more remains to be found than one might expect. The discovery of battle scenes depicting Ahmose's defeat of the Hyksos is but one vivid example of the value of returning to a site thought to be long-since exhausted. Finally, entirely new and surprising discoveries await archaeologists at Abydos. Blocks of a lost temple

Digging in the Ancient Town of Abydos

Early town sites in Egypt are rarely excavated; Abydos provides an important exception. Today, the site of the ancient town is marked by the presence of massive mud-brick enclosure walls of various periods and by the exposed wall foundations from the 30th Dynasty (380–343 B.C.) temple of Osiris. In the early 1900s, Sir William Flinders Petrie excavated at the site, now partially covered by the modern village of Beni Mansur, and found a series of cult buildings connected with the town's chief temple and spanning more than two millennia.

Our excavations at the site, which began in 1991, have revealed a large area of mud-brick houses. Most were occupied from ca. 2300 to 2000 B.C.—the late Old Kingdom, through the First Intermediate Period, and into the early Middle Kingdom—and most underwent several phases of renovation. The houses produced large numbers of artifacts, including complete ceramic vessels, and well-preserved features, such as bread ovens and grain silos. Interestingly, the inhabitants of Abydos appear to have been rather prosperous during the First Intermediate Period, a time of weak or non-existent central administration that contemporary texts describe as highly troubled.

Nearby we found an open-air workshop where faience beads and amulets were made during the later Old Kingdom, the earliest faience production facility ever discovered in Egypt. We identified several faience kilns, some of which had been cleaned out and renewed several times. Although the workshop was near the remains of the late Osiris temple, there is no evidence that it was associated with the Old Kingdom temple, the exact location of which is as yet undetermined. We found little faience in contemporary levels in the nearby houses, and it is likely that the beads and amulets were produced primarily for use in burials elsewhere.

—MATTHEW DOUGLAS ADAMS

inscribed with the distinctive art style of King Akhenaten's reign have been found in the ruins of a temple of Ramesses II at Abydos, and archaeologist David Silverman believes these perhaps indicate an as-yet undiscovered shrine to the Aten existed at Abydos. No doubt, continued work by the combined Abydos projects, as well as by the German Archaeological Institute, will continue to yield new discoveries and insights at one of ancient Egypt's most important sacred and urban centers. ▲

SEAT OF ETERNITY

Excavations at Abydos reveal an elaborate funerary complex linking a deceased Middle Kingdom pharaoh to the god Osiris.

by JOSEF WEGNER

Nine miles west of the bustling Nile-edge town of Balliana, the limestone cliffs of the high desert form a vast bay that frames Abydos, known to the ancient Egyptians as Abdju. It was here that the first pharaohs were buried, ca. 2900–2700 B.C., and where in later millennia a cult center dedicated to the god Osiris, ruler of the netherworld, flourished. The site's modern name is el-Arabah el-Madfunah (literally, "the buried Arabah"), which aptly describes this windy, sandy place where ancient ruins lie deeply cloaked beneath the desert.

Abydos' most famous standing monument is the magnificent painted temple of Seti I (ca. 1306–1290 B.C.). South of it, the cliffs run eastward to within half a mile of the Nile floodplain, then turn abruptly southward creating a half-mile wide area of flat desert between the cliffs and the floodplain that is called South Abydos. Where they turn, the cliffs form a prominent projection that looms behind the Seti temple and cannot fail to draw the attention of anyone approaching Abydos from the Nile. It was here that Senwosret III (ca. 1878–1841 B.C.), a 12th Dynasty pharaoh of Egypt's Middle Kingdom (11th–13th Dynasties, ca. 2040–1640 B.C.) built a funerary complex, a "seat of eternity," designed to link himself in death with Osiris, lord of Abydos. When Senwosret III came to the throne, the power of the monarchy had lessened and regional governors were unchecked by a strong central authority. He reined in the governors and, having addressed the internal situation, campaigned to the south, securing the Nubian frontier.

Senwosret III's funerary complex was first identified between 1899 and 1902 by the Egypt Exploration Fund's David Randall-MacIver, Arthur Weigall, and Charles T. Currelly. They investigated a royal burial complex centered on a vast subterranean tomb, more than 600 feet in length, within a T-shaped mud-brick enclosure directly below the prominent projection of the cliffs, and an associated temple at the edge of the Nile floodplain. Their descriptions of the tomb and temple suggested the core elements of an extensive complex, but provided little substantive information about the site and its role in ancient Abydos, so I initiated excavations there in 1994. True to its name, "the buried Arabah" has exceeded all expectations I had when beginning work in the area. In addition to work on the temple and tomb of Senwosret III, we have discovered an extensive, well-preserved town that housed a community involved in maintain-

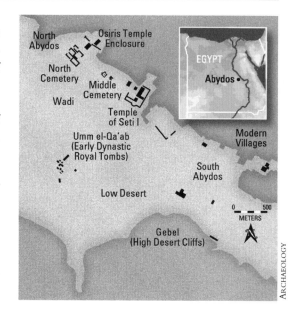

ARCHAEOLOGY

ing the deceased king's mortuary cult. The combination of elements—royal tomb, temple, and town—provides a rare opportunity to use archaeology to look at multiple facets of religious and social life in ancient Egypt.

Senwosret III's tomb has been something of an enigma since its discovery at the turn of the century. The first royal sepulchre to be built at Abydos since the burials of 1st and 2nd Dynasty kings nearly a millennium before, it is also Egypt's largest underground tomb. The burial chamber has an elaborate system of blocked passages, deep wells, and dead ends for protecting the royal interment. Nevertheless, it has rarely been mentioned since its initial discovery as anything more than a cenotaph, or symbolic burial place. In 1997, I decided to excavate a series of structures inside the T-shaped tomb enclosure. One of the assumptions I had made based on the early reports of Currelly and Weigall was that structures connected to the enclo-

Secrets in the Skeletons
Disease and deformity attest the hazards of daily life.

If Abydos is known for anything, it is its cemeteries. Thousands of people were buried here between the Predynastic period and Greco-Roman era, giving Abydos the potential to provide us with a portrait of a population over some 3,500 years. So far, we have excavated and analyzed more than 100 burials and huge concentrations of disturbed and commingled human remains. Already some surprising specimens have come to light.

In 1991, six burials of infants and young children were discovered under the floor of a house dating primarily to the First Intermediate period (2134–1797 B.C.). Three were newborns interred in pots. Another burial was of a newborn lying atop a toddler about 16 to 18 months old, both beneath a bowl. Cross-sections of this infant's arm and leg bones, which are normally tubular, showed no marrow cavities; they were completely solid! An infant without space for bone marrow cannot produce red and white blood cells and cannot survive. A rare congenital disease, this condition is known as osteopetrosis, or "stone bones."

Burials from the nearby Middle Cemetery provide further evidence of congenital abnormalities among the First Intermediate period residents of Abydos. One young woman displays a suite of anomalies—absence of permanent second premolar teeth, fusion of two bones in each foot, an extra right rib, an unusual sternum (breastbone), and only 23 vertebrae in her spine rather than the usual 24—suggesting she may have suffered from a congenital syndrome that contributed to her death in her late teens. A woman in her thirties buried nearby had an extra pair of ribs. Known as cervical ribs, they occur in only 0.5 to 1.0 percent of modern humans. Thus, I was astonished to find two cases in two-weeks' time. The abundance of developmental defects in the burials implies that the townspeople were exposed to as yet to be determined environmental hazards that triggered abnormalities or had a high degree of genetic relatedness.

Middle Kingdom burials from the North Cemetery have also yielded a wealth of information. Childhood nutritional stress was ubiquitous, contributing to short adult stature. Men averaged 5 feet, 5 inches tall, and women, 5 feet, 1 inch. People in their late teens show wear and tear in their skeletons associated with repetitive stress such as carrying heavy loads. Infectious disease was prevalent. Skeletal lesions in a few individuals indicate they had tuberculosis, which is not surprising for people living in settlements with a high population density and close proximity to animals harboring diseases or parasites.

Particularly disturbing are the remains of a Middle Kingdom woman who died in her early thirties. There are healed fractures in her left hand, right wrist, and both sides of her rib cage. Possible trauma to the right side of her jaw caused arthritis in her temporomandibular joint. Most of the fractures are well healed, and she lived long after those injuries. An infected fracture of her right wrist, however, was a more recent trauma. This type of fracture occurs in a fall when the outstretched hands absorb the impact. The final injury—a stab wound to her left ribs—was one she did not survive. Under magnification, the wound's edges show only slight evidence of new bone formation. This lack of healing indicates she died within days of the stabbing. The cut on her ribs and the pattern of fractures suggest the woman was battered throughout much of her life and, ultimately, may have been murdered.

—BRENDA J. BAKER

sure were permanent buildings that had been used after the completion of the tomb. In 1997, however, our work inside the enclosure exposed areas of razed and purposefully toppled walls. Surprisingly, all had been intentionally removed at the time of the tomb's completion. The enclosure and associated structures are the remnants of a vast construction site. I realized that the whole site had been methodically dismantled and left to be reclaimed by the desert sands—there was never intended to be any formal superstructure over the king's tomb once it had been completed. This evidence indicates that the tomb was intentionally built as a concealed royal burial place—the first in Egyptian history.

One of the most basic facts taught to students of Egyptian archaeology is that at the beginning of the New Kingdom (ca. 1550–1070 B.C.) pharaohs abandoned the royal pyramid in favor of the hidden tombs in the Valley of the Kings at Thebes. It is now clear that the tombs of the New Kingdom pharaohs are presaged by the underground tomb of Senwosret III at Abydos. The concept of the hidden royal tomb may have been developed again during the early New Kingdom by pharaoh Ahmose, who also constructed an underground burial place at Abydos, not far south of Senwosret III's. Standing on the site of Senwosret III's tomb in 1997, and wondering about the choice of location, I observed what I believe to be a crucial defining feature of the tomb site. Where the tomb is positioned, the line of the cliffs on either side recedes from view, leaving the visual impression of a massive natural pyramid looming over the tomb site. I believe this 700-foot-tall natural pyramid

served as the focal point for Senwosret III's tomb. This distinct profile of the cliffs of Abydos so visible to travelers approaching from the Nile may have been intentionally chosen by the architects of the complex as a substitute for the pyramid form that had marked tombs of pharaohs for nearly a millennium.

Despite discoveries around the tomb, the major focus of our current work is the remains of the mortuary temple and nearby town that housed the community involved in maintaining the mortuary cult. Both temple and town were destroyed in antiquity, but the desert environs and lack of significant later disturbance have preserved mudbrick architecture as well as organic remains and objects as delicate as unfired clay seal impressions in a condition rarely found for a period as remote as the Middle Kingdom. The recovery of thousands of impressions made with scarab and stamp seals bearing the names of people and institutions is especially significant as this evidence allows us to reconstruct institutional and administrative organization. Among the clay impressions are ones that bear the name of the Senwosret III complex: Enduring-are-the-Places-of-Khakaure-True-of-Voice-in-Abydos (Khakaure was the throne name of Senwosret III).

The temple included a multi-roomed limestone cult structure at its core, flanked by room blocks employed in the maintenance of the material and personnel involved in the king's mortuary cult. The core structure, profusely decorated with carved and painted relief, was built on a raised platform. Between 1994 and 1999, we devoted three seasons to excavating this temple, initially exposed and described by

Quest for Weni the Elder
An Old Kingdom cemetery yields the tomb of a "True Governor of Upper Egypt."

Everyone who has studied ancient Egyptian history knows the autobiographical inscription of Weni the Elder, an enterprising individual who lived during the 6th Dynasty (ca. 2323–2150 B.C.) of the Old Kingdom. The inscription, carved on a limestone slab, describes Weni's service under three kings, culminating in his appointment as governor of Upper Egypt. Scholars have hailed it as one of the most important texts from ancient Egypt and have used it to illustrate the rise of a class of self-made men in the Old Kingdom, whose upward mobility rested on their abilities and not on noble birth. The slab bearing the inscription had been excavated on behalf of the Egyptian government by Auguste Mariette in 1860, from a tomb in the low desert, in an area he called the "Middle Cemetery." Until recently, the precise location of the middle cemetery, and thus the location of Weni's tomb remained unknown.

In 1995, the Abydos Middle Cemetery Project, of which I am director, began surveying an area we believed to be the most likely candidate for Weni's burial. Our surface survey documented numerous 6th Dynasty ceramics and ruined mud-brick mastabas (surface chapels), including one we thought had promise as belonging to Weni. It was badly damaged, in a manner consistent with the removal of architectural elements, such as those taken by Mariette. Armed with that information and a survey of Mariette's finds in the Egyptian Museum, Cairo, we returned to the site in September, 1999.

Excavations revealed that the mastaba did not belong to Weni. Instead, the grave was that of a prince and chief priest, Nekhty, and it was the focus of a large complex and a number of subsiderary monuments constructed around it in the late Old Kingdom, the First Intermediate Period, the Middle Kingdom, and the Late Period. North of Nekhty's complex, however, lies an even larger structure, and it was here that we found the most compelling evidence

for Weni. In 1996, we had documented a mud-brick structure 53 feet long on its north face. Excavation revealed it to be a massive enclosure 95 feet on each side, 10 feet thick, and more than 16 feet high. Within this enclosure was a great burial shaft along with two smaller shafts, and the whole structure would have been filled with clean sand and roofed over to give it the appearance of being a solid mastaba. The mound is at the highest point in the Middle Cemetery, and its visual impact on inhabitants of the town below would have echoed that of the Early Dynastic funerary enclosures across the wadi in the North Cemetery.

Early in the season, we excavated inscribed relief fragments from this area bearing the name "Weni the Elder," and a title, "True Governor of Upper Egypt," the highest promotion recorded in Weni's autobiography. A damaged false door bore an inscription recording Weni's final promotion to the office of vizier. A series of shaft and surface burials, ranging in date from the later Old Kingdom to the First Intermediate period, lay north of this false door, suggesting that Weni's grave may have became the focus of a group cemetery—perhaps a kinship network.

Near the east face of the mastaba we discovered a massive limestone door jamb, inscribed for a vizier Iww. On one side of the jamb, a male relative presents offerings to Iww and is identified as: "His eldest son. The governor of Upper Egypt, Weni the Elder." So despite the stress laid by Weni on merit as the sole means of his upward mobility, it is clear that he was born into a powerful family—although he chose not to reveal this fact.

A small chapel with thick walls was attached to the east wall of the great mastaba. Entered through a narrow doorway, the chapel was originally completely decorated with painted reliefs depicting offering bearers; some had been removed by excavators and looters, others remained in situ. An exterior door jamb

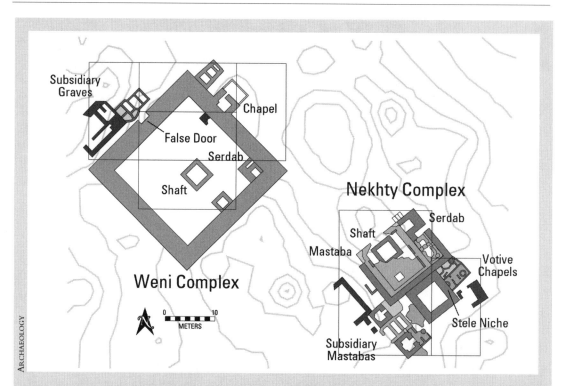

ARCHAEOLOGY

bore a standing representation of the tomb owner, preserved from the waist down. The top of the relief, which depicts Weni, is in the Egyptian Museum.

The final connection to Weni the Elder came from a rectangular serdab, or hidden chamber, in the southeast corner. This structure contained the deteriorated remains of more than 30 wooden bases for statues and statue fragments such as arms and hands, and limestone components of production scenes, including miniature basins capped with basket strainers for the production of beer. The best preserved and most significant artifact was a beautiful-

ly executed limestone statuette of the tomb owner as a young boy, identified by an inscription on its base as Weni.

We believe the half-destroyed chapel is the source of Weni's autobiographical inscription. Upon his promotion to vizier at the end of his career, he installed the false door recording that achievement along with another false door, found by Mariette. Both false doors align with the location of Weni's burial chamber, which lies north of the great shaft at a depth of more than 40 feet. We began excavation of the chamber this spring. —JANET RICHARDS

Randall-MacIver in 1899. We discovered thousands of architectural and decorative fragments that provide the basis for reconstructing the temple on paper. The building, which celebrated the association between

the deceased pharaoh and Osiris, contained statuary of the king as well as private dedicatory objects.

Deep deposits of pottery, refuse, and small objects discarded from the temple interior have been especially informative about how the temple functioned. In this rubbish, we discovered in 1997 and 1999 thousands of identical clay seal impressions that had been used to seal doorways inside the temple. All were stamped with the hieroglyphs: "Nefer-Ka," or Beautiful-is-the-Ka. This appears to be the ancient name of the temple; the *ka* referred to is the royal *ka* or spirit of the deceased pharaoh.

To maintain his mortuary temple at Abydos, Senwosret III created an economic endowment and built a settlement to house the personnel necessary to keep the temple operating in perpetuity. Entirely designed by royal architects, the town site, 1,000 feet south of the temple, is a beautiful example of early state-planning in Egypt. Houses are arrayed in blocks separated by regular streets, all laid out using the cubit measure (one cubit equals 1.72 feet). Our exposure of the town has revealed blocks of elite residences along the desert, occupying the highest elevation in the town, while lower-status housing extends down the sloping edge of the desert running below the modern level of the Nile floodplain. Limestone and wood were used for fittings such as door frames, thresholds, and columns, while the walls were of mud brick that was plastered. Townspeople included priests, administrators, and those involved in food production, such as the "keeper of the chamber of beer" or the "overseer of the cattle stalls," and unskilled laborers.

We have also examined about one-half of a palatial building measuring 175 by 270 feet that forms the town's northwest corner. In 1997, the discovery of dumps containing clay impressions stamped with seals bearing the names and titles of a series of mayors identified this structure as a mayoral residence. The only known house of a mayor from ancient Egypt, it provides an unusual chance to look at the organization and administration of a Middle Kingdom town. A core of nine rooms used as the main living space is surrounded by extensive blocks of supporting rooms and courtyards that were used for activities including storage, cooking, and administration. Huge granaries were integrated into the building and constructed behind it, showing that the mayor's residence served as a important central point for collection and distribution of grain. It appears probable that a major proportion of the wealth and administrative activity that sustained the town and mortuary complex was funneled through the mayor's residence.

As our excavations have expanded during four seasons we increasingly appreciate the manner in which the town, designed on papyrus by master architects, was adapted and changed after its initial construction. Carefully built doorways, colonnades, and courts of the initial plan were often altered for apparently mundane requirements such as expanding living space or storage areas or given over to use by animals. The ancient architects did not create a design that fully matched the needs of an evolving community and so the town was gradually altered to meet changing requirements of its population. As work continues at the site, I anticipate being able to reconstruct in considerable detail the development of this ancient community, whose inhabitants lived and worked in the town named for and dedicated to the deceased pharaoh Senwosret III. ▲

PART III:

MARVELS OF GIZA

THE SPHINX

Who Built it, and Why?

by ZAHI HAWASS AND MARK LEHNER

The Great Sphinx of Giza is more than a national symbol of Egypt, ancient and modern. It is an archetype of antiquity whose image has stirred the imaginations of poets, scholars, adventurers, and tourists for centuries. In recent years the Sphinx has become conspicuous for the rate at which it is deteriorating. Twice in the last decade stones fell off the statue: masonry veneer from the left hind paw in 1981, and a sizable piece of bedrock from the right shoulder in 1988. We have all heard that the surface of the Sphinx is flaking and crumbling while experts search for solutions. More recently, writer John Anthony West and geologist Robert Schoch have claimed that the shape and amount of surface erosion indicate that the monument is much older than Egyptologists think, originating not ca. 2500 B.C. but more like 5000 to 7000 B.C. The Sphinx, they believe, is the remnant of an advanced civilization that is otherwise lost to archaeology. The careful reader may well ask: if the surface of the Sphinx erodes so rapidly, why would we need it to be so much older to explain its present state of deterioration?

The Sphinx sits within the Giza Necropolis, which is dominated by the pyramids of Khufu (Cheops), Khafre (Chephren), and Menkaure (Mycerinus), pharaohs of the

4th Dynasty (ca. 2575–2467 B.C.). Each pyramid had a long causeway running from a Mortuary Temple at its eastern side, down to the level of the Nile floodplain, where a Valley Temple served as an entrance to the pyramid complex. The Sphinx is intimately connected to the Khafre causeway and Valley Temple, which suggests that Khafre had it built as part of his pyramid area. He was, after all, perhaps the greatest maker of statues of the Pyramid Age. There are emplacements in his pyramid temples for 58 statues, including four colossal sphinxes, each more than 26 feet long, two flanking each door of his Valley Temple; two colossal statues, possibly of baboons, in tall niches inside the entrances of the Valley Temple; 23 life-size statues of the pharaoh in the Valley Temple (fragments of several have been found with his name inscribed on them); at least seven large statues of him in the inner chambers of his Mortuary Temple; 12 colossal Khafre statues around the courtyard of his Mortuary Temple; and ten more huge statues in the Sphinx Temple. No other Old Kingdom pyramid temple floor plans indicate so many statues at such a scale. The Sphinx, the largest of all, was carved to a scale of 30:1 for the head and about 22:1 for the lion body.

The pyramid complex was a sacred port from which the god-kings embarked for the Netherworld. A harbor fronted each Valley Temple where, as some Egyptologists have suggested, the king's body was embalmed, or at least ritually purified, before the journey up the causeway to the Mortuary Temple, where the burial ritual was performed. The sacred ships for the funeral and the trip beyond were, in Khafre's case, symbolically docked outside the Mortuary Temple and

alongside the pyramid in the form of great boat-shaped pits quarried from the rock. In the case of Khufu real boats were buried in the pits. The complex served as a temple for the resurrected god-king after his funeral. Each pharaoh ruled as an incarnation of the falcon god Horus, king of the living. After death he transformed into Osiris, king of the dead. By the 4th Dynasty, kingship was also imbued with the life-giving power of the sun, an association symbolized by the pyramids, whose sides of newly polished white limestone must have shone brilliantly in the sunlight.

Officials and relatives of the pharaohs built their tombs in cemeteries east and west of the Khufu Pyramid, and southeast of the pyramids of Khafre and Menkaure respectively. Digging at Giza for nearly two centuries, archaeologists have retrieved an abundance of material dating to Egypt's Old Kingdom. Hundreds of tombs have yielded the mortal remains and artifacts of people who composed the state administration of the Pyramid Age. From hieroglyphic inscriptions we learn their names, titles, and family relationships. Both of us currently direct excavations south of the Sphinx where we are discovering evidence of the working class and everyday life of the society that built the Sphinx and pyramids. Our finds include a large cemetery of workers and petty officials, campsites, storage buildings, and bakeries. We have evidence of the ruins of an ancient city spread out along the valley for the entire length of the Giza Plateau. All this is part of the vast archaeological context of the Sphinx, one that allows us to see it and the pyramids as very human monuments, built by real people whose society we

Pat Remler

The Great Sphinx at Giza was built by the 4th Dynasty pharaoh Khafre.

can and do trace in the archaeological record.

The Sphinx is carved directly from the natural limestone of the Giza Plateau, which is part of the Mokattam Formation, formed from marine sediments deposited when waters engulfed northeast Africa during the Eocene period (see page 1 of color insert). According to geologist Thomas Aigner, formerly of the University of Tubingen and now with Shell International, as the sea retreated northward about 50 million years ago an embankment developed along what is now the north-northwest side of the plateau. (The 4th Dynasty builders aligned the three pyramids along this embankment from northeast to southwest.) As the water

receded, a shallow lagoon formed above a shoal and coral reef in what is now the south-southeast part of the plateau. Carbonate mud deposited in the lagoon petrified, becoming the layers from which the ancient builders quarried their limestone blocks, hauling them up the slope to build the pyramids.

The ancient quarrymen fashioned the Sphinx from the lowest layers, those lying directly on the harder reef. They cut deep into these layers, isolating a huge rectangular block of limestone within a horseshoe-shaped ditch. After sculpting the lion body, they levelled the natural rock floor between the Sphinx and the sides of the ditch. The ditch opened to the east where they had already cut out a broad terrace from the hard and brittle reef limestone. On the south end of this terrace the builders created the Khafre Valley Temple from huge blocks of limestone, some weighing more than 100 tons, that were quarried from the upper layers of rock corresponding to those of the Sphinx head and possibly higher. Stone quarried from the Sphinx ditch was taken to the east to build the Sphinx Temple.

The lowest stratum of the Sphinx is the hard, brittle rock of the reef, which we call Member I, following the work of geologist Lal Gauri of the University of Louisville. Since these layers slope about three degrees from northwest to southeast, Member I is found to a height of 12 feet at the rump and only two to three feet at the front paws. The surface of Member I has not appreciably weathered compared to the layers above it. Tool marks and small cuttings left by the original Sphinx builders still show in the Member I surface around the base and on the north side of the ditch. Most of the lion body and the south wall and the upper part of the ditch were carved in Member II, seven layers that are soft near the bottom, becoming progressively harder near the top. The neck is carved in the base of Member III, which is softer than the upper part from which the head is sculpted. Member III is good building stone, which is why the ancient Egyptians quarried most of it away from the area around the Sphinx. The durability of Member III is also why the details of the face are so well preserved after thousands of years, while the bedrock surface of the lion body has been ravaged by weathering.

We believe the Sphinx belongs to Khafre's Pyramid complex for several reasons. The south side of the Sphinx ditch forms the northern edge of the Khafre causeway as it runs past the Sphinx and enters the Khafre Valley Temple. A drainage channel runs along the north side of the causeway and opens into the upper southwest corner of the Sphinx ditch, suggesting that the ancient quarrymen formed the ditch *after* the Khafre causeway was built. Otherwise they would not have had the drain empty into the ditch. Khafre's Valley Temple sits on the same terrace as the Sphinx Temple. The fronts and backs of the temples are nearly aligned, and the walls of both are built in the same style of large limestone blocks with harder red granite added as a finish.

The Valley Temple was roofed; its chambers led via a corridor to the causeway that ran up the plateau to the Mortuary Temple at the base of the pyramid. The Sphinx Temple had an open central court surrounded by ten colossal statues of Khafre. Herbert Ricke, who carried out a detailed study of the Sphinx Temple from 1967–1970 for the Swiss Archaeological Institute, pointed out

THE PYRAMID COMPLEX WAS A SACRED PORT FROM WHICH THE GOD-KINGS EMBARKED FOR THE NETHERWORLD.

that its court was nearly an exact copy of the one in the Mortuary Temple (another reason to link the Sphinx to Khafre's Pyramid complex), except the latter had 12 colossal statues instead of ten.

The Sphinx Temple offers clues to the meaning of the Sphinx for its Old Kingdom builders. Ricke believed it was perhaps an early sun temple, and that the Sphinx was a depiction of the sun god. The court was surrounded by a covered colonnade whose roof was supported by 24 square granite pillars. There were two sanctuaries, one on the east and another on the west, aligned on the center axis of the temple. Ricke understood the arrangement as symbolic of the sun's circuit, the eastern sanctuary for the rising sun *(Khepri),* the western for the setting sun *(Atum),* with each colonnade pillar symbolizing one of the 24 hours of the day and night. If Ricke's interpretation is correct, the Sphinx Temple embodied the divisions of time. It is interesting to note that on the equinoxes the east–west axis of the temple aligns, over the Sphinx's shoulder, with the sun's setting point at the south foot of the Khafre Pyramid. This alignment is yet another element tying the Sphinx to the Khafre Pyramid complex and one of several indications that the Sphinx is not an ad hoc creation from a block of unused stone in a quarry of Khufu as some Egyptologists have suggested.

Other scholars believe the Sphinx represented the king, the incarnation of the god Horus, in a posture of giving offerings to the sun, Ra. The Sphinx Temple is built on a terrace eight feet lower than the floor of the Sphinx, which looked down into the temple's open court. Offerings would have been presented on an altar in the court, which was paved with white alabaster; the reflected light must have been brilliant if not blinding. In either interpretation, the association with the sun god might relate to a general Egyptian term for "sphinx": *shesep ankh Atum,* "Living image of Atum," known from later texts. Atum is the creator of the world in the Pyramid Texts, Egypt's oldest religious literature, inscribed on the walls of burial chambers in pyramids of the later Old Kingdom. All matter in the world evolved from his being, as did kingship, which he passed down through Shu (atmosphere), Geb (earth), and Osiris to Horus and to each living king.

Alan Gardiner, the great English Egyptologist, has noted that the question of whether the generic Egyptian sphinx represents the king as a powerful lion, a god as a powerful lion, a king in the leonine form of a god, or a powerful god revealed in the person of the king, is one that the Egyptians might have answered "all of the above." The creation of the Sphinx must have had something to do with an increased emphasis on the sun in royal ideology. After all, it was in the reign of Djedefre, who ruled briefly between Khufu and Khafre, that pharaohs adopted the title "Son of Ra."

We are left to speculate about the meaning of the Sphinx for its builders because there are no known Old Kingdom texts that refer to it or its temple. It is possible that inscribed blocks from the Sphinx Temple remain to be discovered. We know that granite from Khafre's temples and pyramid was reused in later monuments, such as the 13th Dynasty Amennemhet I pyramid at Lisht and the New Kingdom Ptah Temple at

Memphis. The absence of Sphinx Temple priests and priestesses from the hundreds of Old Kingdom tombs at Giza may be because the temple service was never begun, for it is clear that Khafre's builders did not finish his grand design. Although the Sphinx Temple was stripped of its granite casing and alabaster flooring in antiquity, anyone who visits it today can see cuttings in the floor at the base of the walls and court pillars, where the builders had finished covering with red granite casing the gigantic limestone core blocks of the walls. The colossal statues that graced the court fit into deep sockets cut into the floor in front of the court pillars. There are also sockets for the smaller pillars of the colonnade. Ricke pointed out that these traces indicate the workmen had finished the interior of the temple. They were about to begin work on the exterior when they quit the job.

In 1978 we found other evidence that Khafre's builders had not quite finished the Sphinx complex. By cutting the temple terrace lower than the Sphinx floor the builders left a tall vertical bedrock ledge. To the west, the ledge forms the north side of the Sphinx ditch, but here the quarrymen did not finish cutting the line. The point at which they stopped is just opposite the left forepaw. From here to the back of the ditch, the unfinished part is a rock shelf of decreasing width. Behind the Sphinx, the workmen were nowhere near finishing the outline of the ditch. When they stopped work they left a huge massif of hard Member I rock, separated by only a few yards from the rear of the Sphinx.

We cleared the top of this shelf and found rectangular humps, depressions, and channels.

This kind of pattern is found in many places at Giza where work was left unfinished; it shows how the ancient masons worked a stone surface from the top down. They would channel to isolate humps that they would then knock away with heavy hammer stones. The channels and depressions on the north ledge were filled with very compact sand and gypsum that we had to remove with small pick hammers. Embedded in the fill we found fragments of pottery, including half of a common 4th Dynasty jar used for beer or water, and hammer stones, one of which still had copper flecks on the end where it was used to strike a chisel. These must be bits and pieces of the builders' tools, abandoned when they stopped work cutting the north side of the ditch.

Later in 1978 we found more evidence of the builders in a small mound of debris in the northeast corner of the Sphinx ditch. Left by previous excavators, this mound supports a corner of the 18th Dynasty mud-brick temple of Amenhotep II, built 1,200 years after Khafre, when the lower Sphinx Temple was buried. One corner of the mud-brick temple juts out over the north ledge of the ditch and over the northwest corner of the Sphinx Temple. At the base of the mound we found three large limestone core blocks where the ancient builders left them as they were dragging them over to complete the core work on the corner of the Sphinx Temple. One block rested upon debris containing numerous pieces of 4th Dynasty pottery. The other two rested on a layer of desert clay, called tafla, that the builders used as lubrication for dragging. Just under the clay layer, we found cuttings in the rock floor that were used as lever sockets for maneuvering the ends of the blocks.

In what condition did the builders leave the Sphinx itself? It is our conviction that the head has never been recarved and that the features we see today are those left in the Member III rock. Much of the original surface of Member II has eroded, but if all the recesses were filled in it would make up a complete lion body. The lower part of the body, carved out of Member I, has weathered relatively little. Emile Baraize, the French engineer who supervised the clearing of the Sphinx in 1925–1926, found the front of the north hind paw bare of its ancient restoration veneer masonry, which had fallen off. Although the surface of the bedrock is rough and gnarled, the toes had a claw carved in relief, suggesting that, like the head, this paw was finished without a coating of masonry. During the recent removal of veneer masonry on the front paws, we saw claws carved in the toes of Member I. On the other hand, when Baraize, and again recently the Egyptian Antiquities Organization (EAO) restoration team, treated the south hind paw, they found an enormous gap in the rock (part of what we call the Major Fissure, which cuts through the entire Sphinx). The greater part of this paw was built almost entirely of large masonry blocks. However, the bottom of the toes are finished, each with a claw, in the sound rock of Member I that rises here only a couple of feet above the floor.

THE SPHINX WAS NEVER MEANT TO BE VIEWED FROM THE SIDE, AS MODERN TOURISTS SEE IT.

We had another good look at the bedrock surface of the Sphinx in a passage that we reopened in 1980 in the rump. Baraize found the passage, but closed it with limestone slabs and cement and never reported it. Part of the passage winds its way down into bedrock and comes to a dead end about 15 feet below floor level. The other part, covered by layers of ancient restoration masonry, is an open trench in the upward curve of the rump. The passage appears to be an exploration cut along the bedrock rump of the Sphinx and down below its floor made at a time when the rear had sanded up, but before the first restoration masonry had been applied. Profiles along the sides of the passage show that the curve of the rump is carved into Member I. The bedrock surface is rough and uneven but against its surface there is an inner casing of large blocks of fine quality limestone quarried from places like Turah, across the Nile Valley, which was used for finishes of stone buildings.

Would the builders have left serious gaps in the left hind paw and a fissure cutting through the body without filling or covering the flaws with masonry? It is possible that some of the larger blocks encasing the lower parts of the Sphinx may represent the beginning of a 4th Dynasty casing that masked these flaws. Alternatively, they may have left these flaws, considering the evidence that they quit before completing work on the sides of the ditch and on the temple. One should remember that the Sphinx was meant to be seen from the front—commoners saw it from outside the Sphinx Temple and priests from the temple court. It was never meant to be viewed from the side, as modern tourists see it, from the shoulder of the Khafre causeway, since the causeway was walled and roofed. The claws carved into the bedrock suggest that the builders did not intend to finish the lion body with a casing of fine limestone.

The Sphinx beard is relevant to this question. Captain Giovanni Battista Caviglia, a Genoese merchant-turned-explorer, found several fragments of the beard at the base of the chest in 1817, the earliest recorded modern excavation of the Sphinx. The fragments were part of a long braided "divine beard," curled at the end, that gods and deified kings wore. Statues of living kings sported short, square beards. Egyptologists have questioned whether the beard was original or a later addition. On both sides of the flat limestone that connected the outward thrusting beard to the chest, there were relief figures of a kneeling pharaoh offering up a gold collar toward the Sphinx's chin. This is certainly

Conversations: Master Of The Sphinx

A reluctant student, Zahi Hawass is now Egypt's archaeological ambassador. He recently spoke with ARCHAEOLOGY'S *executive editor Mark Rose.*

"I need the sand and the dust the way others need water and food. Archaeology is my life, my love, my passion," says the ebullient Zahi Hawass, who was recently made Director-General of Egypt's Supreme Council of Antiquities. He recently talked to executive editor Mark Rose about the challenges facing his country's heritage, his favorite visitor, and a buried statue's fateful stare.

How did you decide to become an archaeologist?

When I finished high school, I wanted to be a lawyer. I had seen lots of lawyers in the movies and admired them and wanted to be like them. At the University of Alexandria, I bought many law books. I started to read them and did not like it. I realized that I did not want to be a lawyer. I heard about a new department called archaeology. I had no idea what this was, but joined and stayed four years. During my study, I found that this was also not something that I really liked or wanted to do. After graduation, I joined the Department of Antiquities in 1968, but even then I wanted to change my career. I decided to become a diplomat, studied for one year, and passed the written exam, but couldn't pass the oral one, and went back to my old job. A year later, I was assigned to an excavation in the Delta. One day, I found a tomb with a beautiful statue. I took a brush and started to clean the sand from the statue—at that moment, I found that the eyes of the statue were looking at my eyes and this touched my heart. I had found my love, and my love is archaeology!

Is the ancient past relevant to the average Egyptian?

When I first started my career, most Egyptians were not interested in ancient history, but over the past 30 years I have had the privilege to witness the ever-growing interest in our extraordinary past. Now, Egyptians come to hear my public lectures and are intrigued with our new discoveries. We are currently developing a program to teach children archaeology. We are copying 20 artifacts from the

New Kingdom in style (1550–1070 B.C.). One of these connecting pieces is lost, but an examination of the other in the Cairo Museum shows that it is like a broad plate, only about one foot thick, with the backside roughed up to assist bonding with gypsum mortar. So the beard seems to be an addition. On the other hand, the limestone of all the beard fragments seems to match the natural limestone layers of the monument's chest and neck, as though the beard was once carved from the rock like the rest of the Sphinx. It is certainly possible that the beard was originally carved from the bedrock along with the head, but had detached, fallen, and broken to pieces. During a later restoration, the pieces that connected it to the chest were recut as thin slabs and reattached.

Another feature that suggests the divine beard may be original is the prominent boss, or bump, formed in the bedrock near the bottom center of the Sphinx's chest. The boss only makes sense as a support for a long divine beard. The sculptors could not extend the thin supporting plate below the curl to the base of the chest, nor could they simply leave the beard and its plate suspended. Both

---

Egyptian Museum, and these copies will be exhibited permanently at every primary school in Egypt.

Your television program "Mysteries of the Pyramids" was popular and there's a new one coming up. Do you worry that people will think archaeology in Egypt is only mummies and pyramids, or they'll see you as a showman, not a scholar?

I am highly respected in my field and love my work. However, I have a wonderful talent. I can speak to the people and bring ancient Egypt into their homes and their hearts. I have been able to inspire young people all over the world, who now dream of being Egyptologists. I receive the most wonderful letters [from them] all the time and always answer them. My lectures, media coverage, and my books have stopped New Age notions [about the past] because people see that the true history is more exciting and incredible than anything they could imagine. By showing people the magic and mystery of Egypt, tourism has increased, and this is vital to the economy of Egypt.

What challenges face Egypt and its cultural heritage today?

One challenge concerns the guards protecting our monuments. Can you imagine that the guards only make about $20 a month? These underpaid men are in charge of guarding the world's greatest monuments. This is ridiculous! How can we expect the average guard to care about the monuments when they don't even know the history of what they are protecting and they make such a small salary? We need to open an institute to train qualified people to protect the monuments. Also, we must establish the best program in the world to train our future archaeologists. Egypt's treasures—our world's shared heritage—must be left in safe and competent hands.

You've shown many famous people around Giza, from Bill Clinton and Tony Blair to Dr. Ruth. Who was your favorite?

I felt honored to give Princess Diana a private tour of the pyramids. She had a beautiful smile and was fascinated by the pyramids. To prepare for her visit, she studied for one month at the British Museum. She was very well read and asked many interesting questions. It was a wonderful visit.

options would have made the beard even more fragile, so they left a thicker column of rock from the bottom of the beard to the base of the chest. Once again, the study of the beard suggests that the original sculptors did attempt to finish their work in the rock.

It appears certain that where the bedrock was sound enough—the head, the north hind paw, and the bottoms of the other paws—the builders did finish the sculpture in the natural rock. They probably intended to fill in flaws, like the Major Fissure, and may have intended and begun to build over weaker rock with a casing. During recent restoration work we found very large blocks of fine limestone casing at the northwest rear haunch. Unless we get better exposures of the lower part of the core body, there is just not enough evidence to determine whether the 4th Dynasty builders began, or how far along they had progressed, filling in and building up with masonry the weak spots in the Sphinx. It is clear that they simply stopped work shortly after Khafre's death to turn their attention to the monuments planned for his successor, Menkaure.

What we call the Phase I restoration was begun, we believe, by the 18th Dynasty Pharaoh Thutmose IV about 1,100 years after Khafre. Phase I filled in the body after the surface formed from Member II bedrock had eroded drastically into a profile of deep recesses and rounded protrusions. At that time, large chunks of natural rock were about to fall off the Sphinx, just as in recent years. At the upper part of the rump, just above the rump passage, we found a wide ledge formed by the curve of Phase I slabs. Baraize filled the space between these slabs and the bedrock body with cement and

packing in 1926. But as the photographs of his work show, a huge boulder of bedrock had detached from the body in ancient times and was held in its tipped position by the Phase I restoration slabs. There is another large boulder shored up by Phase I masonry at the rear left haunch. Phase I limestone is fine-grained and homogenous—characteristic of Turah or Turah-quality limestone. In time the Phase I stone developed a brown patina that has protected it against weathering.

Prior to the recent restorations, we could trace the Phase I cladding from the rump to the front of the Sphinx where it wraps around both of the shoulders. A wide gap at the center of the chest corresponds to the remains of a small open-air chapel tucked between the forepaws. The chapel was built by Thutmose IV, whose 12-foot tall, 15-ton granite stele is the center piece of the back wall, for his intimate worship of the Sphinx which towered above as a symbol of primeval kingship. Thutmose IV was the son of Amenhotep II, who built a mud-brick temple dedicated to the Sphinx as Horemakhet, "Horus in the Horizon," at the north east corner of the Sphinx ditch. Views of the chapel were drawn by the British Consul, Henry Salt, when it was first excavated by Caviglia in 1817. Ramesses II placed smaller stelae that show him worshiping the Sphinx on the side walls of the chapel. The north wall stele had toppled inward, but the south wall stele was intact. The floor was paved with masonry of small slabs dating to the Greco-Roman period (Phase III). On the paws, this masonry covered the larger Phase I blocks that encased the bedrock. Much of the chapel was stripped away soon after Caviglia's dig. The two Ramesses stelae were taken to the Louvre, the north side wall was dismantled, and someone removed all the Phase I masonry from the inner side of the north forepaw, exposing the soft crumbly bedrock. It was possibly Caviglia who removed the front walls and the pavement between the paws. What remains today are the lower part of the south side wall and the granite "Dream Stele" of Thutmose IV.

The stele is named for the hieroglyphic story it tells. Thutmose was a prince, apparently not the crown prince, when he went on a hunting expedition in the vicinity of Giza. Thutmose calls the Sphinx "this very great statue of Khepri," god of the rising sun; and *"Khepri-Ra-Atum,"* the sun god in all its aspects—rising, zenith, and setting. Thutmose also calls the Sphinx *Horemakhet,* "Horus-in-the-Horizon" as do the inscriptions in the Amenhotep II Temple and on numerous smaller New Kingdom stelae. The name may derive from the fact that in the early 18th Dynasty, anyone approaching from Memphis to the southeast saw the huge head of a pharaoh, the incarnation of Horus, framed by the two large Giza Pyramids, which look like the two mountains in the hieroglyph for "horizon," but here the Sphinx head substitutes for the sun disk.

Toward noon Thutmose sleeps in the shadow of the monument. The Sphinx appears to the prince in a dream and tells him that its body is in a ruinous state and that the sand of the desert has invaded its lair. It then offers Thutmose the throne in exchange for his assistance. What must have been a good part of the remainder of the story is missing, but Thutmose did indeed become king in the year 1401 B.C. At the top of the stele he etched a double scene of himself giving offerings and libations to the Sphinx, dated to the first year of his reign.

The relationship between the Dream Stele and the Phase I masonry is preserved only on the south side of the stele, where the wall that framed the stele and fit against the inner curve of the forepaw remains. The forepaw was reconstructed with Phase I masonry that filled in a deeply eroded recess in the lowest layer of Member II in the side of the paw. Phase I masonry could be traced to the right shoulder where it runs up against the chest and also fills in deeply eroded recesses. The broad patterns and structural details suggest that all this masonry, while laid in a definite sequence, was part of a single project that cloaked and reconstructed the body, covered the south forepaw, and framed Thutmose's Stele.

In addition to the continuity of the masonry, there are other small clues that Phase I belongs to the 18th Dynasty. The lower part of the south side wall of the chapel that supported the Ramesses Stele is still intact against the side of the forepaw in front of the Dream Stele. This wall was built of small limestone blocks set around a core of taller and broader limestone slabs arranged as an open box and filled with brown sandy soil and limestone chips. Underneath a layer of modern (1926) sand within the core we found ancient debris that earlier excavators had not cleared. This debris consisted of brown sandy soil containing many small chips and fragments of red granite and flint; worked pieces of sandstone or sand consolidated with gypsum that had been used as polishers or abrading tools; many small fragments of Egyptian blue pigment adhering to a gypsum backing; several fragments of ceramic jars with more traces of Egyptian blue on their interior walls; abundant traces of red paint powder; and minute traces of yellow pigment. Although the wall later supported the 19th Dynasty stele of Ramesses II, this debris suggests it was made in the 18th Dynasty when the Dream Stele was erected. The granite chips may derive from inscribing the stele and beveling its outer edge. The red, blue, and possibly yellow pigment traces may be left from the 18th Dynasty painting of the Sphinx following its reconstruction with Phase I masonry. We found small bits of Egyptian blue in the interstices of all the masonry configurations between the Dream Stele and the Phase I masonry against the chest.

Thutmose also covered the sides of the Sphinx ditch with massive mud-brick walls more than 24 feet tall that encircled the Sphinx like a giant cartouche. Baraize removed most of this covering in 1926, but he left a section along the north ledge of the Sphinx ditch. When Selim Hassan continued excavations in 1936, he removed more of these walls, and recorded that some of the bricks were stamped with the name of Thutmose IV.

There were at least two more major restorations of the Sphinx in antiquity. We believe Phase II dates to the 26th Dynasty, ca. 664–525 B.C. It is essentially a patching of the Phase I exterior. The face of the Phase I slabs was cut back over large areas to lay in the new, smaller slabs. Elsewhere the Phase II masons laid their casing directly over the original surface of Phase I. The limestone used in Phase II is the same fine-grained,

homogeneous limestone employed in the first restoration. Phase III, of Greco-Roman date (332 B.C.–A.D. 395), patched and replaced parts of the Phase I and II veneer using small blocks of white, relatively soft and friable limestone.

Although Baraize's excavations were never published, 226 photographs of the 11-year project record the enormous deposits and superimposed architecture that surrounded the Sphinx precinct in New Kingdom, Late Period and Greco-Roman times. A complete Phase I reconstruction in the 18th Dynasty fits with the picture of the site that emerges from the Baraize photographs and from the notes of Pierre Lacau who was then Director General of the Egyptian Antiquities Service. A whole complex of terraces, enclosures, resthouses and temples was built as a kind of royal national park upon and around the ruins of the 4th Dynasty stone temples. The New Kingdom inscriptions call the Sphinx enclosure, *Setepet*, "The Chosen." Given the fact that Amenhotep II, Thutmose IV, and Ramesses II made dedications to the Sphinx in the first year of their reigns, the name of the site must refer to its role as an image of primeval authority that could ordain and confirm the privileged position of princes and kings. The Amenhotep II Temple in the northeast corner of the Sphinx ditch was only a part of this 18th Dynasty arrangement. In this period a broad viewing platform and stairway fronted the Sphinx. This was the first and lowest of several platforms, each with shrines and podiums, built one on top of the other, until the latest in the Roman period. There was a royal villa attached to the front of the Khafre Valley Temple. Tutankhamen built a kind of resthouse behind the Valley Temple that Ramesses II took over, superimposing his name over those of Tutankhamen and his queen, Ankhesenamen, on the doorway. In addition to the massive enclosure walls around the Sphinx ditch, Thutmose IV built a bastioned wall forming an enclosure that encompassed a much wider area. Emerging from their resthouses over by the old Khafre Valley Temple, royalty descended a stairway to the broad viewing platform that covered the Sphinx temple. After ritual stops at shrines and podiums, another stairway led down into the heart of the cult—the small chapel at the chest of the giant statue. Standing there, a newly ascended king like Thutmose or Ramesses might feel that he could trace his descent to ancient kings like Khufu and Khafre, indeed, back to the primeval god-king, Horus-in-the-Horizon, whose image towered above him.

There is strong evidence that, at the same time as they reconstructed the Sphinx, the New Kingdom pharaohs quarried granite from Khafre's pyramid complex. Granite casing blocks, probably from Khafre's pyramid, have been found in the New Kingdom Ptah Temple at Memphis. The Overseer of Works for Ramesses II was brazen enough to leave his name, May, etched into the rock walls beside the northwest corner of Khafre's Pyramid. Uvo Hölscher, who excavated the Khafre temples in 1909, found a New Kingdom mud-brick ramp on the south side of Khafre's Mortuary Temple that was probably used for hauling away its granite pillars and sheathing. Finally, the 15-ton Dream Stele of Thutmose IV is a reused lintel from a doorway in one of Khafre's temples. The back of

the Dream Stele has the same ledge that forms the top of the door frame, and the same two sockets and pivotholes for a standard Egyptian double-leaf swinging door. Since the bottom sockets of such doors were cut into the bedrock floor of the temples we can determine where Thutmose got the lintel. The space between the sockets only fit three doors in the Khafre Mortuary Temple, one being the entrance to that temple from the causeway. This suggests an explanation for the similarity of the Phase I restoration blocks to Old Kingdom masonry. The range of thickness of the Phase I slabs match very closely those slabs that form the walls of the Khafre causeway. Only a small part of these original walls are left near the exit of the causeway from the Valley Temple. It is very possible that Thutmose had his workmen utilize Khafre's causeway blocks to restore the Sphinx. After they had worked their way up the causeway taking blocks for the Sphinx, Thutmose had them drag the lintel from the Mortuary Temple to the forepaws where he erected it to inscribe the story of his selection by the Sphinx for the throne of Egypt.

It may seem strange and inappropriate to us that these New Kingdom pharaohs would strip the complex of Khafre to repair the Sphinx. But each pharaoh was just another incarnation of Horus, each had his own special Horus-name, Khafre's being User-ib, "Strong Hearted." As part of a revitalization of the kingdom and the cult of kingship during Egypt's period of greatest empire, Thutmose IV may have seen nothing wrong with recycling material from the ruins of Horus User-ib to give rebirth to the Sphinx as Horus-in-the Horizon. ▲

BUILDERS OF THE PYRAMIDS

Excavations at Giza yield the set-tlements and workshops of three generations of laborers.

by ZAHI HAWASS AND MARK LEHNER

For centuries adventurers, scholars, and tourists have been drawn to the wonders of Giza—the pyramids of Khufu, Khafre, and Menkaure, the Sphinx, and tombs of Old Kingdom nobles (2551–2152 B.C.). But what of the workers and artisans who built these great monuments?

When the Greek historian Herodotus visited Egypt in the fifth century B.C., he was told by his guides that 100,000 workers had labored for 20 years to build Khufu's pyramid. Even 20,000 workers, a number closer to recent estimates, is comparable to the populations of large cities in the Near East during the third millennium B.C. An enormous support system must have existed at Giza for at least 67 years, the combined minimum lengths of Khufu, Khafre, and

Menkaure's reigns. Such support would have included production facilities for food, ceramics, and building materials (gypsum mortar, stone, wood, and metal tools); storage facilities for food, fuel, and other supplies; housing for workmen, their families, and priests responsible for services in pyramid temples that remained in use long after the main building phase was completed; and a cemetery for workers who died in the employ of the royal necropolis. Officials and noblemen continued building tombs at Giza until about 2152 B.C. A smaller permanent settlement must have existed there for more than 350 years until the final abandonment of the necropolis.

From hieroglyphic inscriptions and graffiti we infer that skilled builders and craftsmen probably worked year-round at the pyramid construction site. Peasant farmers from the surrounding villages and provinces rotated in and out of a labor force organized into competing gangs with names such as "Friends of Khufu" and "Drunkards of Menkaure." Each gang was divided into groups Egyptologists call phyles (the Greek word for tribe). There were five phyles, whose names, always the same in each gang, bear some resemblance to ancient Egyptian nautical terms such as "great" or starboard and "green" or prow. Each phyle was divided into groups of ten to 20 men, each named with single hieroglyphs sometimes representing ideas such as "life," "endurance," and "perfection."

The pyramid projects must have been a tremendous socializing force in the early Egyptian kingdom—young conscripts from hamlets and villages far and wide departing for Giza where they entered their respective gangs, phyles, and divisions in scenes reminiscent of the most dramatic cinema spectacles of Cecil B. de Mille.

For years the support facilities, residential areas, and cemeteries of the workers who created and maintained the pyramids remained among of the least explored areas of ancient Egypt. But 20,000 people, or three generations of pyramid builders, cannot have disappeared without leaving a trace. Where to look?

We began our search for the pyramid workers' settlement by checking two areas that had been previously investigated: an enclosure west of the Khafre pyramid dubbed the "workmen's barracks" by British archaeologist Sir William Flinders Petrie and a large sandy basin south of the pyramids where the Austrian scholar Karl Kromer discovered a huge deposit of settlement debris.

The so-called workmen's barracks is an area nearly 1,470 feet long and 261 feet wide enclosed by walls built of irregular limestone pieces set in clay. A series of 73 galleries, each about ten feet wide and 94 feet long, is attached to the enclosure's west wall. The space in front of the galleries was left open, and today an asphalt road winds through it. At the end of the last century, Petrie found fragments of many statues in the area of the galleries. Despite such finds he concluded that the galleries had served as lodging for about 4,000 men, presumably those who worked year-round during construction of the pyramid. On the surface there are many pieces of granite and other hard stones brought to Giza for use as architectural blocks and statuary, but where wind had blown away the overlying sand we found no evidence that people had lived here over an extended period—no heaps or scatters of sherds, ashes, or animal bones. Furthermore, the galleries resemble storage magazines attached to New Kingdom royal residences and temples such as those at Tel el-Amarna and Thebes.

In 1989, with Nicholas Conard of the University of Tübingen, we began investigating the galleries. The sand within contained stones that had tumbled from the walls and little else. It appeared that they had been emptied in ancient times, perhaps when work moved south to the pyramid complexes at Saqqara and Abusir at the end of the 4th Dynasty, or later, at the end of the Old Kingdom, when Giza was abandoned as an elite necropolis. Another possibility is that the galleries were never fully used. We did find bits of copper, unworked feldspar, malachite ore, and several small flints. Then, in the last days of our excavation season, we found deposits at the front of two of the southernmost galleries, close to the Menkaure pyramid. They included potsherds, animal bone, and bits of wood charcoal, barley, emmer, and lentils—all material we might expect in a residential area. They also contained pieces of small royal statues and limestone human and lion figurines, suggestive of a sculptor's workshop. One figurine shows a king wearing the tall conical crown of southern Egypt and a shendyt, or kilt. The eyes and beard are painted black. Where one arm is missing at the shoulder, the cut is flat and smooth. Small sculptures with carefully truncated limbs have been interpreted as sculptor's models or trial pieces. Another set of fragments belongs to a figurine of a king wearing the conical crown set against a pillar and a projection that may represent the roof of a colonnade. The whole was painted red and stippled black to imitate granite. The sculptor had begun recarving the face and one side of the crown when the head broke off. This small piece must be part of a model for a granite statue in front of a set of pillars around an open court, with a surrounding covered colonnade whose ceiling projects out over the pillars and statues. There are two temples at Giza that had exactly these features: Khafre's mortuary temple against the eastern base of his pyramid and the temple, probably also built by Khafre, directly below the paws of the Sphinx.

These finds suggest that the enclosure was for storing and working materials and not a barracks for large groups of workmen as Petrie believed. Furthermore, the layout— an open courtyard in front of covered galleries or magazines—corresponds with later wooden models and tomb scenes depicting workshops.

Next we turned to a sandy basin enclosed by peaks and ridges about 1,500 feet south of the Khafre pyramid. Here, in the early 1970s, Kromer excavated part of a huge dump of settlement debris—pottery, animal bones, mud bricks, flints, ash, fishhooks, and mud sealings impressed with the names of Khufu and Khafre—just behind a knoll on the basin's northeastern edge. We found no evidence for a settlement in the bottom of the basin, where the bedrock, a claylike marly limestone (tafla), is covered only by a thin layer of loose sand. The ancient builders may have deepened the basin by quarrying for tafla, a major component of construction ramps, roads, and embankments at Giza, and any settlement here would have been razed in the process. This might explain the debris excavated by Kromer.

We then considered what clues the landscape might offer. A valley separating the Mokattam Formation, on which the pyramids stand, from the Maadi Formation to the south probably served as the route by which building materials, such as granite from Aswan and fine limestone from quarries across the Nile, were brought to Giza. The valley leads to a horseshoe-shaped quarry about 1,000 feet south of the Khufu pyramid, from which a volume of stone comparable to that in the pyramid was removed. This quarry, as well as areas later mined by Khafre and Menkaure, is filled with millions of cubic yards of limestone chips, gypsum, sand, and tafla. This debris, probably remains of construction ramps, was dumped into the quarry after the pyramid was finished. There may also have been a large harbor at the mouth of the valley.

On the south side of the valley a colossal stone wall, called the Heit el-Ghorab (Wall of the Crow), extends about 600 feet eastward. In 1991 we dug into the sand and stone construction debris banked against it and found that the wall was about 33 feet high and more than 39 feet thick at its base. At the wall's center is a gate, 23 feet high and capped with enormous limestone lintels, that seems to have been planned as a great entrance to the Giza necropolis but was never finished. The wall itself may have been intended to separate the sacred precinct of the pyramids and Sphinx, the great stone mastaba tombs, and the temples to the north from whatever lay to the south, perhaps the workers' settlement.

South of the wall is a 39-acre desert tract that, except for a soccer field built in the 1980s, has not yet been engulfed by Cairo's expanding suburbs. In 1934 the Egyptian archaeologist Selim Hassan found mud-brick walls and pottery in test trenches here. Since 1988 we have opened three major excavations in this area. Just off the northwest corner of the soccer field, Scottish archaeologist Fiona Baker has supervised the investigation of a building complex, the centerpiece of which is a structure made of irregular limestone pieces and mud mortar with tafla-plastered walls and floors. The building is rectangular, about 29 by 20 feet, and is divided by a wall running through its center. On each side of the wall is a series of low rectangular pedestals, also made of limestone and mud. In a narrow trench in front of these pedestals, potsherds and small stones laid in circular patterns suggest sockets for poles.

The building resembles granaries depicted in Old Kingdom tomb scenes. During this period small silos were set up on benches, platforms, or pedestals to keep the grain away from rodents and dampness and to allow its extraction from outlets at their bases. The pole sockets in our structure suggest the presence of a light canopy, which is often shown covering rows of silos in late Old Kingdom granary depictions.

There are, however, problems with this interpretation. Silos shown in Egyptian art are round and made of mud brick, but the pedestals are rectangular and bear no traces of mud brick. Furthermore, there are faint traces of thin walls on some of the pedestals, apparently forming the sides of storage compartments of some kind. Toward the end of the 1991 season Baker began excavating some largely intact compartments attached to the building's back wall similar to those that once stood on the pedestals. Other discoveries led us to postpone further investigation of this area, but this year we will return and hope to learn whether these compartments contain clues about the building's use.

For now the most important clues to the purpose of this structure are small, hard bits of mud with hieroglyphic impressions broken from seals on doors, bags, and pots and deposited with other trash in a corridor along the east side of the building. When the mud seal was fresh, a small cylinder carved with the name of the king, an official, or an institution was rolled over it. When the seal was broken, the pieces were discarded. Several sealings from this building mention the Wabet of Menkaure. Wabet, from the root for "pure," is a term for an embalming workshop. Our building complex does not look like a place for making mummies, but a wabet dealt with many things relating to the tombs and their burial goods. In its workshops, metalworkers, joiners, painters, and draftsmen created tomb furnishings for the royal household and its dependents.

INSIDE EACH ROOM LAY A PILE OF BROKEN BREAD POTS DISCARDED AFTER THE LAST BATCH OF BREAD WAS REMOVED 4,600 YEARS AGO.

Just before our 1991 season a backhoe digging sand for use in a construction project dug through ancient walls, floors, and thousands of potsherds about 820 feet northeast of the pedestal building. In cleaning out the trench we discovered a series of stone-rubble wall foundations. The walls had formed about a dozen rooms attached to the larger mud-brick sides of a massive building. The backhoe had dug into the southeast corner of the building, just missing two complete ceramic vats situated in two adjacent, parallel rooms. Excavation of these rooms, under the supervision of Michael Chazan of Harvard University, made it clear that they were bakeries like those shown in Old Kingdom tomb scenes and models.

Each bakery was about 17 feet long and eight feet wide. Inside each room lay a pile of broken bread pots discarded after the last batch of bread was removed 4,600 years ago. Though Egyptian written records attest at least 14 types of bread, we found only small and large bell-shaped pots and flat trays. Along the east wall were two lines of holes in a shallow trench, resembling an egg carton. The holes had held dough-filled pots while hot coals and ash in the trench baked the bread. A hearth in the southeastern corner would have been used to heat pots before they were inverted as lids on dough-filled containers in the trench. Low walls of stone and mud around the rooms were used as counter space to store pots and finished loaves.

The bakeries were attached to the back of a much larger mud-brick building enclosed by a five-foot-thick wall. In 1991 we cleared part of this building's floor. Here we found low partition walls and two sets of low benches, formed of black alluvial mud and covered with tafla, separated by troughs. In one place we found a group of complete jar stands and lids (but no jars) on the benches. In early 1995, with John Nolan of the University of Chicago, we explored the building further, exposing more sets of long parallel troughs and benches, which ran across the floor of a broad court and continued north and west beyond our excavation. Embedded in the floor were fibrous bits and pieces, the remains of fish gills and fins. Only by dripping consolidant on these bits could we excavate them with a small spatula and preserve their forms. We found more fin, gill, and cranial parts strewn along one of the benches and tiny bits of fish bone in the dirt filling the troughs.

We believe this was a food processing installation. We found an assortment of flint blades and flakes alongside the benches. These may have been used for cleaning fish that were then dried and perhaps smoked and salted. One of the benches had been built around two limestone bases for wooden columns. Tomb scenes show meat being dried on lines tied between small columns. The thin deposit covering the floor, in which the fish bone was embedded, had an ashy quality, but we have not found an obvious place where the fish might have been smoked. Old Kingdom depictions of fish processing cataloged by Dina Faltings of the German Archaeological Institute show that head, tail, and skeleton were left intact when fish were splayed and gutted for drying. Men clean the fish on small tables with short legs while they sit on what might be mats or low platforms similar to our benches. In modern Egypt, dried and salted fish are left with head, skeleton, and tail

intact, so the bones could have been left by people eating fish. The extent of fish processing suggested by the troughs and benches, if that is what they were used for, could indicate that the Egyptians were preserving and storing fish, perhaps in the jars whose lids and stands we found.

Food-processing facilities are labeled Per Shena in tomb scenes. The name translates as "House of Shena," but the exact meaning of shena, written with the sign of a plow, is uncertain. Used for storerooms, bakeries, and breweries, it probably meant something like "commissary." A sherd from the bakery discard deposit was inscribed with this term. We began to think that we were excavating royal institutions, perhaps a Wabet and a Per Shena. The period is Menkaure, judging from numerous seal impressions that bear his name. As yet, however, we had no direct evidence that these were part of the workers' support facilities. And we were still left with the question, where are the residential areas?

In the past century there were only a few scattered villages along the foot of the Giza plateau, the closest being Nazlet es-Samman, only 800 feet from the Sphinx. Since then Cairo has expanded to the foot of the plateau. In the late 1980s construction began on a sewage system for the entire Cairo west bank, including Nazlet es-Samman, now a suburb with a population of 300,000. The system required 73 core samples to test subsurface conditions for a network of sewage-pipe trenches (notably one along the Mansouriyah Canal, which runs through the town's center) to be dug into the valley floor east of the Sphinx and pyramids.

As expected, ancient remains were encountered, including the causeway of the

Khufu pyramid complex, and basalt slabs probably from Khufu's valley temple, which had not previously been located. The work, monitored by Michael Jones and members of the Inspectorate of Antiquities at Giza, revealed a continuous layer of mud-brick buildings starting about 165 feet south of the Khufu valley temple and extending about one mile to the south. Among the artifacts are thousands of fragments of everyday pottery, bread molds, cooking pots, beer jars, and trays for sifting grain and flour. Medium to large pieces of charcoal suggest that trees once grew here. East of the south side of the Khufu pyramid the Mansouriyah Canal trench cut through limestone-lined mud-brick walls of a building more than 300 feet long. Was this a palace? Unfortunately the section view of a sewage trench—less than ideal for archaeology and quickly refilled so the project could continue—leaves such questions unanswered.

In 1994, elsewhere in Nazlet es-Samman, a large stone wall was found 1,600 feet east of the Khufu valley temple during construction of new apartment buildings on Zaghloul Street. Toward the south side of the lot the builders scooped out the wall's limestone and basalt blocks and poured a cement foundation before antiquities inspectors were notified. A long segment of the wall spared from construction has a 13-foot-thick limestone foundation. While it is generally straight, neither side is finished with a straight edge or flat face. This is the foundation for a wall that rose with inclined sides of basalt and limestone slabs encasing a core of packed limestone chips. About 50 feet above sea level, the foundation is at a level corresponding with the base of the Wall of

the Crow and the basalt blocks of the Khufu valley temple.

Two years earlier, in 1992, Michael Jones documented parts of basalt and limestone walls in the sewage trench along Zaghloul Street, about 820 feet south and 656 feet north of the long stretch of wall in the building lot. These could belong to parts of the wall running east-west, perpendicular to the north-south stretch, the whole perhaps forming a rectangular enclosure.

The wall must be considered in relation to two conflicting views of the ancient landscape along the foot of the Giza Plateau. These views are crucial to understanding the size of the settlement underneath the modern town. Settlement deposits were observed in the sewage trenches or indicated in core drillings over 494 acres. Could this immense area have been entirely covered with housing? Or was much of the land taken up by waterways, flood basins, or desert-edge lakes that might have served as harbors for the three pyramid complexes?

One approach to reconstructing the ancient landscape begins with the assumptions that the massive amounts of building materials used in constructing the pyramids were brought close to the plateau on waterways and that the completed pyramid complexes had harbors located at the front of their valley temples. In 1995 and 1996 the Giza Inspectorate cleared the area in front of the Khafre valley temple, revealing evidence that there had been such a harbor. The lower ends of two ramps leading to the temple are pocked with small dishlike depressions that may have been caused by water erosion. Tunnels run beneath each of the two ramps, and under the southern ramp there is a well shaft, still covered by a limestone slab with holes for lifting ropes, that even today holds groundwater. The tunnels were originally framed by mud-brick walls that formed a channel. If water rose to the bottom of the ramps during the Nile's annual flood, it might have filled the channel and the tunnels. If it rose higher, it would have been discharged through a narrow channel between mud-brick platforms in front of the Sphinx temple, heading east to where digging and drilling in the 1980s indicated a buried drop-off. When the water receded, some would have been retained in the tunnels and the well shaft, perhaps for use in a symbolic water crossing in a funeral ritual associated with the valley temple. If this explanation is correct, it indicates water once reached the front of the valley temple. The buried drop-off may be the edge of a harbor basin.

Before the sewage project began, we investigated the possibility that subtle depressions and older channels in the relatively flat floodplain might indicate a pattern of canals, catchment basins, and harbors from the time of the pyramids. The level of the floodplain has been built up by ten or more feet of fine silt deposited during annual inundations since the time of the Old Kingdom, but this may not have obliterated the outlines of the deepest and largest ancient features. For example, in his reconstructions of the ancient landscape around Memphis, David Jeffreys of the University of London has confirmed that an old channel called Bahr ("river") el-Libeini may be the remains of the main Nile channel or a major branch during the Old Kingdom. Although today the Libeini is a small stagnant stream, the contours of the valley floor show it runs in a

subtle but unmistakable wider channel.

At Giza, surface contours indicate a large depression extending about 975 feet east-west and 1,650 north-south from the Khufu valley temple. The edge of the depression is defined by a contour line 59 feet above sea level. The Zaghloul Street wall lies along the east side of the depression. Perhaps the wall ran along the edge of a basin that served as the Khufu harbor. The orientations of the Zaghloul Street wall and some of the older canals and basins correspond, reinforcing the possibility that the modern floodplain reflects the ancient terrain. The wall is oriented slightly more than 15 degrees west of true north, roughly parallel to an old drainage canal called Zerayet Zaghloul and part of another old canal farther east called Collecteur el-Sissi. If one extends the line of the wall south for another 1,300 feet, it reaches the higher ground of the modern village of Nazlet el-Sissi, where more Old Kingdom settlement remains were found during the sewage project.

This orientation is nearly perpendicular to a second low area outlined by the 59-foot contour south of Nazlet el-Sissi, extending 650 feet between Amirah Fadya Street and part of the Collecteur el-Sissi, which turns to the west, heading toward the Khafre valley and Sphinx temples. Could these features be vestiges of a flood basin and channel that fed the harbors of Khafre and Menkaure, or a general delivery area at the low southeastern corner of the Giza plateau in use when the Khufu pyramid was under construction? Or is it only coincidence that the two major low areas are directly in front of the Khufu and Khafre valley temples? The picture of ancient land use and pyramid locations at

Memphis and Saqqara, south of Giza, suggests that the pyramid builders took advantage of desert-edge lakes and discharge channels. We might expect settlements to cluster on adjacent high ground and levees.

A second, conflicting view implies that the present landscape has little or nothing to do with the floodplain along the base of the Giza plateau during the 4th Dynasty. The suggestion that the Zaghloul Street wall marked the edge of a basin that could have served as the Khufu harbor might lead us to expect that it was built on higher ground that remained dry during the inundation, or perhaps along the levee demarcating the basin. Yet there is no obvious high spot in the surface contours today that corresponds to the position of the wall, which is actually six to ten feet lower than the lowest part of the depression east of the suggested location of the Khufu valley temple. Of course the wall could have been built on low ground during the dry season, and risen above the shallow inundation waters. The results of the core drilling and sewage trenches, however, led Michael Jones to suggest that the low desert sand extended a considerable distance east of the Khafre and Menkaure valley temples in the Old Kingdom, as it did in the early part of this century. This can be seen in old photographs, such as those of Harvard archaeologist George Reisner, taken before the spread of

the modern city. The sewage trenches showed an Old Kingdom settlement built upon this sand, making it appear unlikely that any waterway could have penetrated all the way to the valley temples, which would have had only symbolic harbors, docking places for the "voyage to the netherworld."

The evidence needs to be studied further before either picture is accepted. A possible resolution of the two views might depend on stratigraphy and chronology. There is abundant evidence at Giza, as noted by previous excavators, including Reisner, that huge amounts of sand blew over the necropolis before the end of the Old Kingdom. In our own excavations we have seen how wind filled the galleries west of the Khafre pyramid with clean sand and dumped nine to 15 feet of sand over the tombs of the working class south of the Wall of the Crow. The sand came down fairly quickly, preserving the small mud-brick tombs in excellent condition. Drilling cores at Memphis indicate that a massive deposit of sand blew in from the west over Old Kingdom and possibly Archaic levels (2900–2150 B.C.), areas below the Saqqara Plateau. When the German Archaeological Institute excavated the 5th Dynasty Userkaf Sun Temple at Abusir, they found that the temple's causeway had been rebuilt after an enormous deposit of wind-blown sand had banked up against it. The

> THERE IS ABUNDANT EVIDENCE AT GIZA...THAT HUGE AMOUNTS OF SAND BLEW OVER THE NECROPOLIS BEFORE THE END OF THE OLD KINGDOM.

evidence points to a more humid climate in the early Old Kingdom, and to greater aridity, desiccation, and windblown sand beginning perhaps as early as the middle of the 5th Dynasty. At Giza, this could have resulted in the filling and choking of the 4th Dynasty harbors and waterways, which were subsequently built over with the housing of those who served the temples after the pyramids were completed. From Reisner's excavations, we know that in the late Old Kingdom the front of the Menkaure valley temple housed tax-exempt priests and caretakers who eventually invaded the temple's court itself, turning it into a kind of sacred slum.

Ancient texts actually give us two names of settlements at Giza, the "Northern Gerget [settlement] of Khufu" and the "Southern Tjeniu [bank marker or cultivation border] of Khafre." Perhaps the settlement extending from the Khufu valley temple, glimpsed in the sewage trenches, is the Northern Gerget of Khufu. We now believe the area south of the Wall of the Crow is a good possibility for the Southern Tjeniu of Khafre. A royal residence probably would have been one of the major components of an Old Kingdom pyramid town. No palace of this date has ever been found, although one of the Archaic period was partially cleared at Hierakonpolis. According to David O'Connor of New York University's Institute of Fine Arts, New Kingdom palaces tended to be to the right and in front of the exit of major temples, as at Karnak and Amenhotep III's festival city of Malkata. The east-west temple axis and the north-south palace axis represented the axes of the world. The Old Kingdom pyramid complexes were essentially temples, and our excavation area is just to

the right and in front of the valley temple entrances of the Khafre and Menkaure pyramid complexes. Some substantial institution in this area seems to be hinted by the colossal stone Wall of the Crow with its large gateway, which forms the northern boundary of the area.

Old Kingdom food-production facilities, unlike modern bread factories and fish-packing plants, probably did not exist in isolation. Production in early Egypt was household based. Barry Kemp of the University of Cambridge has pointed out how Middle and New Kingdom granaries, bakeries, breweries, and carpenters' and weavers' shops were attached in modular fashion to large households, even when they were part of overarching "state" (that is, royal household) enterprises. Smelly fish-cleaning and smoky bread-baking must have been downwind from any large household or institution to which such activities might have been attached. Our bakeries are attached to the southeast corner of an unidentified large mud-brick building. The prevailing wind is from the northwest.

As we prepare for our next season and think about the greater context of our bakeries, a question has begun to influence our strategy—to what large household were our food production installations attached? Although we began with a search for the commoners of the pyramid workforce, by the time this article appears we will hopefully be south of the Wall of the Crow, clearing away the modern overburden in order to open a series of excavation squares over a wide area north and west of the bakeries, with both the common workers and palaces of the Giza kings on our minds. ▲

TOMBS OF THE PYRAMID BUILDERS

by Zahi Hawass

The cemetery of the laborers and artisans south of the Wall of the Crow at Giza reveals as much about life and death in the Old Kingdom as do the burials of royalty and noblemen north of the wall and surrounding the pyramids. A lower part of the burial ground contains small mud-brick and stone-rubble tombs of common laborers, while a higher tier is dominated by larger, decorated stone tombs of craftsmen and overseers.

The first tomb came to light during our 1988–1989 excavation season, just uphill from a building with sealings bearing the name Wabet (embalming workshop) of Menkaure of the 4th Dynasty. Formed of mud brick and stone rubble, the tomb was built after the structure's west wall collapsed, suggesting that it, and much of the rest of the lower cemetery, might be later. The tomb had two vaulted chambers, each containing a human skeleton in fetal position, head north and face east, with no grave goods. A small gabled opening in the east wall of each chamber was blocked by stone rubble retaining walls. At first we thought the chambers might have been granaries, later reused for poor burials. We did not know that hundreds of tombs lay buried in the sand around us.

On April 14, 1990, the chief of the pyramid guards, Mohammed Abdel Razek, reported that an American tourist was thrown from her horse when the animal stumbled on a previously unknown mudbrick wall. The next month we began excavating there, only about 100 feet from the 1988–1989 American excavation area. The wall turned out to be another tomb, with a long vaulted chamber and two false doors through which the dead could commune with the living and receive offerings. Crude hieroglyphs scrawled on the false doors identified the tomb owners as one Ptah-shepsesu and his wife. At the back of the chamber were three burial shafts for the man, his wife, and, probably, their son. In front of the tomb was a square courtyard with low walls of broken limestone. While not in the style of the great stone mastaba tombs of nobles beside the pyramids, Ptah-shepsesu's tomb and courtyard are grand in comparison to others that we uncovered around it. Pieces of granite, basalt, and diorite, stones used in the pyramid temples, had been incorporated into the walls. Such material suggests that some tombs in the cemetery may belong to the pyramid builders or succeeding generations of workers who made use of stone left over from the construction

THE TOMBS COME IN A VARIETY OF FORMS: STEPPED DOMES, BEEHIVES, AND GABLED ROOFS.

of the pyramids, temples, and tombs. Attached to Ptah-shepsesu's tomb were small shaft burials of people who probably worked under him.

The lower part of the cemetery contains about 600 such graves for workmen and 30 larger tombs, perhaps for overseers. The tombs come in a variety of forms: stepped domes, beehives, and gabled roofs. Two to six feet high, the domes covered simple rectangular grave pits, following the configuration of the pyramids in an extremely simplified form. One small tomb featured a miniature ramp leading up and around its dome. Could the builder have intended it to represent the construction ramp of a royal pyramid? Other tombs resemble miniature mastabas with tiny courtyards and stone false doors with the names and titles of the deceased inscribed on them.

We dubbed one remarkable grave the "egg-dome" tomb. An outer dome, formed of mud brick plastered smooth with tafla, enclosed an egg-shaped corbelled vault built over a rectangular burial pit. What was the meaning of the double dome? Egyptologists believe that mounds left inside large 1st Dynasty (ca. 2920–2770 B.C.) tombs and rock protrusions in the pyramids themselves represented a primeval mound of creation that magically ensured resurrection. The same idea may have been in the minds of those who built this tomb.

We have found many false doors and

some stelae attached to these tombs. Inscribed in crude hieroglyphs, they record the names of the people whose skeletons lay below: on one stela a man named Khemenu is depicted sitting at an offering table in front of his wife, Tep-em-nefret; a false door is inscribed with a woman's name, Hetep-repyt (Offering to Presiding Goddess, or Hathor); another belongs to Hy, priestess of the goddess Hathor, Lady of [the] Sycamore Tree, and her son Khuwy. These women, the wives of the pyramid builders, served as priestesses of Hathor, goddess of love, music, dance, and the necropolis, and a counterpart to Horus, god of kingship.

Small stone figurines in a rectangular niche attached to a little mud-brick mastaba represent a household of these workers. One of the statuettes depicts a woman seated on a backless chair with her hands on her knees. An inscription on the chair identifies her as Hepeny-kawes. She wears a black wig with hair parted in the middle and reaching to her shoulders. She has large eyes typical of Old Kingdom depictions. Her body is well modeled under a white robe that covers all but her feet. A second statuette, badly damaged by salt, depicts her husband, Kaihep. A third statuette is of a kneeling woman, possibly a servant, grinding grain. She wears a beaded collar and a short black wig with carefully rendered locks held in place by a band of white cloth tied around her forehead. Her arms and shoulders suggest the strength needed for her work, and she wears a red bracelet on her right wrist. The oval grinding stone has traces of red paint, probably to represent granite, and is painted white in the middle to indicate flour, which is being collected into a sack held between her

legs. The statues represent a simple household: man, wife, and servant. Alternatively, the woman grinding grain could be the wife doing her own chores. Similar sets of statues representing larger households include potters, butchers, brewers, and bakers.

Women in the lower cemetery were either buried with their husbands or in tombs next to them. Two women, however, were found in their own tombs. One is identified as Repyet-Hathor, a priestess of Hathor, by an inscription on a small offering basin placed in front of her false door. The tomb of the second, named Nubi, was considerably grander than Repyet-Hathor's. She was a priestess of Neith, goddess of Sais, an important cult center in the Nile Delta. Two especially interesting burials were those of dwarf women, little more than three feet tall, one of whom who had apparently died in childbirth—we found the skeleton of an infant within her remains.

As we excavated the lower cemetery, we came upon a ramp that ran up the slope to the west to an upper level of burials. These upper tombs, so far numbering 43, are larger and more elaborate than those of the lower part of the cemetery. Many are completely rock-cut or have a stone facade in front of a low cliff face. Others are built of limestone and mud brick in the mastaba style. We found higher quality artifacts and statuary in these tombs, and the painted and inscribed false doors are also superior to the scrawled texts from the lower tombs. The skeletal remains, as in the lower cemetery, were found in shafts two to three feet underground, most in a fetal position, and many in wooden coffins.

Titles such as "overseer of the side of the

pyramid," "director of the draftsmen," "overseer of masonry," "director of workers," and "inspector of the craftsmen" are another indication that those buried in the upper part of the cemetery were of higher status than the people buried below. Perhaps the most important title we found was the "director for the king's work." I believe some of these are the tombs of the artisans who designed and decorated the Giza pyramid complexes and the administrators who oversaw their construction. We need, however, to analyze the names, pottery, and decoration of the tombs further to be sure they date to the time when the Giza pyramids were being built.

The ramp from the lower cemetery led to a small rectangular court with walls of broken limestone. A shorter second ramp, its floor paved with mud and stone rubble and its side walls made of limestone and granite pieces, extended from the west wall of the court. Pottery from this ramp and court dates to the end of the 4th Dynasty and the beginning of the 5th Dynasty. A mud seal impression found in the bed of the ramp can be read as Djed-khau (Enduring of Diadems), one of the official names of Djedkare Isesi, a pharaoh of 5th Dynasty. This is another chronological indicator suggesting that much of this cemetery dates a few generations after the kings who built the Giza pyramids.

At the end of the second ramp were two

WOMEN IN THE LOWER CEMETERY WERE EITHER BURIED WITH THEIR HUSBANDS OR IN TOMBS NEXT TO THEM.

children's graves with no offerings, and a mastaba tomb. Built of limestone and similar in style to those of the 4th Dynasty, the tomb had six burial shafts sunk through it and two false doors carved on its eastern face. The ramp from the lower cemetery reminded us of the causeways that led from the Nile Valley to the pyramids on the high plateau. The court could be compared to the pyramid valley temple, while the mastaba took the place of a pyramid.

Attached to the mastaba tomb, but separate from it, was a room cut into the bedrock. Inside was an intact burial with pottery. A niche carved into the west side of the chamber was sealed, except for a small hole, with limestone, mud bricks, and mud mortar. We peered inside and were astonished to see the eyes of a statue staring back at us. We were even more surprised when we removed the mud bricks and limestone blocks and found not one but four statues: a large one in the middle flanked by two smaller ones to the right and one to the left. There had been two on the left, but one, made of wood, had disintegrated into a heap of powder. All four surviving statues are inscribed, "the overseer of the boat of the goddess Neith, the king's acquaintance, Inty-shedu." It seems that Inty-shedu was a carpenter who made boats for the king or the goddess Neith. The middle statue shows Inty-shedu at the time of his death. The standing statue to the right and the surviving statue to the left depict him in his youth. The seated statue to the right depicts him at an older age. The artist carved each face to indicate a stage of life and sculpted muscles and shoulders to show corresponding strength. This group of five statues recalls the five statues of the pharaohs placed in most pyramid temples from the time of Khafre to the end of the Old Kingdom.

One of the more interesting artisans' tombs is that of Nefer-theith and his wife Nefer-hetepes. Though simple, it is inscribed with beautiful hieroglyphic writing. It contains three limestone false doors and stelae with the name of the deceased, his two wives, and his 18 children. The false doors of his tomb are unique for their scenes of grain grinding, and bread and beer making. Was Nefer-theith the supervisor for the bakery recently found in the plain below? There is also a list of feast days and offerings for the deceased including bread, beer, birds, and oxen. On the false door of Nefer-hetepes, his primary wife, is a list that records offerings of natron (a combination of baking soda and salt used in mummification), sacred water, oil, incense, kohl (black eye paint), 14 types of bread, cakes, onions, beef, grain, figs and other fruits, beer, and wine. Nefer-hetepes held the titles "one known by the king, weaver." On the third false door, two stelae represent Nefer-theith standing while below him a man makes beer and another person pours it into four jars.

The tomb of a man named Petety has a unique form with three open courts. In contrast to Nefer-theith and his wives, Petety and his wife Nesy-Sokar are depicted separately. A priestess of the goddess Hathor, Nesy-Sokar is also described as beloved of the goddess Neith. She is shown standing on the doorjamb of the chapel in the traditional pose: one arm raised on her breast and the other behind her back. She wears a tight dress that leaves the breasts bare, a collar, and a broad bead necklace. Her hair is divided in front and behind her shoulders. The artist has portrayed her with her head tilted slightly up and forward, perhaps a realistic touch caused by wearing the wide, tight collar. This gives her face a bold and confident expression enhanced by the darkly outlined eye. On either side of the entrance to the tomb we found hieroglyphic curses to protect it. Petety's curse reads:

> Listen all of you!
> The priest of Hathor will beat twice any one of you who enters this tomb or does harm to it.
> The gods will confront him because I am honored by his Lord.
> The gods will not allow anything to happen to me.
> Anyone who does anything bad to my tomb, then [the] crocodile, [the] hippopotamus, and the lion will eat him.

Based on the pottery, names, and titles found in association with the tombs, the cemetery was begun as early as the reign of Khufu in the 4th Dynasty and continued through the end of the 5th Dynasty, from ca. 2551 to 2323 B.C. The cemetery probably extends across the escarpment above the low desert plain where we have found production and storage facilities. It seems to be an Old Kingdom version of the New Kingdom (ca. 1500–1163 B.C.) cemetery at Deir el-Medineh, where workers who excavated and decorated the royal tombs in the Valley of the Kings were buried. We believe that so far we have found only 20 percent of the tombs buried under the sand along this slope.

None of the workers was mummified, a prerogative of royalty and nobility, but many tombs in this cemetery contained skeletal remains that tell us much about the lives of these people. Study of the remains by Azza Sarry el-Din and Fawziya Hussein of Egypt's National Research Center reveals that males and females were equally represented, mostly buried in fetal positions, with face to the east and head to the north. Many of the men died between age 30 and 35. Below the age of 30 a higher mortality was found in females than in males, a statistic undoubtedly reflecting the hazards of childbirth. Skeletons from the great mastaba cemetery west of the Khufu pyramid, in which members of the upper class were buried, reflect a healthier population whose women lived five to ten years longer than those of the artisan and worker community. Degenerative arthritis occurred in the vertebral column, particularly in the lumbar region, and in the knees. It was frequent and more severe than in the skeletons from the mastaba cemetery. Skeletons of both men and women, particularly those from the lower burials, show such signs of heavy labor.

Simple and multiple limb fractures were found in skeletons from both the lower and upper burials. The most frequent were fractures of the ulna and radius, the bones of the upper arm, and of the fibula, the more delicate of the two lower leg bones. Most of the fractures had healed completely, with good realignment of the bone, indicating that the fractures had been set with a splint. We found two cases, both male, that suggested amputation, of a left leg and a right arm. The healed ends of the bones indicate that the amputations were succesful. Few other cases of amputation have been recorded in Egyptian archaeology. Depressed fractures of the frontal or parietal skull bones were found in skulls of both males and females. The parietal lesions tended to be left-sided, which may indicate that the injuries resulted from face to face assault by right-handed attackers.

We should contrast the evidence of the tombs and of medical treatment with the notion that pharaohs used slave labor to build the giant pyramids, an idea as old as Herodotus. The scenario of whip-driven slaves received support from the biblical account of Moses and the Exodus and the first-century A.D. historian Josephus. In our era, Cecil B. de Mille's galvanizing screen images reinforced this popular misconception. The pyramid builders were not slaves but peasants conscripted on a rotating part-time basis, working under the supervision of skilled artisans and craftsmen who not only built the pyramid complexes for the kings and nobility, but also designed and constructed their own, more modest tombs. ▲

DATING THE PYRAMIDS

How tiny organic bits in the ancient gypsum mortar offer evidence of age as well as clues to the fabric of Egyptian life.

THE DAVID H. KOCH PYRAMIDS RADIOCARBON PROJECT

It was an odd sensation climbing over the Great Pyramid, looking for minute flecks of charcoal or other datable material, loaded down with cameras, scales, notebooks, and forms with entries for sample number, site, monument, area, feature, material (charcoal, reed, wood, etc.), matrix (gypsum mortar, mud brick, etc.), date, time, notes on details, extracted by, logged by, photograph numbers, and sketches. It was 1984 and the Edgar Cayce Foundation, named for an early twentieth-century psychic who claimed that the Sphinx and Khufu's Great Pyramid were built in 10,500 B.C., was paying for the analysis of our samples (see page 1 of color insert). Old friends and supporters of the deceased psychic had visited Giza in the early 1980s and several of them were willing to put their beliefs to the test by radiocarbon dating the Great Pyramid. Archaeologists believe it is the work of the Old Kingdom

4th Dynasty society that rose to prominence in the Nile Valley from ca. 3000 B.C. and built the Giza Pyramids in a span of 85 years between 2589 and 2504 B.C.

When the Great Pyramid was built is not an open question for Egyptologists because they have a detailed chronological framework—based on king lists, regnal dates of the pharaohs, and the ancient Egyptian civil calendar—with which they date this and other monuments. The civil calendar, used for all official dating, had three seasons: Akhet or Inundation, Peret or Sowing and Growing, and Shemu or Harvest. Each season had four 30-day-long months with five additional days after the end of Harvest for a total of 365 days. The Egyptians used their civil calendar to date most events, but the astronomical year, the time it takes the earth to orbit the sun, is actually 365¼ days and the Egyptians did not compensate for the extra ¼ day as we do with Leap Year. So the Egyptian calendar constantly slipped about one day every four years and a whole month every 120 years. As a result, the civil seasons often had no relation to the natural events after which they were named, but every 1,460 years the civil and astronomical years would coincide, and the official New Year's day would come back to the traditional beginning of the year marked by the rising of the star Sirius (called Sothis by the Egyptians) in the eastern horizon just before daybreak. We know from the Roman author Censorinus that the rising of Sirius and New Year's day coincided in A.D. 139, and from this we can calculate that it also coincided in 1317 B.C. and 2773 B.C. Hieroglyphic texts that record risings of Sirius anchor the Egyptian New and Middle Kingdom regnal years and civil dates to our own calendar.

> ## THE EGYPTIAN CALENDAR CONSTANTLY SLIPPED ABOUT ONE DAY EVERY FOUR YEARS AND A WHOLE MONTH EVERY 120 YEARS.

While Middle Kingdom dates are thus precisely fixed, there is a problem in just counting back kings' reigns into the Old Kingdom. Separating the Middle Kingdom—marked by national unity and culture, including a pyramid revival—from the Old Kingdom is the First Intermediate Period, a time of local principalities along the Nile, and then war between rival ruling houses in the north and south. We are not sure how long the First Intermediate Period was because king lists are unreliable and the sequence of regnal years and royal monuments is interrupted. It was perhaps less than a century, maybe more than 150 years. Beyond this chronological chasm the pyramid age stretches back into the third millennium B.C. with no astronomical footholds.

We hoped that radiocarbon dates from secure contexts in a series of pyramids, mortuary temples, and other structures at Old Kingdom sites like Dashur, Giza, Lisht, Meidum, and Saqqara, southwest of Cairo, would confirm or adjust the entire time frame of the extraordinary developmental phase of Egyptian civilization that saw the biggest pyramids built, the nomes (administrative districts) organized, and the hinterlands internally colonized—that is, the first consolidation of the Egyptian nation state. Our 1984 work raised questions that led to a second project in 1995, funded by the David H. Koch Charitable Trust.

Eye on the Mortar

The pyramids were originally cased with fine white limestone brought from quarries to the east across the Nile Valley, cut into blocks and laid with exquisitely fine joins. Today one sees the stepped, slumped, or eroded cores of pyramids, left after the outer casing was stripped away to be used for building stone or made into lime in later centuries. Smaller pyramids had cores of small stone and mud retaining walls and dumped fill, or, in the later Middle Kingdom pyramids (1897–1797 B.C.), mud brick tempered with large quantities of straw. The cores of the largest pyramids, like those at Giza, were made of crudely cut limestone blocks. Builders filled the large seams between the blocks with irregular limestone pieces and globs of gypsum mortar. This mortar includes fired reddish clay particles, and occasionally fragments of stone tools, green copper flecks from chisels, and pottery sherds. More often it contains small bits of charcoal, probably derived from fires used to heat the gypsum. Given that the Giza pyramids were built with great quantities of such mortar, we have to imagine many smokey fires dotting the work area. We believed that

suitable samples for radiocarbon dating could be extracted from secure contexts within the fabric of these pyramids, the mortar or mud brick, material that was probably deposited during the reigns of kings for whom the pyramids were built.

In principle radiocarbon dating is simple. Cosmic radiation striking the upper atmosphere converts a small amount of nitrogen into the unstable radioactive isotope carbon-14 (14C). Bound in carbon dioxide gas molecules, it is absorbed by plants and, from plants, by animals. When organisms die, the 14C in their cells is no longer replenished and begins to revert back to nitrogen at a constant, measurable rate. The amount of 14C remaining in a sample can thus be used to date when it stopped absorbing 14C. For example, dating wood charcoal found in the ashes of an ancient hearth will date the death of the tree or reed, that is, when it was cut (not the year in which it was burned as fuel).

Flies in the radiocarbon ointment include calibration, old wood, contamination, and error margins. The 14C content in the atmosphere, and thus in plants and animals, has not been constant, and in some periods organisms will have absorbed more or less 14C than in others. Fortunately, some trees, such as California's bristlecone pine, live thousands of years. Each annual growth ring can be dated by a direct count, and this can be compared to the exact amount of 14C, or radiocarbon date, of each ring. This comparison allows us to calibrate the raw radiocarbon dates to account for fluctuations in atmospheric 14C.

Remains of short-lived plants, such as grain, are ideal for dating. With wood there is always the chance that the tree from which the sample came was cut down long before it was incorporated in a site. If so, it could give a date centuries older than the real age of the hearth or structure in which it was found. And dates from a single log of a long-lived tree can vary greatly depending on where the samples came from—deep in the interior and hence earlier, or near the exterior and thus more recent. Samples can be contaminated with younger or older carbon from groundwater or carbonate rocks such as limestone. Contamination can be eliminated by chemical cleaning prior to dating. Even if these problems are controlled, the date obtained for a sample is not really a date but a probability that the sample is from a range of time, hence the plus or minus figure appended to radiocarbon dates.

In 1984 we extracted 80 samples from ten pyramids, including those of Khufu, Khafre, and Menkaure at Giza, and six mortuary temples all thought to be from the Old Kingdom (ca. 2686–2181 B.C.). We also took one sample from a tomb of the 1st Dynasty (ca. 3100 B.C.). We obtained 73 radiocarbon dates, mostly from fragments of charred wood. Other samples ranged from wood beams projecting from the core of Djoser's Step Pyramid to unburnt straw from mud-brick walls associated with some of the pyramid complexes. We dated the larger samples at the Radiocarbon Laboratory of Southern Methodist University, and the smaller ones at the Eidgenossische Technische Hochschule (ETH) in Zurich. We calibrated these dates with the most recent methods. All samples were chemically treated to remove carbonates, and the two laboratories compared their accuracies by dating several split samples.

1984 Results

We compared the 1984 radiocarbon dates with historical age estimates derived from the Cambridge Ancient History. Ten radiocarbon dates were younger than the historical chronology, but we had doubted the samples were contemporary with the monuments from which they were taken. We removed from consideration these ten, and ten others that were single dates from monuments (agreement between multiple dates is needed for reliable dating). The remaining ones, from monuments spanning the 3rd Dynasty (Djoser) to the late 5th Dynasty (Unas), averaged 374 years older than the Cambridge Ancient History dates of the kings with whom the pyramids are identified. In spite of this discrepancy, the radiocarbon dates confirmed that the Great Pyramid belonged to the historical era studied by Egyptologists, though this scientific evidence may not have shaken the convictions of our Cayce Foundation sponsors.

In dealing with the 374-year discrepancy, we had to consider the old wood problem. In 1984 we thought it was unlikely that the pyramid builders consistently used centuries-old Egyptian wood as fuel in preparing mortar. Ancient Egypt's population was compressed in the narrow confines of the Nile Valley with a tree cover, we assumed, that was sparse compared to less arid lands. We expected that by the pyramid age the Egyptians had been intensively exploiting native wood for fuel for a long time and that old trees had been harvested long before. If so, the trees used in Egypt would likely have been cut when quite young.

Could we be dating charcoal that derived from wood fuel that had been long used for other purposes? The Egyptians did reuse wood from large trees in a variety of ways. At the Middle Kingdom pyramids at Lisht, the Metropolitan Museum excavations uncovered tracks of acacia and tamarisk wood beams laid at intervals like railroad ties with an overlay of mud and gypsum for hauling stone blocks and other materials. The beams were reused parts of boats. It is also well-known that the Egyptians imported long-lived cedar trees from Lebanon. It is conceivable that they used them for more than one generation as parts of boats or other structures, reused the wood as transport levers and tracks, and eventually broke up the wood and used it for fuel in the fires of gypsum preparation. However, it seemed highly unlikely that this was occurring with the regularity suggested by our study.

The 1984 results left us with too little data to conclude that the historical chronology of the Old Kingdom was in error by nearly 400 years, but we considered this at least a possibility. Alternatively, if our radiocarbon age estimations were in error for some reason, we had to assume that many other dates obtained from Egyptian materials were also suspect. This prompted a second, larger study.

The 1995 Project

During 1995 more than 300 samples were collected, mostly by team members Robert Wenke and John Nolan. We sampled monuments ranging from the 1st Dynasty tombs at Saqqara to the Djoser pyramid, the Giza Pyramids, and a selection of the 5th and 6th Dynasties and Middle Kingdom pyramids.

Samples were also taken from excavations on the Giza Plateau where two largely intact bakeries were discovered in 1991. In a provisional laboratory at our field house near the Giza Plateau, Wilma Wetterstrom of the Harvard Botanical Museum identified selected samples. An abundance of acacia in the mortar was not surprising. One of the few common trees in Egypt, acacia burns slowly and at high temperatures, making it an ideal fuel for manufacturing mortar or other tasks requiring high, steady heat.

We ended up with 163 new dates. For 1984 and 1995 we now have a total of 235 dates, including 42 for Khufu's Pyramid. In general, the calibrated dates from the 1995 Old Kingdom pyramid samples tended to be 100 to 200 years older than the historical dates for the respective kings and about 200 years younger than our 1984 dates. The disparity is particularly glaring for Khufu's Pyramid. In 1984, 20 dates on charcoal produced a calibrated average age of 2917 B.C. In 1995 we had 18 dates on charcoal from this pyramid giving an average date of 2694 B.C., closer to the pharaoh's historical dates, 2589–2566 B.C., but still a century older.

The number of dates from both 1984 and 1995 was only large enough to allow for statistical comparisons for the pyramids of Djoser, Khufu, Khafre, and Menkaure. There are two striking results. First, there are significant discrepancies between 1984 and 1995 dates for Khufu and Khafre, but not for Djoser and Menkaure. Second, the 1995 dates are scattered, varying widely even for a single monument. For Khufu, they scatter over a range of about 400 years.

By contrast, we have fair agreement between our historical dates, previous radiocarbon dates, and our radiocarbon dates on reed for the 1st Dynasty tombs at North Saqqara. We also have fair agreement between our radiocarbon dates and historical dates for the Middle Kingdom. We sampled the Middle Kingdom pyramids of the 12th Dynasty pharaohs Amenemhet I, Senwosret II, and Amenemhet III. Two samples from mud bricks and mud layers on the ruined core of the pyramid Amenemhet I produced dates more than 800 years younger than the end of his reign in 1962 B.C. As Dieter Arnold of the Metropolitan Museum later informed us, there was settlement from the 13th Dynasty through the New Kingdom Ramesside Period (19th and 20th Dynasties) at this pyramid. Here the radiocarbon dating gives a loud and clear signal of a mistaken sampling—apparently these two samples were material from the later settlement. We had better luck with eight calibrated dates on straw from the pyramid of Senwosret II, which ranged from 103 years older to 78 years younger than the historical dates for his reign, with four dates off by only 30, 24, 14, and three years. Significantly, the older date was on charcoal.

Old Kingdom Problem

If the Middle Kingdom radiocarbon dates are okay, barring mistaken sampling, why are the Old Kingdom ones from pyramids so problematic? We should be aware of evidence that the pyramid builders used older cultural material whether out of expedience or to make a conscious connection between their pharaoh and his predecessors. In galleries under the pyramid of the 3rd Dynasty pharaoh Djoser more than 40,000 stone ves-

sels were found. Inscriptions on many of these vessels included most of the kings of the 1st and 2nd Dynasties, but Djoser's name occurred only once, on a clay sealing of a linen wrapping that might have been used to bring some vessels down into the pyramid. Rainer Stadelmann, a leading authority on the pyramids, suggests that Djoser gathered up the stone vases from the 200-year-old Archaic tombs at North Saqqara. In the 12th Dynasty, Amenemhet I actually took bits and pieces of Old Kingdom tomb chapels and pyramid temples (including those of the Giza Pyramids) and dumped them into the core of his pyramid at Lisht. The burial of older material in the mass of the pyramid may explain six dates on straw from mud bricks in the 6th Dynasty pyramid of Teti. They ranged between 2792±84 B.C. and 2543±85 B.C., the historical time frame for the 3rd Dynasty and early 4th Dynasty, 447 to 198 years before the beginning of Teti's reign. Teti's builders may have taken whole bricks from 3rd and 4th Dynasty mastaba tombs from the nearby cemetery and dumped them into the pyramid core as fill. Dieter Arnold reports that most of the pottery from the mud-brick core of the Senwosret III pyramid is Old Kingdom. We know from texts that there was an Old Kingdom settlement nearby, attached to the two large stone pyramids of the 4th Dynasty king Sneferu. Apparently, Senwosret's builders were forming bricks with earth and 300-year-old settlement debris.

At Giza, although a few tombs of the Archaic Period have been documented about a mile south of the pyramids, there is no other definite evidence of an older Archaic settlement. In the early 1970s the

Austrian archaeologist Karl Kromer dug a half mile south of the pyramids into a huge mound of settlement debris, apparently the dumped debris of a village that had been razed. Kromer thought that some of the material suggested the settlement had been occupied since the Archaic Period, but the evidence is weak.

South of the Sphinx we are excavating extensive remains of facilities for storage and production of fish, meat, bread, and copper that date to the middle and end of the 4th Dynasty, when the pyramids of Khafre and Menkaure were under construction. The royal names in impressions on mud sealings suggest that the production center was in its heyday during the reign of Menkaure, dated historically to 2532–2504 B.C. Three of the eight dates from samples taken here are almost direct hits on Menkaure's historical dates (one of these is from a charred tuber and grains, which we would expect to be short-lived). The other five, however, range from 350 to 100 years older. If any part of our site was that much older in real time, the ceramics would be screaming this fact loud and clear. But that isn't the case. On the other hand, two samples from the same small, charcoal-rich deposit produced calibrated dates 163 years apart. Our radiocarbon dates from the site are limited in numbers compared to the series from the pyramids, but those done so far suggest that, like those from the pyramids, the dates on charcoal from the settlement scatter widely in time with many dates older than the historical estimate. The pyramid builders need not have been recycling Archaic settlement debris to give us the old dates on the pyramids; they could have done so by recycling

their own settlement debris!

The more we work at Giza, and the more we dig our site, the more impressed we are at the vast amounts of wood fuel the 4th Dynasty Egyptians must have consumed. At first it was the amount of wood charcoal in huge pyramid building waste dumps. Then we began to find deep and extensive deposits of ash and charcoal in contexts like the Old Kingdom bakeries in our 1991 season. We found similar deposits in a copper-working facility in 1998. In some cases, the excavators were working ankle- to knee-high in dense black ash- and charcoal-laden soil.

This evidence, combined with the pyramid radiocarbon dates, suggests it may have been premature to dismiss the old wood problem in our 1984 study. Do our radiocarbon dates reflect the Old Kingdom deforestation of Egypt? Did the pyramid builders devour whatever wood they could harvest or scavenge to roast tons of gypsum for mortar, to forge thousands of copper chisels, and to bake tens of thousands of loaves to feed the mass of assembled laborers. The giant stone pyramids in the early Old Kingdom may mark a major consumption of Egypt's wood cover, and therein lies the reason for the wide scatter, increased antiquity, and history-unfriendly radiocarbon dating results from the Old Kingdom, especially from the time of Djoser to Menkaure. In other words, it is the old wood effect that haunts our dates and creates a kind of shadow chronology to the historical dating of the pyramids. It is the shadow cast by a thousand fires burning old wood.

Samples randomly collected from many trees without knowing from which part of the tree they originate—older near the heart of the wood, or younger toward the bark—

will yield dates scattered within a range defined by when the trees began growing and when they were cut. The older parts of long-lived trees will pull the average of these dates older. Most of the identifications that Wilma Wetterstrom could do on wood or charcoal were acacia. The acacia variety that grows today in Egypt and the Sudan is said to grow rapidly, although we have not yet learned of maximum recorded ages for this or other Egyptian trees. It is also reputed to be resistant to decay, and herein lies another confounding old wood effect.

In a 1986 article, University of Arizona archaeologist Michael Schiffer pointed out that "firewood is commonly collected as dead wood." Iron wood and mesquite that he collected in the Sonoran desert radiocarbon dated from 200 to 1,500 years before present! Schiffer thought that old wood contributed to "the great dispersion exhibited by any extensive series of radiocarbon dates on wood, as well as many 'anomalous dates.'" The various aspects of old wood, he concluded, generally bias "archaeological chronologies toward an excessive antiquity."

For dates on charcoal, we cannot eliminate culturally induced old wood effect—a charcoal industry, for example. We might imagine ancient people hacking down trees and bushes, then building a crackling fire for cooking, smelting, or roasting gypsum. But it is possible, if not probable, that they used prepared charcoal which, like wood, could have been stored a long time. When we replicated one of the ancient bakeries we discovered at Giza, the villagers who worked with us scoffed at the idea of using freshly cut wood or dead wood as fuel in the open baking pits. They would only use ready-made charcoal from the village market.

If the fair agreement of our 1995 results with historical dates and previous radiocarbon dates for the Archaic Period and with the historical dates for the Middle Kingdom hold, the problematic Old Kingdom dates are boxed in. And therein may lie a hint of multifaceted old wood effects for a period, especially from Djoser to Menkaure, when any and all wood resources may have been consumed at a whole other order of magnitude than before or after the giant pyramid-building projects.

While the multiple old wood effects make it difficult to obtain pinpoint age estimates of pyramids, our project has proved valuable beyond the narrow goal of dating monuments. The David H. Koch Pyramids Radiocarbon Project now has us thinking about forest ecologies, site formation processes, and ancient industry and its environmental impact—in sum, the society and economy that left the Egyptian pyramids as hallmarks for all later humanity. ▲

MIXED MESSAGES

A tomb on the Giza Plateau yields chewing-gum wrappers, Cairo tram tickets, a 1944 newspaper, and a 4,500-year-old burial.

by W. B. HAFFORD

As I chipped away the final seal on the entrance to the burial chamber, I was gripped by both anticipation of what might lie inside and a sense of mystery. The other chambers of this tomb, lying in the shadow of Khufu's monumental pyramid at Giza, had been opened in the 1930s by George Reisner, Harvard's highly respected archaeologist, but for some unknown reason this one had escaped his notice.

Standing in a shaft only 20 inches wide, I rocked the long limestone slab covering the chamber's entryway back on its base. It took a good deal of effort, but finally the stone slid back, kicking up fine sand. As the dust settled I peered into the darkness, only to find myself face to face with…modern garbage: shredded newspaper and bits of plastic and foil. Anticlimactic perhaps, but archaeology can be just that at times.

I was at a loss to determine how modern material had gotten into the ancient tomb. It certainly hadn't come in the way I had; there'd been a heavy, unbroken mud-plaster sealing at the entrance. To find out just what had happened, I wadded myself up into a ball and gingerly began investigating the small, low chamber. It extended south beyond the shaft opening, and there, reaching to the ceiling, was a large pile of sand.

Over the next few days, I returned again and again to my cramped position, carefully excavating the sand pile, documenting its contents despite the fact that much of it was modern debris. I found many things of chronological interest in that pile, including a 1940s or 1950s chewing-gum wrapper and Cairo tram tickets of the same period. Finally the definitive time frame for the "invasion" of the chamber appeared. Nestled in the sand was a torn piece of the *Egyptian Mail,* an English-language newspaper, dated April 28, 1944. Its partially preserved headline read "…Hit Germans By Night," and on the reverse were pictures of SS head Heinrich Himmler and Luftwaffe chief Hermann Goering. I hadn't expected to come up against the Nazis at this dig, but now perhaps I could claim a kinship with the action-adventure archaeologists of motion-picture fame.

Slowly, I pulled the remaining sand away from the ceiling and began to understand what had happened. Reisner's team had found three burial shafts and chambers in this tomb, and during excavation they had weakened a fourth. Not long after they stopped work, a minor collapse had occurred, leaving a small hole in the unexcavated chamber's southwestern corner. Over the next five to ten years, sand and wind-

blown trash had filled it, sealing the burial once more.

Nazis aside, most exciting of all was the fact that the chamber's original occupant remained intact. As I continued to work in the small area, I found her, still in the position in which she had been placed so long ago. Curled into the tiny space, her knees were at her chin and her hands beneath her head, resting on a stone pillow in her eternal sleep. There were no burial goods, apart from the much later newsprint, so we had nothing more than her bones to tell us how she had lived.

Why had this woman's burial chamber escaped Reisner's notice? Let me roll back the clock to 1939, when the spectre of World War II was beginning to cast its shadow over the world. At that time, Reisner and his crew were busy excavating a group of tombs in the western cemetery at Giza for Harvard and the Boston Museum of Fine Arts. The season's endeavors were part of ongoing research that Reisner had conducted in his four decades at Giza. With a large workforce and a rail system to carry away the overburden, "Papa George," as he was known, moved more than 11,000 cartloads of sand, and excavated 22 mastaba tombs, low rectangular brick or stone structures. He investigated a hundred burial shafts and chambers and recovered 42 skeletons as well as a few small statues and other artifacts. One of the tombs, designated G2061, included the burial chamber in which I was now working.

The 1939 season was particularly difficult. Reisner was plagued by increasing blindness—caused by cataracts and a detached retina in his left eye—and the possibility of war was on everyone's mind. The work log kept by his Egyptian foreman, Mohammed Said Ahmed, records the preparation of the most stable tombs as bomb shelters, the beginning of the war with Hitler's invasion of Poland on September first, and these entries three days later: "Mr. Frank Allen went in town and brought Gas Masks for all the Egyptians, guards, house boys and the children" and "At 5 P.M. we went to the rock cut tombs after hearing the [air-raid] whistle…it finished after 15–20 minutes." One cataloger even scribbled a caricature of Adolf Hitler on an inventory card while recording the finds. With the outbreak of war, Reisner called an end to the year's excavation, and the woman's burial chamber was never found. Three years later, at age 74, he died at the Harvard camp at Giza, where he had lived and worked for four decades, and most of the tombs excavated in 1939 remain unpublished.

A new expedition, the Howard University Giza Cemetery Project, led by Ann Macy Roth and including myself, has returned to the site to record what Reisner had seen and done in that last prewar season. Most of our work is concerned with mapping, drawing, and documentation to bring the old field notes and Reisner's manuscript up to par with modern archaeological publication standards. The discovery of the unopened burial chamber in G2061 was an unexpected dividend of these efforts.

When Reisner's team was working in the funerary chapel attached to the G2061 tomb, they uncovered a small statue—now in the Egyptian Museum in Cairo—of a husband and wife. They sit together and the woman holds her arm about her husband's shoulders in an affectionate manner. Almost undoubtedly, this statue represents the couple who owned and built the funerary chapel and tomb with its four burial chambers. Judging from inscriptions in the nearest cluster of tombs, one or both of them may have held the title "Palace Attendant." We are uncertain what duties such officials performed, but they were honored enough to warrant burial in a sacred place near the Great Pyramids. They were probably the parents of the woman whose skeleton I had just uncovered, and would have occupied the tomb's two deepest chambers. Unfortunately, both had been emptied long before Reisner found them. The third chamber Reisner investigated contained a complete burial, but his notes do not record the individual's gender, age, or stature. They do provide a scale drawing, however, and the bones are shown small, perhaps from a teenager.

The statue of the mother and father gives us some idea of what the woman in the fourth chamber may have looked liked, but because there were no inscriptions anywhere in the tomb, we don't know her name. Her bones, however, tell a great deal. They reveal not only her gender but also that she was between twenty-five and thirty-five years of age when she died and that she had lived a relatively hard life. Lack of calcium caused her bones to be thin and brittle, and her lower back was in a deteriorated condition. She'd broken a finger during her lifetime, and patterned wear on her teeth might be an indication of habitual work, such as processing leather or stripping reeds for basketmaking.

Scientific techniques for studying human bones have improved greatly since the 1930s, and we are fortunate to have obtained a complete skeleton for comparison with the sometimes scantily recorded data about those that Reisner found six decades ago. Recovering the body was not a quick or easy task. After I excavated her fragile remains, I still had to draw them, take a multitude of photographs, and collect, label, and store the bones. Such painstaking disinterment and investigation is time-consuming and costly, but the information gained is substantial. Positioning of the body and lack of burial goods provide indications of burial customs, and in this, we are adding to what Reisner documented. But finer detail, such as tooth wear and the development of muscle attachments on the bones, gives us an idea of the sort of work she may have conducted, and her thin bone walls and compacted vertebrae tell us about her diet and health. Such information was not noted and perhaps even sought in Reisner's day.

At the same time, we've learned something about the archaeologist who first investigated her family's tomb. Much of our personal knowledge of Reisner comes from the copious written material he left behind—an unpublished manuscript and notes and the daily record kept by Mohammed Said Ahmed. Although Reisner worked at a pace much faster than archaeologists today, clearing many tombs in one or two days where now several weeks are spent on each, he was extremely careful for his time. His photographic record was meticulous, and he is sometimes cited as the first to excavate by

systematically following the natural layers of deposits rather than arbitrary levels, beginning as early as 1909 in his work at Samaria.

Reisner's unfinished Giza monograph is filled with information and shows both his love of the work and his attention to detail, but the diary of his Egyptian foreman contained more personal entries. As I read through this log, mostly recording the number of cartloads of sand removed each day, I stumbled across an entry that began "What a day!" It went on to describe the great pride felt by the entire crew at Reisner's latest award, an honorary doctorate to be given by Harvard. At the same time, there was a note of sadness that he would be away for two months making the long trek back to Boston to attend the ceremony. His return received an equally excited entry in the diary, describing the joyful preparations—the outfitting of his quarters with new linens and flowers, and the stocking of the kitchen for a welcome-home feast—made in expectation of his arrival.

POSITIONING OF THE BODY AND LACK OF BURIAL GOODS PROVIDE INDICATIONS OF BURIAL CUSTOMS...

Such love and respect came from Reisner's equal show of admiration for his fellows, including his local workers. Indeed, he had a great respect for the Egyptians, both modern and ancient. This devotion was often remarked upon by his students, his foreman, and crew, and was echoed in the moniker "Papa George" given him by his many friends. His genuine concern for the crew was reflected in his arrangements to keep them safe in the event of war. He was dedicated not just to archaeology but to Egypt as a whole, and he was prepared to do what he could for its living people even while he researched its dead.

The double slice of history we uncovered in this one small tomb among thousands on the Giza Plateau demonstrates that we archaeologists experience history at the same instant we study it, as Reisner's work here on the eve of World War II shows. And I like to think our work is akin to the rebirth the ancient Egyptians sought. They believed they would carry on in the afterlife, and their hope was that they would continue to be remembered in the physical world as well. Perhaps it is something that, thousands of years later, we remember and honor this woman by trying to learn more about her and her people. ▲

Giza's Sphinx (above left). The Great Pyramids (above right) are the only surviving structures of the Seven Wonders of the Ancient World. Archaeological, geological, and radiocarbon evidence all indicate that they were built by the 4th Dynasty pharaohs Khufu, Khafre, and Menkaure. Photographs show the Sphinx and Pyramids today; the engraving is from the *Illustrated London News* of July 26, 1862.

Aerial photograph shows tomb entrances in the Valley of the Kings (above left), the principal burial ground of the pharaohs of Dynasties 18–20 (ca. 1551–1069 B.C.). Tomb 55 in the Valley yielded a coffin of Akhenaten's wife Kiya (above right) that was adapted for a male burial. In Amenhotep III's tomb, the wings of a vulture deity encircle cartouches with the pharaoh's names (below left). His son Akhenaten (r. ca. 1350–1333 B.C.) was a central figure of the final generations of the 18th Dynasty (below right).

In Nubia, royals built pyramids to mark their tombs at Meroe from around 270 B.C. until the end of their kingdom ca. A.D. 350.

Pyramids, built on a small scale, were used for private burials in Egypt after they went out of use as royal tombs. This reconstructed New Kingdom pyramid is at Deir el-Medineh, in the cemetery of the workers who labored in the Valley of the Kings.

Dominique Vivant Denon, one of the scholars who accompanied Napoleon to Egypt, described many ancient monuments, such as these ruins of a temple at Hermopolis, in his book *Voyages in Upper and Lower Egypt* (1802).

A highly romantic nineteenth-century depiction shows **Napoleon inspecting a mummy at the pyramids**. The well-dressed men in the background holding umbrellas are some of the savants the general brought with him to Egypt.

TALES FROM THE CRYPT

A Descent into the Tomb of Osiris

by ANGELA M.H. SCHUSTER

It has often been said that only mad dogs and English-men go out in the noonday sun. I believe the same holds true for archaeologists. Taking advantage of an extended lunch break during the Eighth International Congress of Egyptologists, held in Cairo this past April, five of us—Aidan and Diana Dodson of the University of Bris-tol, Salima Ikram of the American University in Cairo, Veronique Verneuil of the Institut Français d'Archéologie Orientale, and I—ventured out into the searing heat to visit the so-called Osiris Tomb on the Giza Plateau, the "discov-ery" of which had created an international media stir only weeks before.

Armed with written permission from Zahi Hawass, [then] director of the Giza Plateau monuments, and accom-panied by Mohammed, who served as both inspector and keybearer, we headed out toward Khafre's Pyramid, built ca.

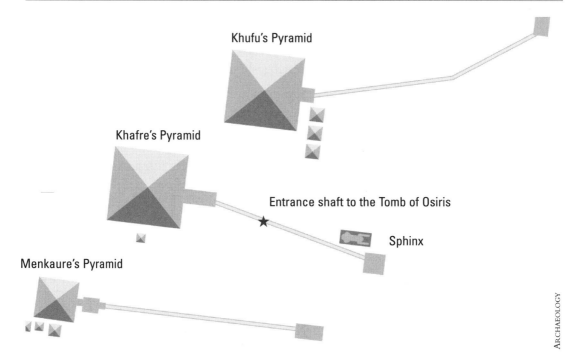

Khufu's Pyramid

Khafre's Pyramid

Entrance shaft to the Tomb of Osiris

Sphinx

Menkaure's Pyramid

2500 B.C. and the second largest on the plateau. The Osiris Tomb lies among a number of deep shaft graves belonging to Egyptian nobility dug more than a millennium after Khafre's Pyramid was built. The tomb is 100 yards or so down the causeway that connects Khafre's Mortuary Temple, at the base of the pyramid, with the Sphinx and his Valley Temple.

An eight-foot-long tunnel beneath the causeway leads to a shaft. Mohammed unlocked an iron gate and one by one we descended a metal ladder some ten feet down into an empty tomb chamber, roughly 30 by 15 feet. At the far end of this room, a second shaft, measuring five by five feet, plummeted 40 feet down into total darkness. We divided up flashlights and began our

descent, taking care not to brush against the walls, showering those below us on the ladder with sand. At the bottom was another burial chamber, about the same size as the first, with six burial chambers, two of which contained large granite sarcophagi executed in classic Saite style of the 25th Dynasty (664–525 B.C.). We explored the cool, moist chamber, illuminating our feet as we walked so we would not step on the scattered piles of potsherds and human bones.

A somewhat narrower shaft had been dug into the floor of what appeared to be a seventh chamber, its walls alive with the mundane activities of scorpions and the largest waterbugs I have ever seen. After a brief and animated discussion as to who would go first—Salima graciously volunteered—we began a second 40-foot descent. Clenching a small flashlight in my teeth, I surveyed each rung carefully before stepping onto it.

Nearly 100 feet below the Giza Plateau, we finally reached the Osiris Tomb, a damp grotto hewn from the rock. The floor was covered with broken slabs of stone that rocked as we stepped on them. At the center of the chamber, roughly 30 feet square, were the eroded remains of four columns surrounding a rectangular pit containing a granite sarcophagus, its lid askew, resting on two heavy wood beams. A moat filled with crystal-clear water surrounded the pillars on three sides. A splendid sight even by flashlight, the chamber would have been a fitting architectural tribute to Osiris, Egypt's master of the underworld and god of fertility, whose annual death and resurrection rituals symbolized the renewal of nature. But was this mysterious grotto really an Osirion, a cenotaph or ceremonial tomb of the god, or was it simply another shaft tomb belonging to a noble family?

According to Hawass, who had recently alerted the press and scholarly community to the presence of the tomb, it has architectural parallels with the Osirion at Abydos, commissioned as part of a mortuary temple complex by the New Kingdom pharaoh Seti I (r. ca. 1306–1290 B.C.). Indeed, the Osirion at Abydos has much in common with the Giza grotto. Both contained sarcophagi surrounded by pillars that are ringed on three sides by groundwater-fed reflecting pools. Moreover, says Hawass, the shape of the pool surrounding the pillars is a rendering of the hieroglyph *per*, "9," meaning "house." The Giza Plateau, which had a highly developed Osiris cult in the New Kingdom, was once known as the *per wesir neb rastaw*, or "House of Osiris, Lord of Rastaw." According to Hawass, Rastaw may refer to underground chambers.

Early Exploration of the Tomb

While the six-chambered hall had been known to archaeologists for nearly a century—it was published by Egyptologist Selim Hassan in 1935—fluctuating groundwater on the plateau had prevented scientific exploration of the lower, four-pillared hall. Nevertheless, Hassan, as well as several intrepid travelers, saw enough of the chamber to know that it was colonnaded and that it contained at least one if not more sarcophagi. Confusion over the number of caskets (there is only one) may have been caused by the fact that the lid of the sarcophagus had been removed, perhaps by looters in antiquity, and left near the chamber's entrance. It has been put back atop the sarcophagus.

Early descriptions of the tomb vary in detail and contain information that can only be described as pure fantasy; one tells of magnificent sculptures of young maidens, colorful murals, and finely wrought alabaster vessels. The reports, some of which appeared in quaint local English-language publications, do agree on several key points, most notably that the chamber contained human bones. This has been confirmed by Harvard archaeologist Mark Lehner, who in the early 1980s used the shaft to gauge the depth of the Giza water table and determine its effect on the stability of the Sphinx. If the bones are contemporary with the tomb, rather than being from a later period, it would suggest

The shaft leading to the so-called Osiris Tomb lies directly below the causeway that connects Khafre's Pyramid to the Sphinx. The shaft leads to an empty hall, at the far end of which is a 40-foot-deep shaft.

At the base of the shaft is a six-chambered hall, which was used for burial during Dynasty 26 (664–525 B.C.) and in the later Greco-Roman period (332 B.C.–A.D. 642). Two of the chambers contain large granite sarcophagi; the floor is littered with piles of potsherds and human bones. A 40-foot-deep shaft cut through the floor of what may have been a seventh burial chamber leads to the Osiris Tomb.

The remains of four eroded pillars cut out of rock surround a rectangular pit, which contains a granite sarcophagus. Crystal-clear water surrounds the pillars on three sides.

ARCHAEOLOGY

that the chamber was used as a real rather than symbolic burial place, arguing against an interpretation of the chamber as an Osirion. Shallow burial pits carved in the floor of one of the rooms in the six-chambered hall show that at least that level was reused as a tomb in the early years of the Greco-Roman period (332 B.C.–A.D. 642).

WHAT HERODOTUS SAID ABOUT THE TOMB

Many media reports invoked Herodotus in connection with the tomb, claiming a full description of it, including details such as its sarcophagus being of granite, can be found in his *Histories*. Unfortunately, none of the reporters had read the fifth-century B.C. Greek historian's work. Herewith is exactly what Herodotus had to say:

> *Cheops [Khufu] reigned (so the Egyptians said) for 50 years; at his death he was succeeded by his brother Chephren [Khafre], who bore himself in all respects like Cheops. Chephren also built a pyramid, of a less size than his brother's. I have myself measured it. It has no underground chambers, nor is it entered like the other by a canal from the Nile, but the river comes in through a built passage and encircles an island, in which, they say, Cheops himself lies....*

> —*Book II: 127, Loeb Classical Library, volume 1*

Herodotus says nothing of the sarcophagus, much less of what it was made.

WHEN WAS THE FOUR-PILLARED HALL BUILT?

In light of the evidence presented so far, it is difficult to determine a precise date for the construction of the four-pillared hall. If, in fact, Herodotus is refering to this grotto when he tells us Khufu was buried on an island surrounded by water, it would place the construction of the tomb in the early years of the Old Kingdom, ca. 2500 B.C., which seems highly unlikely.

According to Hawass, the tomb belongs to the New Kingdom, based on pottery and bones found in the lowest levels of the shaft, which he says date to around 1550 B.C. (18th Dynasty).

Architecturally, the four-pillared hall appears to be an afterthought. It looks as if the shaft leading to the grotto was dug into the floor of a seventh burial chamber in the 26th Dynasty construction 40 feet above. Moreover, as splendid as the chamber looks, some have noted that the crystalline moat surrounding the pillars is little more than a visual accident, resulting from rising groundwater on the Giza Plateau, the very water that had until recently prevented scientific exploration of the tomb itself. That the chamber would, in fact, resemble an Osirion in shape, is no surprise, according to Lehner. A cult of the god was practiced throughout Egyptian history and is attested in the architecture of a number of tombs, namely those of the Middle Kingdom pharaoh Mentuhotep (r. 2061–2010 B.C.) at Deir el Bahri and the New Kingdom pharaoh Ramesses III (r. 1194–1163 B.C.) in the Valley of the Kings.

So what are we to make of all of this? Clearly, the tomb, perhaps the deepest on the plateau, is an impressive feat of engineering, whatever its construction date, and I marvel at the fact that the massive sarcophagi within it could have been lowered down the 40-foot sandstone shafts seemingly without incident. Whether the four-pillared hall has any connection to the worship of Osiris will only be determined with further research, including the proper excavation of the chamber and careful analysis of the pottery and human remains found within it. Hawass has his work cut out for him. ▲

PART IV:

FARTHER AFIELD: *Other Sites and Finds*

EXPLORING THE VALLEY OF THE KINGS

by DONALD P. RYAN

The Valley of the Kings is well-known to travelers and Egyptologists as the principal burial ground of the pharaohs of the New Kingdom (Dynasties 18–20, ca. 1552–1069 B.C.). Most often remembered as the site of the discovery of Tutankhamun's tomb by Howard Carter in 1922, the Valley held the remains of some of the most notable rulers of Egyptian history—including Hatshepsut, Thutmosis III, Seti I, and Ramesses II. Located across the Nile from modern-day Luxor, this royal necropolis sits in an arid valley surrounded by high cliffs. Though intended as quiet and secure resting places for the Egyptian god-kings, the tombs, like the highly visible pyramids of earlier periods, suffered greatly at the hands of plunderers. Some of the pharaohs' tombs were robbed within a few years of their closing; even the tomb of Tutankhamun appears to have been broken into at least once.

During the past two centuries, the large, elaborately decorated royal tombs have been the most obvious targets for archaeological activities. Their relation to historical personages, and their enlightening texts, decorations, and inscribed stone sarcophagi offer a wealth of information. Yet nearby are many modest uninscribed tombs. In fact, of the 60 or so known tombs in the Valley of the Kings, about half contain little or no decoration and are typically quite small compared to the great royal tombs. Most of these smaller tombs were discovered at or before the turn of the century by early excavators and have only been briefly studied.

My own interest in these neglected tombs began in 1983 during a study tour of the Valley. With map in hand, I attempted to relocate each of them. It was easy to find most of the large decorated monuments, several of which have conspicuous doorways or were open to tourists. But for many of the smaller, uninscribed tombs, a small pit or depression was all that could be seen of an entrance. Others were completely buried, and the exact locations of a few had never been recorded.

Who owned these tombs and why were these people sufficiently special to warrant burial in this most sacred of places? How are these tombs related to the bigger tombs in the Valley? What is the meaning of their small size and lack of decoration? To address such questions, I organized the Pacific Lutheran University Valley of the Kings Project to examine, document, and preserve some of these forgotten tombs. Although each of these burials had been entered before, we would conduct the first systematic study of them. We would reopen the tombs, map them, and examine any remaining artifacts for whatever they might reveal about the tombs and their occupants.

Each tomb in the Valley bears an identification number, assigned by early excavators or surveyors, and we were to examine numbers 21, 27, 28, 44, and 45. These tombs seemed to form a group and were located in a seldom-visited area behind a hill east of the main tourist thoroughfare (see page 2 of color insert). In addition, I had been urged by the late Elizabeth Thomas, a distinguished Egyptologist, to try to relocate Tomb 60, an 18th Dynasty burial thought to be in the general vicinity of the others.

Howard Carter had discovered Tomb 60 in 1903 while digging in the entranceway of Tomb 19, which belonged to Prince Montuhirkopeshef of the 20th Dynasty. Undecorated and robbed of its funerary goods in antiquity, Tomb 60 contained two female mummies, one within a decorated coffin, the other lying on the floor, and some mummified geese (funerary provisions). Apparently uninterested in the tomb, Carter closed it and published only a brief description with no plan or map.

While clearing Tomb 19 in 1906, English archaeologist Edward Ayrton reopened Tomb 60, and removed the mummy in the decorated coffin to the Cairo Museum. The coffin bears the name and title of Sitre, a royal nurse of Queen Hatshepsut. The other mummy was left lying on the floor of the burial chamber and the exact location of the tomb was soon forgotten.

I recall our first day in the field, June 27, 1989. We arrived at the site in the late morning to drop off a few tools. Unable to start any serious work in the heat of the noonday sun, we hiked up to the vicinity of Tomb 19 to search for clues to the location of Tomb 60. I harbored few hopes of finding it, but looked over the terrain around Tomb 19 and reconsidered Carter's brief notes. Grabbing a broom, I swept back the dusty surface covering the limestone bedrock at the entranceway of Tomb 19, and soon encountered an unnatural fracture in the rock. Work with a trowel revealed two edges of a pit that would prove to be the entrance to Tomb 60. Over the next several days we cleared a steep flight of crudely carved stairs leading to a door that was blocked with large stones. When we removed the stones and opened the tomb we found a corridor that led to the square door of a burial chamber. On each side of the corridor near the entrance was a niche filled with smashed funerary goods, including an intriguing face-piece from a wooden coffin lid. The face-piece had been roughly adzed by looters to remove its gilded surface and inlaid eyes of precious metal or stones.

The floor of the corridor was littered with burial debris: coffin fragments, linen wrappings, pottery, and lamp wicks. We also found a small side chamber not mentioned by Carter. On a sill at its entrance lay a partially unwrapped portion of a mummified side of beef. Smashed mud bricks in the corridor and the remains of mud plaster on the edges of the chamber doorway indicated that it had once been sealed. Inside the room was a large pile of linen wrappings and a wrapped bovine leg.

The floor of the burial chamber at the end of the corridor was likewise littered

INSIDE THE ROOM WAS A LARGE PILE OF LINEN WRAPPINGS AND A WRAPPED BOVINE LEG.

with scattered burial debris. Across from the entrance lay small packages of mummified bird and bovine food provisions. A large coffin fragment lay near another wall as did fragments of a ceramic pot. On the floor near the center of the burial chamber was an excellently preserved female mummy lying on her back. It was mostly unwrapped, having been stripped by tomb robbers in their search for jewelry. Strands of reddish blonde hair lay on the floor beneath the head.

The mummy's left arm was bent at the elbow, a loosely clenched hand over the center of the chest. The right arm lay against the right side of the body with fingers extended. The nails of the left hand were painted red and outlined in black. This arrangement of the arms and hands is intriguing because it is a pose characteristic of 18th Dynasty royal female mummies.

In her book *Royal Necropoleis of Thebes*, Thomas cautiously speculated that if Tomb 60 were ever rediscovered, the mummy found therein might prove to be that of Hatshepsut, the famed 18th Dynasty queen who ruled as a female pharaoh. She wrote, "Of the...mummy nothing can be said without examination. It is merely possible to ask a question with utmost temerity: did Thutmosis III [stepson and successor of Hatshepsut] inter Hatshepsut intrusively in this simple tomb below her own?"

The idea is not entirely fanciful—Hatshepsut's mummy has never been identified and few royal mummies in the Valley of the Kings have been found in their actual tombs. Once a tomb had been broken into, priests of the necropolis usually moved the royal mummies from their original resting places to spare them further abuse by grave robbers. Perhaps Hatshepsut's tomb (which lies directly above and adjacent to Tomb 60) was plundered, and her mummy was removed by relatives or priests and secretly cached in the nearby tomb of her royal nurse, Sitre. There is, however, no evidence linking the mummy from Tomb 60 to any specific individual. We found only two pieces of inscribed wood in the tomb, and these bear only a few legible hieroglyphs that offer no clues to the mummy's identity. So there is an excellent chance that we may never know who she was.

My colleague Mark Papworth examined the body and concluded from the dramatic folds of loose skin on its backside that the woman had been quite fat. The teeth were well-worn, suggesting an older person. The body seems to have been eviscerated through its pelvic floor and not through its side as was the standard procedure in the mummification process. Perhaps this was necessary because of its obesity.

Of particular interest were some small clay seals that we found in different locations within the tomb. Two of the seals bear the stamp of the necropolis, a recumbent jackal over nine captives. Such seals were typically used to officially close important jars, boxes, and papyrus rolls.

The coffin lid face-piece found in the niche by the door came from the lid of a very expensive coffin that had once been gilded. The chin sported a notch for a false beard, but there was no trace of a royal uraeus (headdress insignia) on the forehead. The general style is that of the 18th Dynasty, and it was probably made for the burial of a high-status nonroyal male. The question is, why would such a coffin, or just its lid, appear in a tomb which held two female mummies?

During the 20th Dynasty, the approach to Tomb 19 was cut over the top of Tomb 60. Though the mummies and the general architectural style of Tomb 60 indicate the burials were of the 18th Dynasty, our pottery analysts, David and Barbara Aston, determined that the ceramic material from the tomb dated to around the 20th Dynasty. The pottery could represent a 20th Dynasty intrusion into Tomb 60, perhaps by Valley workmen during the construction of Tomb 19. On the other hand, there is no complete record of what Carter and Aryton may have put into or removed from it.

Apart from the absence of formal decorations, we were struck by signs of hasty construction throughout. The Egyptians were masters of symmetry, and straight lines predominate in most of their tombs. In the case of Tomb 60, however, there were few straight lines, and even the carving of the burial chamber had been left unfinished. Perhaps the tomb was commissioned at the death of someone important and quickly hacked out of the rock for immediate use. That the mummy of Sitre was found in a tomb near that of Hatshepsut suggests an association between the uninscribed tombs and nearby royal monuments.

Although the location of the 18th Dynasty Tomb 21 had never been forgotten, its entrance had long been buried. This tomb was originally discovered by the famous Italian adventurer Giovanni Battista Belzoni in 1817, who noted its lack of decoration and wrote that two female mummies with long hair were in the burial chamber. A few minutes of careful probing in the vicinity with a trowel revealed the top of an ancient cut in the rock marking the entrance. We cleared old excavation refuse and flood debris from 18 steps that led to a doorway more than 20 feet below the surface. Tomb 21 was open from 1817, when Belzoni discovered it, to at least 1826, the date of graffiti on its ceiling. Debris from flash floods covered the tomb entrance sometime thereafter, and according to an old survey of the Valley it was inaccessible in 1893. Around 1896, a trench was dug to the top of the doorway and the tomb was reentered by unknown parties. The trench gradually filled with debris and windblown materials including a steady fill of newspapers and other tourist garbage. As we excavated, we noticed that the papers became increasingly older. Those at the entrance and inside the doorway were from the mid-1890s, thus providing a general date for the intrusion. The trench appears partially filled in 50-year-old pictures we found in a Luxor photography studio.

Tomb 21, unlike Tomb 60, was well constructed. Its upper corridor was filled with a sloping heap of debris from previous excavations and flooding. Amidst this material were a few potsherds, and some broken remains of the mummies described by Belzoni. Parts of these were also recovered from atop the interior stairs and on the floor of the burial chamber where their snapped-off hands and feet presented a grotesque display.

Honoring Belzoni

Italian adventurer Giovanni Battista Belzoni (1778–1823) is one of the most controversial personalities in the history of archaeology. Often branded as a careless thief of Egypt's antiquities, Belzoni has been portrayed as the archetype of the early nineteenth-century treasure hunter, recklessly and competitively collecting the biggest and finest antiquities for export to Europe. His earlier career as a carnival performer in England also left his credentials in doubt. Belzoni traveled, explored, and collected antiquities in Egypt from 1815 to 1819. Some: of his deeds include digging out the temples of Abu Simbel, entering the pyramid of Khafra at Giza, and exploring sites on the Red Sea and in the Wester Desert. Most notably, Belzoni is the first Westerner known to have excavated in the Valley of the Kings. His forays there resulted in the discovery of not only the undecorated Tomb 21 with its two mummies, but also the immense and splendidly dec-

orated tomb of Seti I and Tomb 19 (the tomb of Prince Montuhirkopeshef), and in an adjacent valley the tombs of Ramesses I, Ramesses III, and King Aye.

Despite his modern notoriety as a looter, recent research demonstrates that Belzoni possessed archaeological notions rarely understood or practiced by his contemporaries. For example, he measured, described, and published much of his work in the Valley of the Kings, including tomb plans and a topographic map. His unpublished materials include an impressive and complete record of the decoration of the tomb of Seti I in watercolors, and a sectional plan of the temple of Ramesses II at Abu Simbel. Belzoni's book about his adventures and his exhibitions of antiquities inspired new public interest in Egypt. He died in West Africa in 1823 during a short and ill-fated attempt to find the source of the Niger River. —DONALD P. RYAN

The first corridor led to a steep set of stairs and a second, lower corridor that ended at a burial chamber. The burial chamber was fairly large (about 19 by 21 feet), with a single stone pillar in the center and long, shelf-like niches along two walls. The floor of the chamber was covered with small rocks and wood fragments, bits of pottery, rotted pieces of linen wrappings, assorted human body parts, and some animal bones from decayed burial provisions. Although one English visitor to the tomb (ca. 1825) described it as "a clean new tomb, the water not having got into it," a stain encircling the perimeter of the room indicated that at one time there had been several inches of water in the chamber.

Only a side room, almost two feet above the level of the burial chamber, escaped water damage. This room contained about two dozen big whitened pots dating from the early to mid-18th Dynasty. All of them had been broken by vandals. Graffiti on the ceiling of the chamber read: "ME! 1826" and may date this intrusion. Lying among the pottery fragments were pieces of cloth resembling linen mummy wrappings. On closer examination, however, these "wrappings" proved to be the contents of many of the broken jars, apparently embalming materials stored within the tomb as part of the burials. Mixed in with this debris were dozens of little white linen bags, tied at the top, that probably contained patron, a dehydrating substance used in mummification. Similar embalming materials have been found in other tombs. We also recovered five small jar or box seals in this room, each bearing the stamp of the Valley of the Kings necropolis.

Mark Papworth reassembled the mummies as best as he could. One was missing its head, and the other much of its abdomen. Perhaps the missing head with its long hair became an exotic souvenir for a nineteenth-century visitor or antiquities dealer. After reassembling the bones, flesh, and wrappings, we discovered that one, if not both of the mummies, had been embalmed in the same regal pose as that of the mummy in Tomb 60. Only a few small decorated but badly decayed artifact fragments were found, and these proved insufficient to ascertain ownership of the tomb. Its architectural plan, the mummies, and the pottery, though, point to an 18th Dynasty date. Cracks in the walls had been patched and all seems to have been ready for plastering, yet the tomb was devoid of decoration.

We examined four other nearby tombs, each consisting of a shaft opening to one or more small, approximately rectangular rooms. Tomb 28 had been "excavated" by some unknown diggers, and we were essentially picking through what was left. We found the bones of three individuals, along with fragments of a limestone canopic jar (a container for a mummy's viscera), many fragments of wooden objects, and some early to mid-18th Dynasty pottery. In Tomb 27, adjacent to Tomb 28, there was stratigraphic evidence that the tomb had been flooded at least seven times, filling some areas with rock and muddy debris nearly to its ceiling.

When Carter discovered Tomb 44 in 1901, its door was sealed with mud bricks. Inside he found a single room containing three 22nd Dynasty (ca. 945–712 B.C.) coffins, side-by-side and covered with dried floral wreaths, resting among the debris of earlier burials. The coffins were removed to Cairo. When we entered the tomb, we found its floor strewn with rubble and piles of debris. Protruding everywhere were human bones, presumably the remains of the earlier burials noted by Carter.

As we sifted through the debris, we recovered little other than human remains. Our osteologist, Daris Swindler, determined that seven people were represented, including three children, one perhaps as young as four years old. Among the artifacts we found were what appeared to be an end-piece from a child's coffin, a small wood fragment bearing a few traces of yellow and blue paint, a blue cylindrical bead, and a large, uninscribed piece of a canopic jar. Tomb 44 was apparently built in the early to mid-18th Dynasty and used for the burial of seven individuals. It was subsequently robbed and flooded. The flooding hastened the deterioration of the mummies and remaining burial objects and a thick deposit of solidified mud formed a hardened layer across the floor of the tomb. Ancient wasp nests on the ceiling indicate that the tomb lay open for some

A Walk Through the Valley of the Kings

Egypt's Valley of the Kings is the subject of countless publications, in print and on the web, produced with different purposes and audiences in mind. The newest is the Theban Mapping Project's Web site (www.thebanmappingproject.com), which combines features geared to the general public with an adaptation of a scholarly work.

At its heart is a tomb-by-tomb description, based on a survey of the valley that began in 1978 and is directed by the American University in Cairo's Kent Weeks. Each entry includes basic information, such as the tomb's location and dimensions, summaries of who investigated it and what was found there, its condition, drawings and photographs, bibliography, and more.

You access this information by clicking on tombs designated on a map or by clicking on the "Launch Atlas" button, which also gives you narrated "tours" of the tombs. But many of these are too brief—a few sentences and one or two images—to be real tours. Much more elaborate is the single "3-D" tour in which you move along the length of tomb KV 14, viewing images of the decorated walls in synch with the narration.

If the Web site isn't yet a one-stop source on the tombs for the general public, perhaps that's because it is an outgrowth of the Atlas of the Valley of the Kings, *the project's monumental scholarly publication. For example, the Web site's entry for KV21 has a terse description of the tomb and the mummified remains of two women, possibly royal, found in it, along with data like the tomb's elevation (180.654 meters above sea level) and area (120.29 square meters). By contrast, Nicholas Reeves and Richard Wilkinson's* Complete Valley of the Kings *has a longer description of the tomb, interior photos, and quotes explorer Giovanni Belzoni, who saw the mummies in 1817: "their hair pretty long, and well preserved, though it was easily separated from the head by pulling it a little."*

The Theban Mapping Project's Web site is an outstanding source for basic information, and provides useful stand-alone articles (on tomb robberies, exploration of the valley, and funerary equipment, to name a few), a timeline, and searchable text and image database. Adding more "tours" like the KV14 one and more general descriptions of the tombs, their contents, and decoration, would take it to an even higher level.

—MARK ROSE

time before it was reused and sealed during the 22nd Dynasty.

Tomb 45, about a dozen yards west of 44, was discovered by Carter in 1902. Its shaft provides access to a single chamber. The tomb contained the water-ruined decorated coffins and the mummies of a male and female. As in Tomb 44, these coffins seem to represent a 22nd Dynasty reuse of an 18th Dynasty tomb. A heart scarab (an inscribed funerary amulet in the form of a beetle) recovered by Carter from the male mummy bears the name and title of an individual associated with the powerful cult of the god Amun: Merenkhons, Doorkeeper of the House of Amun. An 18th Dynasty canopic jar fragment that is inscribed with the name Userhet, Overseer of the Fields of Amun, revealed the identity of one person buried there during the 18th Dynasty.

Carter had apparently cleared both tombs 44 and 45 by scooping up the debris and piling it in the corners, probably excavating one half of the tomb at a time. Within these piles in Tomb 45 we found human bones and hundreds of fragments of the highly decayed coffins left by Carter. Many still retained decoration, including several pieces that bear verses from the funerary text known as the Book of the Dead. One of the first fragments we found was the wooden coffin lid facepiece from the female coffin. Its sculptured features were intact but only isolated specks of paint remained to suggest its original finished surface. We also found numerous fragments of ushabti figures (to serve the deceased in the afterlife) made from unbaked clay. Along with the skeletons of the two individuals found by Carter, our work also revealed the scattered remains of

two additional individuals who presumably belonged to the earlier burial. Tombs 27, 28, 44, and 45 all seem to be of similar early-mid-18th-Dynasty date, though the destruction of these burials allowed the reuse of at least Tombs 44 and 45 during a later dynasty. The contents of all had been severely damaged by flash floods, and the lack of intact, inscribed artifacts has rendered many of the tomb's occupants nameless.

Of what value is the study of these small undecorated tombs? Like many sites or areas of inquiry ignored by past archaeologists, the tombs offer exciting avenues of research for the present and future. They show, for example, that the Valley of the Kings is a far more interesting and complex site than we thought. It is becoming increasingly apparent that a greater number and diversity of individuals were interred in the royal necropolis, including nonroyal persons, small children, young adults, and perhaps queens.

Despite our careful sifting of the evidence, many important questions remain unanswered. Who are the mummies of tombs 60, 21, and elsewhere? Can their identities be established by the relationship of their tombs to nearby royal tombs? Why are the walls of these tombs blank while brightly painted private tombs of all manner of bureaucrats can be found just over the ridge from the Valley in the "Tombs of the Nobles"? At present, the mummies, along with cartons of catalogued artifacts we recovered from the burials, remain in the quiet security of the tombs in which they were found, awaiting further study.

As we worked in these tombs, it became clear that the Valley of the Kings has suffered greatly from both human and natural forces.

KV5

A long-neglected tomb proves to be of great importance.

One of the past quarter century's most interesting Egyptological discoveries of is the extent of KV5—generally called the tomb of the sons of Ramesses II—and the tomb's unusual layout. First partially explored in the 1820s by James Burton, the tomb was visited by others during the nineteenth century, including Karl Lepsius, who recorded a cartouche of the pharaoh Ramesses II near its entrance. But other than Burton's note and sketch plan of nine chambers near the entrance, including a large hall with 16 pillars, little work was done to explore or understand the tomb. Its identification as being for some of Ramesses' 50 sons was proposed by Elizabeth Thomas in her 1966 book Royal Necropoleis of Thebes. Thomas based her suggestion on the cartouche and on a papyrus that preserves testimony extracted from tomb robbers caught in the reign of Ramesses III, mentioning the "tomb of the royal children" of Ramesses II, whose own tomb is nearby (as, indeed, KV5 is).

The tomb's entrance, which had become buried under debris from other excavations and flooding that sometimes affects the Valley of the Kings, was relocated in the late 1980s by Kent Weeks, now with the American University in Cairo. It was on February 2, 1995, that Marjorie Aranow, a doctoral student in Egyptology pushed into a corridor extending beyond the 16-pillared room that was nearly choked with debris. Now, a total of 120 corridors and chambers have been found, making KV5 the largest and most complex tomb in the Valley of the Kings. The tomb has not been fully explored, and what else Weeks will find remains to be seen.

KV5 was once finely decorated, but its reliefs and paintings have been seriously damaged by repeated flooding. It has been possible, however, to read the names of several of Ramesses' sons in the texts preserved on the walls. This seems to prove Thomas correct in linking the tomb with the pharaoh's offspring. While it might be tempting to see the many rooms as individual burial chambers for the pharaoh's sons, they are simply too small for stone sarcophagi and large wood coffins known from royal burials.

—MARK ROSE

Tourism, pollution, water, and wind are some of the many factors that have adversely affected the monuments. One of the biggest threats to the tombs in this arid valley is flash flooding, yet many tombs remain wide open. During the summer of 1993, our expedition focused on such preservation issues, mapping the Valley in detail to provide hydrological data and producing a hazard assessment for each tomb. These efforts are a start in the long-term preservation of both the decorated and the uninscribed tombs in the Valley of the Kings. ▲

WHO'S IN TOMB 55?

In a mystery worthy of Agatha Christie, scholars seek clues to the identity of a mummy that could clarify the royal succession at the end of Egypt's 18th Dynasty.

by MARK ROSE

On January 6, 1907, Theodore M. Davis, a wealthy American financier, and his hired archaeologist, a young Englishman, Edward R. Ayrton, opened a most unusual tomb in Egypt's Valley of the Kings. The tomb, designated KV55 or simply Tomb 55, was unimpressive, with a single chamber and side niche, but its contents were extraordinary.

The largest object was a wooden shrine, sheathed in gold, that had been made for the funeral of Queen Tiye, the mother of the late 18th Dynasty pharaoh Akhenaten (r. 1350–1333 B.C.). This pharaoh's name could be read on two of the four clay bricks found on the tomb's floor. In the niche were four jars, originally inscribed for Kiya, a secondary wife of Akhenaten, mismatched with stoppers bearing exquisite portraits, probably of one or more of Akhenaten's daughters. The strangest of the tomb's contents was an elaborate coffin, also originally for Kiya as attested by reworked yet still decipherable inscriptions, but adapted for a male burial by the addition of a beard and the alteration of the inscriptions (see page 2 of color insert). The face on the coffin had been broken off and the royal names on it, which might have identified its occupant, removed.

In the century following its discovery, Tomb 55 has been hotly debated, especially the identity of the remains in the coffin and how that person fit into the royal family and succession at the end of the 18th Dynasty. "It is probably true to say," notes Aidan Dodson of Bristol University, "that there are as many interpretations as Egyptologists who have written about the notorious Tomb 55. But it matters: the tomb provides part of the key to what was actually going on at the end of Akhenaten's reign—and perhaps at the end of Tutankhamun's as well." Results of an examination of the skeleton by British Museum Egyptologist and physical anthropologist Joyce M. Filer (see page 132) may help close the book on Tomb 55's mysterious occupant.

Akhenaten, who came to the throne as Amenhotep IV, promoted worship of the solar disk, the Aten, over Amun, the god of Thebes, alienating that deity's powerful priesthood. In his fifth year he changed his name to Akhenaten ("Servant of the Aten"), and the following year founded a new capital, which he called Akhetaten ("Horizon of the Aten") and which is known today as el-Amarna. Very late (or very early—as usual, scholars disagree) in his reign, Akhenaten

had Amun's name purged from monuments, particularly in Thebes—it was war between the pharaoh and the Theban priesthood. After Akhenaten's death, Tutankhaten reverted to the worship of Amun and changed his name to Tutankhamun. Akhenaten's own monuments were later cast down or obliterated, perhaps in the first years of the 19th Dynasty (1297–1187 B.C.), and he was called the "criminal of Akhetaten."

Debate over who the mummy is or isn't has continued for nearly a century. Is it the "heretic" pharaoh Akhenaten? Could it be Smenkhkare, who some scholars think was co-regent during Akhenaten's last years; husband of Meretaten, oldest of the Amarna princesses; and possibly Tutankhamun's brother? Or is there some other explanation?

Davis believed that the Tomb 55 mummy was that of Queen Tiye, but this was wishful thinking. The shrine was undoubtedly hers; her name could be read on a surviving portion of the gold on it. Akhenaten apparently had it built for her burial at Amarna. When Amarna was abandoned after his death, the shrine, coffin, and other objects from the royal tombs there were moved to the Valley of the Kings, some ending up in Tomb 55. But Davis' identification was soon discredited when examination by anatomist Grafton Elliot Smith showed the mummy was that of a man. Arthur Weigall, Chief Inspector of Antiquities at Luxor when the tomb was found, argued that it was Akhenaten's, which would explain the coffin's defacement—priests or workers of the Valley of the Kings had entered the tomb and obliterated the name and face of the "criminal of Akhetaten." Smith, however, concluded that the man was in his early twenties at death, too young for Akhenaten, who died in his mid-thirties (we know he was in his teens when he ascended the throne and that he ruled for 17 years).

The interpretation of royal names—carved into monuments, engraved on funerary objects, and written on dockets listing commodities—is key to sorting out the late 18th Dynasty succession and identifying the mummy. Egyptian rulers had five names, the most important being what scholars term the prenomen and nomen, written in cartouches. For example, Tutankhamun's full name was Nebkheperure (prenomen) Tutankhamun-Heqaiunushemay (nomen with an epithet). Some queens also used epithets with their single cartouches, so that Akhenaten's principal wife Nefertiti was, in full, Nefertiti-Nefernefruaten. Two other royal names known from the end of the 18th Dynasty are Ankhkheprure Smenkhkare and Ankhkheprure Nefernefruaten. Three basic scenarios have been proposed to account for these names and for Nefertiti's absence from the record after year 13 of Akhenaten's rule:

1. Nefertiti dies in year 13 or later of Akhenaten's reign. Smenkhkare (a.k.a. Nefernefruaten), a male co-regent during Akhenaten's last three years, predeceases him; Tutankhamun succeeds Akhenaten. The Tomb 55 body is Smenkhkare.

2. Smenkhkare, a male co-regent, predeceases Akhenaten, who is succeeded by Nefertiti, ruling under her name Nefernefruaten; Tutankhamun succeeds her. The Tomb 55 body is Smenkhkare.

3. Nefertiti becomes co-regent in year 12–13, as Nefernefruaten; after Akhenaten's death she rules under the name

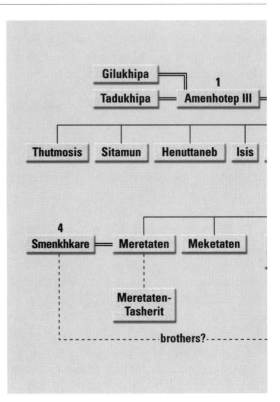

Smenkhkare; Tutankhamun succeeds her. The Tomb 55 body is Akhenaten.

The two basic questions are, is there evidence that a male co-regent named Smenkhkare existed, and, who is the body?

Several objects found in Tutankhamun's tomb bear the name of other royal family members. These include four miniature gold coffins that held jars containing Tutankhamun's internal organs. Names inscribed inside the coffins were reworked, apparently first from Smenkhkare to Nefernefruaten, and certainly then to Tutankhamun. From the way that this was done, it would suggest that Smenkhkare and Nefernefruaten were names borne by the same individual. In addition, the face portrayed on

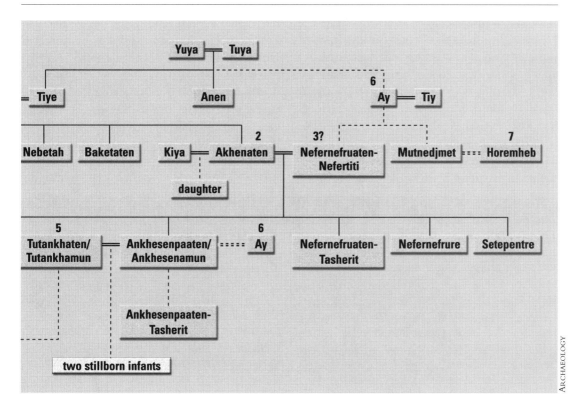

ARCHAEOLOGY

these and on Tutankhamun's middle coffin does not match other representations of him. On the basis of the texts of the miniature gold coffins, this must be the face of Smenkhkare. He also appears in a tomb painting at Amarna; a relief block bears his name, as do some finger-rings and stamped bricks. A battered limestone head from Amarna has also been claimed to represent him.

The Tomb 55 skeleton's age may be key to its identification. Akhenaten was in his mid-thirties at death, but examinations of the Tomb 55 bones from Smith to the 1960s yielded estimates in the early twenties. Then, at a 1988 Egyptological conference, University of Michigan orthodontics professor James E. Harris and Fawzia H. Hussein of

the Anthropological Laboratory, National Centre, Cairo, claimed a mid-to-late thirties age, just right for Akhenaten. That study, however, has never been published. Joyce M. Filer, latest to examine the bones, places the age in the early twenties at most, precluding their identification as Akhenaten's.

In addition to the Tomb 55 body, there are other late 18th Dynasty royal mummies. The best-known is Tutankhamun, which has been linked by blood type and by skull shape to the Tomb 55 body. Mummies found in 1898 have been identified as Amenhotep III and Tiye, Akhenaten's parents and Tutankhamun's grandparents, but both identifications have been questioned, epecially the second. An alternative, speculative proposal is that the supposed Tiye mummy may be Nefertiti, but from the context of the find it is pretty clear that it is of a much earlier lady and has nothing to do with Akhenaten's family. Finally, two mummified fetuses from Tutankhamun's tomb were possibly carried by his wife Ankhesenamun.

DNA analysis might clarify relationships among these mummies, but just before an Egyptian-Japanese team took tissue samples from Tutankhamun's mummy last spring, the Egyptian government abruptly halted the work for what it said were national security reasons. Press reports, however, pointed to concern that some people might misinterpret the results to further claims that Akhenaten was the biblical Moses. This far-fetched link—it assumes, among other things, that our understanding of Egyptian chronology is off by a number of centuries—has been

Royal Coffin Controversy

An old theft and secretive dealings are the latest chapters in the history of an enigmatic royal coffin discovered in the Valley of the Kings in 1907. The tomb in which the coffin was found, known as KV55 and excavated by English archaeologist Edward Ayrton, was small, with a single chamber and side niche. It held the coffin, in ruined condition; a dismantled wooden shrine once covered in gold foil; four canopic jars; and other funerary objects.

The top half of the coffin, along with the gold foil that had been applied to the sides and floor of the bottom half, went to the Egyptian Museum in Cairo. Between a restoration of the objects in 1914 and an inventory in 1931, the gold from the bottom half was stolen. It was later rumored that the gold was in a European museum. Last fall, the journal KMT published two photos of the restored gold decoration from the sides of the coffin's bottom half and named Munich's State Collection of Egyptian Art as possessing it.

The mummy in the coffin was first identified as Tiye, mother of Akhenaten (r. 1350–1334). Her name was on a surviving portion of the gold foil from the dismantled shrine, which Akhenaten apparently had ordered built for her funeral at his capital, el-Amarna. The shrine, coffin, and other objects were later moved to the KV55 tomb. Identification of the mummy as Tiye was soon disproved; examination showed it was that of a man. The mummy's identity has been debated ever

since. Cartouches with Akhenaten's name had been excised from the top half of the coffin and from Tiye's shrine. Many of his monuments were defaced after his heretical worship of the sun disk Aten was abolished by his successor, Tutankhamun. Akhenaten is one possibility, but the mummy is of a man in his twenties, which is too young for him. Yet the mummy's skull shape and blood type are similar to Tutankhamun's. Could it be Smenkhare, co-regent during Akhenaten's last years and possibly his brother?

Now, an article in the German magazine Der Spiegel offers an account, based on a recent lecture by Berlin Egyptian Museum scholar Rolf Krauss, of how the gold came to Munich. It was acquired ca. 1950 by a Geneva-based antiquities dealer. After efforts to sell the gold during the 1970s proved unsuccessful, it went to the museum in Munich, then directed by Dietrich Wildung, in 1980. It was secretly restored there and mounted on a plexiglas shell. In 1994, the dealer's daughter formally donated it.

While cartouches on the sides of the bottom half have been removed, as the KMT photos show, there is hope that its floor was not defaced. According to Der Spiegel, the museum's current director, Sylvia Schoske, refuses access to it and has not made public her own study of it. Negotiations are said to be underway between Munich and Cairo, the German museum asking for a long-term loan in exchange for return of the coffin gold.

—MARK ROSE

made in Moses; Pharaoh of Egypt, authored by Egyptian-born amateur historian Ahmed Osman, and other books. While it is understandable that such creative interpretations might make the government skittish, the more solid evidence there is, the less room there will be for such wild claims.

For now, we can say that there is artifactual evidence for a male ruler from the end of the 18th Dynasty who is not Akhenaten and is not Tutankhamun. We can also say that the body in Tomb 55 belongs to the immediate family of Akhenaten and Tutankhamun, but it is too young to be the former, and we have the mummy of the latter. Returning to the scenarios explaining the royal names, the evidence fits best with the first case: Smenkhkare (a.k.a. Nefernefruaten), a male co-regent during Akhenaten's last years, predeceases him; Tutankhamun succeeds Akhenaten. The second case seems needlessly complex, and is apparently disproved by the evidence of the names in the miniature coffins. The facts fit least well with the third case: there is evidence for a royal male and a body to go with it, so equating Nefertiti with Smenkhkare as Akhenaten's successor before Tutankhamun leaves the body unexplained.

The most straightforward interpretation of the inscriptions, artifacts, and bones is that the body from Tomb 55 is Smenkhkare. This means that Tutankhamun, like his father, came to the throne only through the early death of an older brother. The early deaths of both Smenkhkare and Tutankhamun without heirs spelled the end of the 18th Dynasty. ▲

ANATOMY OF A MUMMY

A close study of the mystery skeleton's bones indicates he was male and in his early twenties.

by JOYCE M. FILER

Cairo, January 2000. I am waiting in a private research room at the Egyptian Museum to examine the skeletal remains found in Tomb 55 of the Valley of the Kings. The identity of this mummy has been debated ever since the tomb was discovered in January 1907. The excavator, Theodore M. Davis, invited two doctors visiting the newly opened tomb to examine the mummy, reduced to a skeleton through poor preservation and mishandling upon discovery. One of the physicians was a Dr. Pollock and the other, whose name appears unknown, is described as "a prominent American obstetrician." Davis was obviously pleased to be informed by them that the mummy was "without doubt" that of an elderly female, for he was convinced he had found the tomb of Queen Tiye, the wife of Amenhotep III (r. 1388–1348) and mother of Akhenaten (r. 1350–1333). The machinery for controversy was set in motion when the remains were sent to the anatomist Grafton Elliot Smith for further examination. Smith identified the individual as a male who was at least in his mid-twenties when he died. Despite these conflicting anatomical views, Davis published the tomb and remains as Queen Tiye's in 1910, while Smith published the remains as male in 1912.

Over the years, the body has been re-examined several times, the majority of researchers agreeing that the body is of a male. The age at death, however, has continued to be a source of controversy as it has considerable bearing on the proper identity. To tie in with historical sources, scholars who favor identifying the remains as those of Akhenaten require the body to be that of a man at least 35 years of age at death. Those accepting the body to be that of a younger man support its identification as a co-regent from the end of Akhenaten's reign named Smenkhkare. Some proponents of the Akhenaten identification look for ties to artistic representations that show the pharaoh with a bizarre physique (spindly limbs, large pelvis, and elongated, angular face), reasoning that the skeleton may preserve evidence of a medical disorder.

As an Egyptologist and physical anthropologist, I hope my examination of the remains will solve some of the mysteries surrounding this body. Key points of the examination will be confirming the sex of the individual, determining the age at death, and looking for evidence of possible pathological conditions.

Ninety-three years later, almost to the day it was discovered, I watch as the protective textile covering the body is rolled back under the supervision of Nasry Iskander, the curator in charge of mummies at the Egyptian Museum. My first task is to establish how much of this famous body actually exists, for some researchers have suggested that the skeleton is incomplete and in poor condition. It is immediately obvious that this is not the case. Apart from a few missing teeth, and hand and foot bones boxed separately, the skeleton is almost complete and is in good condition except for some damage that occurred after death to some of the vertebrae and the tip of the left pubic bone. The bones are dark-colored in places, a feature often seen in Egyptian mummies following the decay or removal of linen wrappings. Unguents used in mummification and complex environmental interactions within the burial place can produce such discolorations. Flakes of an opaque substance adhering to some of the bones are likely remnants of the paraffin wax in which Arthur Weigall, Chief Inspector of Antiquities at Luxor when the tomb was found, soaked the body before sending it to Smith.

My next task is to check whether or not the skull and the bones of the skeleton actually belong to one another. The possibility that parts of this skeleton might have been mixed with those of another (or others) has been raised by at least one researcher, so I feel it is vital to establish the integrity of the body before proceeding any further. Happily, the situation looks good. The upper and lower leg bones articulate together smoothly, and these in turn fit correctly with the two pelvic (hip) bones. All the elements of the spine fit together well and also articulate perfectly with the sacrum, the series of fused vertebrae positioned between the two hip bones. Moving to the top of the spine, I am keen to check if it fits with the base of the skull, as this will determine if the skull and skeleton belong to the same person. It does. So, there we have it—one individual. But what about those crucial questions of sex and age?

To establish the sex of any skeleton, an examination of the pelvis is critical. As I articulate the two hip bones with the sacrum, they form a basin or girdle that is small and heart-shaped, a very male attribute. The angle of the two hip bones, where they meet at the front of the body, is steep: another male characteristic. The greater sciatic notch, a curved hollow area on the lower edge of each hip bone, is neither overtly male nor female in shape, but it is not the most important indicator of sex, so we cannot place too much weight on it. The sacrum is typically male in shape. The skull presents some very strongly male features: large mastoid processes (the bone you can feel just behind your ear) and well-defined brow ridges. The mandible, or lower jaw, is strong and wide and rather square-shaped, all features associated with males. Overall, the skeleton is not overly robust, but neither is it as delicate or feminine as some researchers have claimed. I do find an aperture in both upper arm bones just above the elbow. Such apertures are found more often with gracile individuals, hence females, and are often seen in ancient Egyptian remains. But in light of the other, stronger indicators of sex, they cannot really sway an assessment away from male. Looking on the backs of the upper leg

bones, I find a pronounced ridge (the linea aspera), again supporting a determination as male. In putting the evidence together from the hip bones, the skull and mandible, and other features, I am in no doubt that the skeleton before me is male.

In considering this man's age at death, I need to look at his teeth and assess the maturity of his bones. Apart from one of the four third molars (wisdom teeth) not being fully erupted, he had a full set of adult teeth. The front ones of the lower jaw are missing, but I can see clearly from the empty sockets that they were lost after death. The partially erupted third molar tells me this is a younger adult—no older than the early twenties—although wisdom teeth can erupt at any time from about the age of 18 onward. The teeth show no signs of periodontal disease or tooth decay. Importantly, the molars show only the slightest wear on the chewing surfaces, which again strongly suggests a young adult.

Turning to the bones, I can see that some skeletal elements are immature. As bones reach maturity, various unattached elements (called epiphyses) fuse onto the main section, preventing further growth. Because the bones in the human skeleton fuse in a particular order and within a known time frame, this information can be used to assess an individual's age at death. As I examine the ends of the arm and leg bones of the skeleton, the fusion lines are clearly visible, indicating that this man was not quite a fully mature adult, between 18 and 21 years when he died. Following his examination, Smith stated that the limb bones were "fully ossified and consolidated," but this is not borne out by what I see. One section of the outer edge of the hip bone (the crest of the ilium) is not fused, pointing to an age of no more than 25 years for a male. Generally, the last element of the skeleton to fuse is the end of the collar bone that articulates with the breastbone. Here there is no fusion at all, setting an upper age limit of about 25 years. Interestingly, but not often noted, research conducted in the early twentieth century showed that, skeletally speaking, modern Egyptians tend to mature earlier than their European counterparts. If this was the case in ancient Egypt, the noted lack of fusion in some skeletal elements of the body provides further corroboration of a young age.

Although the fading and obliteration of the sutures holding the bones of the skull together is an unreliable indicator of age by itself, I think it is worth noting that this skull presents no signs of this; it would be expected if the individual were significantly older. Similarly, I see no evidence of osteoarthritis, the arthritis caused by everyday wear and tear, and this, too, tends to suggest a younger person.

Some statues and stelae of Akhenaten show him with an overly long face and head and an exceptionally feminine physique, prompting speculation that he suffered from a pronounced medical disorder. When Smith studied the body, he considered the varying degrees of density in the skull bones as indicating hydrocephalus, an abnormal enlargement of the skull, but others examining the skull later found no such signs. Was Smith influenced by the representations of the king that he'd seen in the Egyptian Museum? Certainly, he felt confident in proclaiming the Tomb 55 body as that of Akhenaten in his 1912 report. With that in mind, I exam-

ine the skeleton for any traces of abnormality. I can see that the skull is large, but well within normal limits and is, in fact, of a shape totally contrasting with that of the hydrocephalic. The pelvic basin or girdle is small and its lack of width rules against its matching the generous dimensions exhibited in some of Akhenaten's statues.

It is also worth noting that there are some depictions of him with a normal stature. It may well be, as has been suggested, that he chose to have himself represented with features of both sexes as an expression of his religious beliefs in which he viewed himself as the mother and father of his people. If this is the case, the presence or absence of cranial abnormalities or female skeletal characteristics may not be significant in establishing the individual's identity.

During my examination of the bones, I have the opportunity to compare the x-ray images of Tutankhamun's skull taken by anatomist R.G. Harrison of the University of Liverpool in 1966 with those of the Tomb 55 skull taken by James E. Harris, a University of Michigan orthodontics professor, in the 1970s. By overlaying one x-ray image upon the other on a lightbox, it is possible to examine and compare the size and shape of both skulls. Several researchers have commented upon the remarkable likeness in size and shape between Tutankhamun's skull and that of the Tomb 55 mummy and I am in total agreement with them. It does seem, from this anatomical similarity, that these two individuals must have been closely related. Perhaps DNA analysis will one day help us clarify the situation.

A question commonly asked about the ancient dead is how did he or she die. Harrison says that he found evidence of periostitis (bone inflammation most often caused by trauma or infection) on x-ray images he made of several of the bones. I see no signs of traumatic injury; thus it is possible that this young man had suffered some form of infection during life. Without taking new x-ray images, it is difficult to comment further on Harrison's findings. As the evidence stands, it is not possible to state a cause of death.

An anatomical examination cannot identify the individual, but it can provide information useful in evaluating the theories various scholars have proposed. The human remains from Tomb 55, as presented to me, are those of a young man who had no apparent abnormalities and was no older than his early twenties at death and probably a few years younger. If those wanting to identify the remains with Akhenaten demand an age at death of more than mid-twenties, then this is not the man for them. As an obviously younger individual, some people might like to identify the remains as belonging to the mysterious Smenkhkare. Might they, in fact, belong to neither of them? Whoever he was, the similarity between the Tomb 55 skull and that of Tutankhamun, Akhenaten's son, certainly suggests he was a member of the royal family. ▲

The Valley of the Golden Mummies

The story varies depending upon who tells it, but in May 1996 an antiquities guard or a guard's donkey made an amazing discovery in the Bahariyah Oasis, 230 miles southwest of Pyramids at Giza. A chance step, by foot or hoof, revealed burial chambers cut into the sandstone three and one-half miles south of Bawiti, the regional capital. The discovery was kept secret to protect the site from looters until it could be excavated. In March 1999, Zahi Hawass, now secretary general of Egypt's Supreme Council of Antiquities, led a team that explored four tombs, possibly family burial vaults, that held 105 mummies. Dated to the first and second centuries A.D., the Bahariyah mummies are typical of the Roman period in Egypt, with gilded and painted cartonnage masks that extend partway down the body and elaborate linen wrappings, the cloth strips covering the body in a pattern of rhomboids. They blend Egyptian and Roman traditions and cultures. The deities depicted on them include the four Sons of Horus, who guarded the viscera; Anubis, the jackal-headed god of embalming and the necropolis; and goddesses like Isis and Nephthys, shown protecting the deceased with their outstretched wings. But they have Roman hairstyles and wear laurel wreaths. Among the other finds were jewelry, scarabs and other amulets, coins, ceramic food and wine vessels, and statuettes of mourning women. Hawass estimates that the cemetery may extend for two square miles and contain as many as 10,000 burials. The site is now known as the Valley of the Golden Mummies after the gilded masks worn by its long-dead inhabitants.

—Mark Rose

EMERALD CITY

Exploration in Egypt's Eastern Desert yields the mines that furnished Rome's elite with coveted gems.

by JEAN-LOUIS RIVARD, BRANDON C. FOSTER, AND STEVEN E. SIDEBOTHAM

E gypt's Eastern Desert has been one of the most isolated and under-explored regions in the country, its
ruins, spanning more than 5,000 years of history, protected by its forbidding climate and mountainous terrain.
Now, rapidly encroaching resorts and villas along the Red
Sea coast, together with mass tourism and a burgeoning
local population, have placed its ancient sites at great risk.

One of the most popular tourist destinations is what
travel brochures call the "emerald city" in Wadi Sikait: hundreds of buildings, temples, graves, and mine shafts associated with the search for emeralds that began in Roman
times and possibly earlier. Groups of tourists arrive by four-
wheel drive vehicles from hotels on the coast, then wander
about unchaperoned, leaving behind plastic water bottles

and juice containers. Their "guides" know nothing about the site and do not care if the tourists climb on walls, dislodging stones, or help themselves to pottery sherds. Worse still, graffiti has been spray-painted and incised on walls of one temple, and portions of an inscription from another have disappeared, undoubtedly stolen, in the past decade.

We know little about the mining operations here and the people who worked and lived in this remote desert area. How large was the population and how did it fluctuate? Where did the inhabitants acquire food, water, and mining tools? What type of goods made their way there? The need for answers to these questions, as well as the growing threat posed by unrestricted access by visitors, makes our mission—the proper documentation and preservation of sites like Sikait—of the utmost importance.

In his *Natural History*, Pliny the Elder (A.D. 23/24–79) brings together facts, lore, and gossip about emeralds, which Romans called smaragdi. He praises the bright green color of the "Egyptian" or "Ethiopian" stones, as he terms the gems from the Eastern Desert, and notes they were "so hard as to be unaffected by blows." Romans prized emeralds above all except diamonds and pearls. Writes Pliny, "I have seen Lollia Paulina, who became the consort of Gaius [Caligula, r. A.D. 37–41]…covered with emeralds and pearls interlaced and alternately shining all over her head, hair, ears, neck and fingers, the sum total amounting to the value of 40,000,000 sesterces." For comparison, the annual salary of a soldier under Domitian (r. A.D. 81–96) was about 1,200 sesterces. Naturally the high value placed on

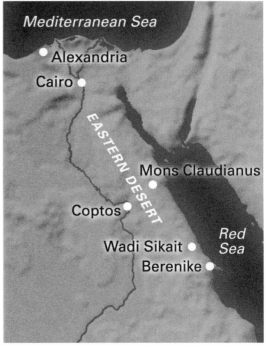

emeralds led to counterfeiting, which Pliny denounced. "There are treatises by authorities," he notes, "describing how by means of dyestuffs emeralds and other transparent colored gems are made from rock crystal…. And there is no other trickery that is practiced against society with greater profit."

Demand for these precious stones prompted the flowering of Sikait in the region called Mons Smaragdus (Emerald Mountain) by the Romans. It was the only source of emeralds known to them. The ruins that tourists see today are what is left of a humming center of industrial activity. Almost unbelievably, the site's location was once lost. When Mohammed Ali Pasha came to power as the Ottoman viceroy of Egypt in the early 1800s, one of his goals was to exploit the mineral wealth of his domain.

This included an effort to locate the mines and reopen them. In 1816, Ali sent out Frédéric Cailliaud, a French goldsmith, mineralogist, and adventurer from Nantes, to find and document the mines. Cailliaud found them in November 1817, and he stayed at the site for two days, making drawings that are now a valuable, if somewhat fanciful, record of what once stood there. Until Cailliaud's discovery of the mines, only a few second-hand reports in European travelogues, vague references in medieval Arab sources, and a handful of the region's Ababda Bedouin preserved knowledge of them. But the mines were never reworked; the heat and terrain were too severe and, although popular with the Romans, the emeralds mined here were less desirable in a nineteenth-century market that had access to superior quality stones from Colombia.

Ancient literary works indicate that the Egyptian mines were most heavily exploited during Roman times. In his Geography, written at the beginning of the Christian era, Strabo states that the Arabs dug deep tunnels to extract the emeralds. Trade routes extended from Coptos, on the Nile, to ports on the Red Sea, such as Berenike, and Pliny recorded that the emeralds were dug at mines a 25-days' journey from Coptos (in reality they are much closer). The historian Olympiodorus in the fifth century A.D. wrote that one needed the permission of the king of the Blemmyes, a nomadic desert tribe then controlling the area, to visit the mines. In addition, an inscription dated A.D. 10/11 found at a Roman quarry farther north in the Eastern Desert records that an imperial official was in charge of emerald mines and "all other mines of Egypt."

During archaeological surveys over the past 15 years, we have recorded the remains of a number of ancient mines. Those in the region of Mons Smaragdus are by far the largest and most impressive. In spite of numerous visits by travelers and scholars to the mines and associated settlements over the past two centuries, nobody has ever drawn a detailed, measured plan of any of them, nor attempted to study what daily life at the mines and related communities was like in antiquity.

So, in the winter of 1998, two members from our main expedition, which was conducting excavations at Berenike, began this monumental undertaking by mapping an emerald-mining camp in Wadi Abu Rashid, not far from Wadi Sikait. We continued in the winter of 2000 with another two-man team sent to survey Wadi Sikait itself. Living in the ancient settlement for 40 days, our crew's only neighbors were Ababda Bedouin who occasionally passed through with their herds or wandered through in search of wayward camels. We returned last summer with a larger team, completing the survey of the main settlement at Sikait, then continuing north to two related sites that we named Middle and North Sikait.

Traveling north toward Sikait from Wadi Gemal, one sees many indications of the settlement: cairns marking the route, lines of stones for tethering the pack animals that shuttled between the mines and the Nile Valley via the main Nile-Red Sea road, outbuildings, and graves on the sides of the wadi. A small rock-cut temple marks the entrance to Sikait. Based on drawings made by French and English visitors in the first half of the nineteenth century, this edifice

Courtesy Mark Rose

The drawings by French explorer Frédéric Cailliaud, who discovered the site of Sikait in 1817, provide a valuable guide to the condition of the site's monuments at that time.

was dedicated to the gods "Sarapis, Isis, Apollo and all the gods sharing their temple." This inscription, which has not survived, was carved sometime during the reign of the emperor Gallienus (A.D. 260–268).

As one continues northward, the immensity of the settlement becomes apparent. To the east is a large temple with a Doric facade, its interior cut into the mountainside. We do not know to whom it was dedicated; only a few letters from a Greek inscription above the entrance remain. Opposite this temple, on an outcrop at the entrance to the site, is a building comprising three-rooms along a central axis of doorways. Its innermost chamber is rock-cut with a stone roof, a common characteristic of buildings in Sikait. To the north and far-

ther up the slope sits another important structure, marked by three doors facing due east and leading onto a large platform overlooking the wadi below. The functions of these latter two structures remain a mystery.

Farther into the valley, narrow steps cut into the rock or built up of quarried stone linked different parts of the settlement, zigzagging through the maze of buildings rising up the mountainsides along the wadi. Many of the hundreds of structures, apparently built of stone from small quarries adjacent to them, have well-preserved doorways, windows, and niches. We discovered more than 20 tunnels and subterranean rooms, most filled with tumbled stone and debris. Possibly exhausted or abandoned mine shafts, these rock-cut features often extend

Drawing shows Frédéric Cailliaud's camp in 1817 in front of a temple dedicated to Sarapis, Isis, and Apollo, and adorned with carved rearing cobras flanking a solar disk.

ers must have been difficult, at times brutal, to judge from our own experience at the site. Winter daytime temperatures range from the 70s to 90s, sometimes higher, but can drop down into the 30s at night. There are occasional downpours; in fact, heavy rains damaged some parts of the site this January. Our thermometer did not go high enough to record maximum daytime temperatures last summer, but the glue of our shower bags melted, and the air was so dry and hot that pages fell out of our paperback books when the adhesive bindings failed. It cooled down overnight only to 95 degrees. We worked from dawn until sunset, but during summer had to rest under a shade tent from 11:00 until 3:00 in the afternoon.

We located several ancient wells in the wadis of Sikait, but whether the inhabitants obtained all their water locally or had to bring in more water from some as-yet unidentifiable source is uncertain. There is plenty of evidence from other desert sites that some fruits and vegetables were grown locally in antiquity. Wine, oil, some meat (on the hoof or dried and salted), and fish would have been imported. Excavators at the quarry site of Mons Claudianus, farther north in the Eastern Desert, found that some transport animals, especially donkeys, were slaughtered for food ("Lure of the Desert Road," ARCHAEOLOGY July/August 1989). This may have been the case at Sikait, too.

The location of Sikait's cemeteries is a mystery. We have found only about 100 graves, all thoroughly robbed, scattered mainly north and east of the main settlement. Usually marked by simple piles of stones or low stone walls, the graves were easy to locate and plunder; human bones

directly into the mountainside a short distance, others spiral beneath themselves or catacomb in multiple directions. Future excavation may reveal what, if anything, was stored in these areas and how deeply the tunnels cut into the mountainsides. Two large shafts found at the northern end of Sikait are obvious evidence of mining. Worn steps had been carved into the steep sides of the largest shaft, which was about 23 feet in diameter and at least 33 feet deep. Large piles of schist and other stone fragments indicate the intensity of activity that once took place here.

Working conditions for the ancient min-

and potsherds litter the ground around the looted ones. Most of the people buried in these places probably had little money, so grave goods would have been minimal. In one instance, a small building, probably an observation post, overlooks the remains of about two dozen graves strewn down a mountainside. Other than these, we noticed only scattered graves between Sikait and the juncture with the ancient route between Berenike and the Nile.

We do not know yet if the emerald mines were exploited before the arrival of the Romans in Egypt in 30 B.C. Initial study of potsherds we found littering the slopes of the wadi suggests that the construction and occupation of Sikait began in the first century A.D. and that it was abandoned some-time in the fifth century, which accords with the historical sources. But does this really provide the earliest and latest evidence of habitation at the site? Small-scale excavations planned for this summer will address this question. In future seasons, we will focus on restoring and reconstructing Sikait's major structures. We also hope to carry out survey work in the region to record other such settlements and the facilities that supported them. Of equal importance, we want to educate visitors of the need to treat sites like Sikait with respect so that future generations might benefit from them. All of us—ourselves, the tourist industry, the local Bedouin, and the Egyptian government—stand to gain from the study and preservation of this ancient emerald-mining city. ▲

Great Was My Astonishment

Frédéric Cailliaud's *Voyage á L'Oasis de Thèbes* traces his travels in the region between 1815 and 1818 following, in part, the texts of ancient authors. This excerpt, from the 1822 English edition of his account, tells of his discovery of Sikait on November 22, 1817:

...we mounted our dromedaries, the master-miner, my Interpreter, and myself, to make some researches in the vicinity. We proceeded in a direction to the south, to about seven leagues from Mount Zabarah. In this track we came to some mountains with emerald quarries and mines far more considerable than those already mentioned. They contain, perhaps, a thousand excavations; there appears to have been long stone causeways constructed under ground, to facilitate the communications. They were so contrived that the camels could convey provisions to the workmen, ascending to the very summit of the mountains where the apertures commence. In fact, we every where discerned vestiges of very extensive labours, evidently the works of the Ancients. With so few men, we found it impossible to enter those galleries, which were almost innumerable.

About half a league to the south of these new mines, I discovered the ruins of a little Greek town, now called by the Ababdeh, Sekket [Sikait] Bendar El Kebyr. About 500 houses of rough hewn stone yet remain: three temples have been partly cut out of rock, and partly constructed of stone. Great was my astonishment to find, in the desert [sic], at so remote a distance, a town in such good repair. It was highly amusing to me to stroll from house to house, from chamber to chamber. In these deserted dwellings, various instruments, utensils, &c., were to be seen, with lamps of burnt earth, and fragments of vases of beautiful form, both of earth and glass; also stones, hollowed and fluted, that served for mills to grind their grain. With unbound satisfaction I greeted and hailed a town, hitherto unknown to all our voyagers, which had not been inhabited, perhaps, for 2000 years, and almost entirely standing.

—FRÉDÉRIC CAILLIAUD

REDISCOVERING ALEXANDRIA

Underwater and underground, archaeologists are exploring the ruins of an ancient metropolis.

by MARK ROSE

Having wrested Egypt from the Persians in in 332 B.C., Alexander the Great marched past Rhacotis, a small village on the Mediterranean coast at the Nile Delta's northwestern edge. Noting the site's promising location, he founded a new city there, unmodestly naming it Alexandria. Under the Ptolemies, the Dynasty established by one of Alexander's generals, the city flourished. It was visited by the Greek geographer Strabo (64 B.C.–A.D. 21) not long after its last Ptolemaic ruler, Cleopatra VII, killed herself in 30 B.C. rather than accept Roman captivity. His description of Alexandria has provided archaeologists with a map of sorts:

In the Great Harbor at the entrance, on the right hand, are the island and tower of Pharos, and on the other hand are the reefs and also the promontory of Lochias, with a royal palace upon it; and on sailing into the harbor one comes, on the left, to the inner royal palaces, which are continuous with those on Lochias and have groves and numerous lodges painted in various colors. Below these lies the harbor that was dug by the hand of man and is hidden from view, the private property of the kings, as also Antirrhodos, an isle lying off the artificial harbor, which has both a royal palace and a small harbor.

Alexandria's lighthouse, built in 285–280 B.C., was one of the Seven Wonders of the Ancient World. It rose in three tiers, some 325 feet, atop which was a statue of Zeus. But this is a seismically active region marked by earthquakes and subsiding land. The lighthouse was damaged by successive earthquakes (23 are mentioned by ancient and Arabic authors in the period from A.D. 320 to 1303), and by 1349 it was in ruins. On its seaside location, and with some of its stones, the Mameluke sultan Ashraf Qaitbay erected a fortress in 1477–1480.

It was long known that ancient remains lay on the seafloor off Alexandria and in its harbors. As early as 1961, the Egyptian navy had pulled up a colossal statue of a Ptolemaic queen dressed as the goddess Isis. In March 1994, the Egyptian cinematographer Asma el-Bakri was working on a documentary about ancient Alexandria and asked French archaeologist Jean-Yves Empereur of the Centre d'Études Alexandrines to help in filming remains on the seafloor near Qaitbay Fort. Diving in the five-acre area just 24 feet below the surface, Empereur saw sculptural and architectural remains all around. Over the next five years, Empereur and his colleagues, working with Egypt's Supreme Council of Antiquities, found fragments of three obelisks of the pharaoh Seti I; papyrus shaped column capitals, some with car-touches of Ramesses II; 25 sphinxes; and hundreds of columns. In October 1995, a stone torso of a third-century B.C. Ptolemaic queen was lifted from the seabed; a colossal king weighing 11.4 tons soon followed. Along with the rest of the finds there are thousands of architectural elements, one of Aswan granite 34-feet-long and weighing more than 70 tons. Empereur believes that some of these are from the collapse of the lighthouse in the fourteenth century.

Empereur has also located a number of Greek and Roman shipwrecks. One mid-first century B.C. vessel is represented by its cargo, hundreds of amphoras that would have been used to transport wine or olive oil. Most of the wreck's amphoras are from southeastern Italy. These were found beneath smaller numbers of amphoras from Crete and Rhodes, suggesting the ship had come eastward from Italy, stopped at Crete and Rhodes, then continued on to Alexandria.

In a separate project, also in conjunction with the Supreme Council of Antiquities, Franck Goddio of the Institut Européen d'Archéologie Sous-Marine mapped remains now submerged on the harbor floor 20 feet below the surface. Beginning in 1992, Goddio recorded columns, capitals, sculpture fragments, paving stones, and amphoras scattered on the seafloor. Of particular interest was the question of whether or not any traces survived of Cleopatra VII's palace on the sunken island of Antirrhodos. Investigations there, however, yielded only remains from the early third century A.D., during the reign of the Roman emperor Caracalla.

Not all of the discoveries in Alexandria have been underwater. In the summer of

1997, Jean-Yves Empereur responded to an Egyptian request for assistance in excavating part of a Hellenistic (323–146 B.C.) cemetery threatened by road construction in Gabbari, western Alexandria. He found intact inhumations and cinerary urns in 42 collective burial chambers. The earlier burials in the cemetery, from the time of the city's founding, are of upper class citizens, the later ones are more middle class. Some of those buried at Gabbari had been mummified, but they are poorly preserved. Strabo's "map" of Alexandria includes a description of a necropolis with gardens and embalming workshops, and the Gabbari cemetery may well be part of it. ▲

HUNTING ALEXANDER'S TOMB

by ROBERT S. BIANCHI

Alexander the Great, dying at Babylon on the banks of the Euphrates River in June of 323 B.C., was explicit in his last wish. He wanted his body thrown into the river so that his corpse would disappear. In that way, Alexander reasoned, his survivors might perpetuate the myth that he was whisked off to heaven in order to spend eternity at the side of the god Ammon, who had allegedly fathered him. His generals, not respecting the wish, concocted elaborate plans for his burial. According to one ancient account, it took two years from the time of Alexander's death to design and construct a suitable funerary cart in which his mummified body could be conveyed to its tomb. En route to its destination, whether Macedonia or elsewhere is moot, the funerary cart and its entourage were met in Syria by Ptolemy, a Macedonian general in Alexander's army. Ptolemy, who in 305 B.C. would proclaim himself king of Egypt as Ptolemy I Soter and inaugurate the Ptolemaic Dynasty, diverted the body to Egypt where it was buried in a tomb at Memphis.

der had had at least three tombs in two Egyptian cities. Whenever someone asks where the tomb of Alexander the Great is located, I assume the query refers to the third and last tomb, although admittedly the question might apply equally to his tomb at Memphis or to his first Alexandrian tomb, neither of which has ever been found.

The literary tradition is clear that the third and last tomb was located at the crossroads of the major north-south and east-west arteries of Alexandria. Octavian, the future Roman emperor Augustus, visited Alexandria shortly after the suicide of Cleopatra VII in 30 B.C. He is said to have viewed the body of Alexander, placing flowers on the tomb and a golden diadem upon Alexander's mummified head. The last recorded visit to the tomb was made by the Roman Emperor Caracalla in A.D. 215. The tomb was probably damaged and perhaps even looted during the political disturbances that ravaged Alexandria during the reign of Aurelian shortly after A.D. 270. By the fourth century A.D., the tomb's location was no longer known, if one can trust the accounts of several of the early Church Fathers. Thereafter, creditable Arab commentators, including Ibn Abdel Hakam (A.D. 871), Al-Massoudi (A.D. 944), and Leo the African (sixteenth century A.D.) all report having seen the tomb of Alexander, but do not specify its exact location.

The Egyptian Antiquities Organization has officially recognized more than 140 searches for Alexander's tomb, and there have been at least four recent attempts to locate it. The first was mounted in 1960 by the Polish Center of Archaeology, whose members continue to excavate an area

A marble portrait now in Instanbul depicts a young Alexander.

Subsequently, in the late fourth or early third century B.C. (whether during the reign of Ptolemy I Soter or that of his son and successor, Ptolemy II Philadelphus, is debated) the body of Alexander was removed from its tomb in Memphis and transported to Alexandria where it was reburied. At a still later date, Ptolemy Philopator (222/21–205 B.C.) placed the bodies of his dynastic predecessors as well as that of Alexander, all of which had apparently been buried separately, in a communal mausoleum in Alexandria. By now, Alexan-

known as Kom el-Dikka in the heart of downtown Alexandria. Reasoning that the crossroads of the ancient city might correspond to the intersection of modern Horreya and Nebi Daniel streets, they obtained permission to excavate a site bounded by these two streets on which stood the remains of a Napoleonic fort and the artificial hill on which it was constructed. Although they have excavated more than 50 feet below the surface, they have not discovered any remains identifiable as the tomb. Their work has produced, however, extraordinary discoveries, including a marble odeum, or small theater, of Roman Imperial date and a contemporary bath complex, both of which have no parallels at any other site in Egypt.

The western limit of the Polish excavation site abuts the Mosque of Nebi Daniel, where Arabic tradition maintains the tomb is to be found. In 1991, Mohammed Abduk Aziz of the Arabic Language Department of Al Azhar University in Zagazig directed excavations at the mosque. He contends that Arabic sources, often overlooked by scholars searching for the tomb, offer good reasons for identifying the mosque with the tomb. His activities have been criticized by Faouzi Fakharani, professor emeritus of the University of Alexandria, who claims that he has already explored every inch of the mosque, including its two sub-basements, and has concluded that the tomb of Alexander is not to be found there. While the two professors have squared off in a battle of accusations and counter-accusations, religious officials charged with the administration of the mosque have obtained a moratorium on excavation, fearing that further digging might undermine the building's foundations and precipitate its collapse.

Whereas efforts by the Polish Center and Aziz are creditable and scientifically grounded, two more fanciful attempts to locate the tomb have recently been launched by Greek nationals. Liani Souvaltzi of the Institute of Hellenistic Studies renewed excavations at the site of the so-called Doric Temple at El Maraqi Bilad el Rum in the Siwa Oasis in 1989. The structure was described when it was still standing by Frédéric Cailliaud (1822–24), Heinrich Minutoli (1826), and Gerhard Rohlfs (1869). Its interior was of an unusual plan, consisting of five rooms, one behind the other. Souvaltzi insists, but without documentation, that she has evidence to suggest that Alexander was buried in the Siwa Oasis because, she claims, "he wanted to be near his father Amun," whose oracle there supposedly proclaimed Alexander his son. She argues that the temple, by virtue of the fact that it is both in Siwa and in the Doric order, must mark the site of Alexander's tomb.

Souvaltzi's theory has been received with skepticism by Egyptologists. She has also managed to alienate the Greek community in Alexandria that steadfastly believes the conqueror is buried in their city. Nonetheless, her contention has received support from Leonardo and Bettina Leopoldo, a Swiss couple, the latter a self-styled ethnologist. The Leopoldos have their own reasons for locating the tomb in the Siwa Oasis—they own a collection of Siwan jewelry and handicrafts that is being exhibited worldwide.

Lastly, there is the claim of Stellio Komotsos, a Greek waiter in Christina Konstantinou's cafe-bar L'Elite in Alexandria.

Obsessed with discovering the tomb, Komotsos would save every piaster he earned and, when not waiting tables, go off and dig holes everywhere he could in the city. Now retired and reportedly living in Athens, he is said to have amassed more notes, maps, and documentation on the subject than any scholar. Who knows what secrets are contained therein? Komotsos once offered to share his data with a patron in exchange for a pension in dollars and a new Mercedes. Such a price, mused one starry-eyed graduate student, would be small indeed if the key to the location of the tomb of Alexander was to be found in the Komotsos "archive!" ▲

Alexander's Tomb...Not

In a flurry of media hype exceeded only by that surrounding the O.J. Simpson trial, Liani Souvaltzi, a self-styled authority on Alexander the Great, and her husband, Manos, have once again conned the press into publicizing their latest discovery of Alexander's tomb in the Siwa Oasis, some 330 miles west of Cairo near the Libyan border.

All competent authorities agree that the great conqueror's final resting place was in Alexandria, although the whereabouts of his tomb has perplexed scholars for centuries. This much is known: After Alexander's death at Babylon in 323 B.C. the Macedonian general Ptolemy, who in 305 B.C. would proclaim himself king of Egypt, transported the body to Memphis (see ARCHAEOLOGY, *July/August 1993). It rested there until the late fourth or early third century B.C., when it was taken to Alexandria and reburied, either by Ptolemy or his son and successor, Ptolemy II Philadelphus. Toward the end of the third century, during the reign of Ptolemy IV Philopater, the body was moved to yet another tomb in Alexandria.*

Several creditable expeditions have recently looked for the tomb in Alexandria, all without success. The Souvaltzis appear driven to discover it in the Siwa Oasis. According to numerous classical sources, including Plutarch, who included the "Life of Alexander the Great" in his biographies of famous personalities, Alexander visited Siwa in 331 B.C. to consult a famous oracle of the god Ammon, which, *tradition maintains, proclaimed him son of that Egyptian god. Six years ago, suggesting that Alexander had always wanted to be buried near his god/father, Liani Souvaltzi began excavating at El Maraqi Bilad el Rum in the Siwa Oasis and "discovered" a Doric temple there. She promptly proclaimed it to be the tomb of Alexander the Great, and reported her discovery at the Sixth International Congress of Egyptology in Turin, Italy, in September 1991. Her paper was immediately challenged by the academic establishment. Her alleged tomb was in fact a temple erected in Siwa during the Greco-Roman period. Still standing in the mid-nineteenth century, it had been described by at least three scholars of the day.*

In the face of such opposition, the Souvaltzis turned their attention to the so-called Oracle Temple, where, according to Plutarch and others, Ammon's oracle had presided. To prove their new case they cited as evidence the text of the Romance of Alexander, *an enigmatic work written ca. A.D. 300 by an unknown person. The Souvaltzis had trotted out this same mixture of history and legend in trying to prove the Doric temple was the tomb. To support their new contention, they also reported finding three tablets inscribed in Greek, and a 16-pointed star (an emblem of the Macedonian royal house). One tablet, allegedly written by Ptolemy, claimed that Alexander had been poisoned and that his body had been brought to Siwa.*

The Souvaltzis announced their "find" at a press conference so carefully orchestrated that all major media attended. The presence of high officials of Egypt's Supreme Council of Antiquities, which regulates archaeological missions in Egypt, encouraged the media to view their claim as a legitimate one. As soon as the sound bites had aired, critics besieged Egyptian officials. This was, after all, the second discovery of a tomb of Alexander the Great at the same place by the same people within five years. Greek archaeologists drove out to Siwa to investigate, but were refused access to excavation records. The Supreme Council of Antiquities quickly called a press conference to distance itself from the Souvaltzis and to dismiss their claim. It reminded the press that, according to ancient historians, both Augustus in 30 B.C. and Caracalla in A.D. 215 had visited the tomb in Alexandria, where they reported seeing Alexander's mummy.

One wonders about the Souvaltzis repeated attempts to find this tomb in the Siwa Oasis. Liani Souvaltzi claimed to have "received mystical guidance in her search, in part from snakes," according to a report in The New York Times. She now insists that she was misquoted, and that her guidance came from "saints." Perhaps more to the point was an article in the Cairo newspaper Le Progrès Égyptien, which characterized Souvaltzi, a Greek national, as an ultra-patriot of extreme political views. According to the article, she believes in the prophecy of an authority identified by her only as "Aristander," who allegedly promised that whoever possesses the mortal remains of Alexander the Great shall rule over a stable and prosperous realm. Accordingly, should a Greek secure Alexander's body, the Greeks might well gain control of Macedonia, Alexander's homeland, which they maintain was, is, and forever after ought to be within the borders of their modern nation-state. Greece would thus no longer be forced to share the designation "Macedonia" with Skopje, a province of former Yugoslavia.

The efforts of the Souvaltzis to find the tomb of Alexander appear to be transparent attempts to politicize archaeology. NBC and other media outlets that broadcast or published the "discovery," in some cases without reservation, should be more cautious the next time the Souvaltzis call a press conference to announce yet another discovery of Alexander's tomb…particularly if it is again in the remote, albeit picturesque, Siwa Oasis.

—ROBERT S. BIANCHI

THE OTHER PYRAMIDS

A tour of ancient Nubia where clusters of steep, topless "tomb-stones" punctuate a remote desert landscape

by BOB BRIER

Last year, I drove twice across 600 miles of Sudanese desert to study the world's most exotic and elegant pyramids at the ancient Nubian site of Meroe (see page 3 of color insert). The desert is different from any I had ever seen before—beautiful dunes, vast areas with scrub vegetation like the American Southwest, and flat, hard sand for hundreds of miles in all directions. The Sudan has double the pyramids of its neighbor, Egypt, but because they are so remote, even the kings who built them and their function were uncertain until American George Reisner's excavations beginning in 1916.

Nubia is a relatively modern name, introduced a mere 2,000 years ago by the Greek geographer Strabo, who met members of the Noba tribe and decided to call their country Nubia. For millennia before Strabo's visit, the Egyptians called it Ta-Seti, Land of the Bow, because of its famous archers. It is Kush in the Old Testament, and the only pyramid builder mentioned in the Bible is the Nubian king Taharqa (r. 690–664 B.C.). It may have been Taharqa's predecessor, Piye (r. 747–716 B.C.), who revived the building of pyramids for royal burials, an Egyptian tradition that had been extinct for more than eight centuries.

To understand this pyramid-building revival, you need to understand Nubia and Egypt's complex love-hate relationship. For more than a millennium, Egypt dominated the Nubians, who are shown in tomb paintings bringing tribute—exotic animals, pelts, and rings of solid gold—to the pharaohs. Depicted as different from the Egyptians, with darker skin and curlier hair, they were a people apart, to be conquered, ruled, and used. At the same time, many Nubians worked as free laborers in Egypt, formed a hired police force, and served in the army. One Nubian general, Mahepri, was even buried in the Valley of the Kings. If he were willing to live like an Egyptian, a Nubian could have the benefits of an Egyptian. Still, it was always clear who was in control. Eventually, the roles reversed as Egypt declined in power and Nubia grew more and more independent. Free of Egyptian control, Nubians nonetheless regarded Egypt as their patrimony, worshiped its main deity Amun, and made offerings to other Egyptian gods. When Egypt was at its weakest, Piye marched north and conquered it ca. 722 B.C., founding the 25th Dynasty. He and his successors did not, however, see themselves as outsiders; they called themselves pharaoh and intended to restore Egypt to its former greatness. When Piye died, he was buried in his homeland, Nubia, but most scholars

ARCHAEOLOGY

believe that above his sepulchre there was an Egyptian-inspired pyramid.

What first strikes you about these pyramids is how steep they are—their sides slope

This small royal pyramid at Meroe, reconstructed by German architect Friedrich Hinkel, was the last built in Africa. A small funerary chapel with a "monumental" entrance is attached to one face of the pyramid.

between 68 and 77 degrees, while Egyptian royal pyramids never exceeded 52 degrees. But, as you look at them, the list of differences gets longer and longer. At 164 feet, Taharqa's is the highest, but most are less than 100 feet high, as compared with 440 feet for the Great Pyramid of Giza. The Nubian pyramids are clustered together, so close that you can literally touch two at the same time, something you could never do in Egypt. But the greatest difference is that unlike Egyptian ones, Nubian pyramids are not tombs, and this confused both tomb robbers and archaeologists for quite a while. It was Reisner who discovered that the burial chambers were separate, unlike in Egypt, where they were built within the body of the pyramid. The Nubians cut their burial chambers into the bedrock, carving out a

stairway that would be filled and concealed after the deceased was interred. The pyramid was often built above the burial chamber, covering part of the entrance passage, something that could be done only after the funeral and in-filling of the passage. In those cases, at least, the king or queen's pyramid must have been built by his or her successor. The pyramids were tombstones, the Nubian kings' tribute to an ancient Egyptian tradition.

Reisner helped piece together a chronology for the biblical kingdom of Kush and gave archaeologists a glimpse of a vanished world. His excavations revealed a unique mix of Egyptian and Nubian burial customs. In Taharqa's tomb, for example, he discovered more than 1,000 *ushabtis*—traditional Egyptian servant figurines intended to work for the deceased in the next world. But in the center of the burial chamber there had been a stone platform unlike anything ever seen in Egypt—a platform on which the king's body rested.

Sudanese pyramids are grouped in four major clusters. Three are around Gebel Barkal, the "Pure Mountain," so-called because of its sacred nature, which is over 600 miles upstream from Aswan. The mountain's distinguishing feature is a dramatic 245-foot pinnacle rising in front of it that resembles a rearing cobra wearing the white crown of Upper Egypt. For the Nubians, Gebel Barkal was their holy of holies, the home of the god Amun. The cobra, personifying Upper Egyptian kingship, showed that the mountain was the primeval source of kingship in Nubia and Upper Egypt, which they had inherited from the pharaohs.

Examining the pinnacle with a small telescope in 1986, Timothy Kendall, then of Boston's Museum of Fine Arts, could see there were hieroglyphic inscriptions near the summit of the cobra's crown, but he couldn't read them. After a year of rock-climbing lessons, he returned to Gebel Barkal, descended 80 feet down the mountain's cliff face to where it joins the pinnacle, ascended the back of the cobra to its top, and then down the front to the inscription. There he read what no one had seen for millennia—an inscription boasting of Taharqa's military prowess. Framing the inscription, Kendall could see, were small nail holes that once held a thin sheet of gold pressed into the inscription. In ancient times, the cobra gleamed. Kendall is now clearing a temple at the base of Gebel Barkal that appears to be where Nubian kings received their crowns.

The first royal burials of the 25th Dynasty are at el Kurru, where Piye was interred, downstream from Gebel Barkal. Subsequent kings and queens built their pyramids there until Taharqa, who was buried at Nuri, on the opposite side of the river from Gebel Barkal. Royal burials continued at Nuri for over three centuries, when pyramids began to be built at Gebel Barkal itself. But Nubia was already in decline. Invading Assyrians expelled Taharqa's successor from Egypt and in 593 B.C. the Nubians were defeated by a resurgent Egyptian dynasty after which they moved their capital from Napata, near Gebel Barkal, to the more distant site of Meroe. The Nubian royals eventually opted for burial at Meroe beginning about 270 B.C. There, in isolation, they continued to build pyramids for more than 700 years.

Meroe is the second home of Friedrich Hinkel, a Berlin architect who has been studying Nubia's pyramids for nearly 50 years. Contrary to most scholars, Hinkel believes from his examination of the foundations of Piye's burial monument that it was not in fact a pyramid, though he could not determine the structure's original form. For him, it was one of Piye's successors who began building pyramids again, possibly Taharqa.

Hinkel's passion, rebuilding the Nubian pyramids, has helped to explain some of the striking differences between the steep Nubian ones and the earlier, broad-based Egyptian royal ones from the Old Kingdom (2686–2125 B.C.). If the Nubian kings and queens were inspired by the royal Egyptian pyramids, why did they build their own with such steep sides?

Almost certainly, the large and dramatic Old Kingdom pyramids at Giza and

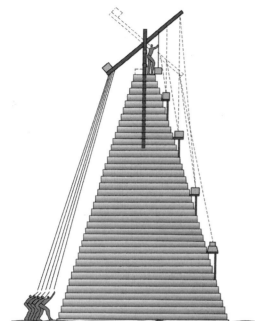

Diagram shows how the pyramids of Nubia were built using the shadouf, the crane of ancient Egypt.

Dahshur inspired the Nubians to take up the flame of pyramid building. But Nubian pyramids, with their steep angles, were clearly not modeled after them. The actual models may have been much closer to home. During the 18th Dynasty (1550–1295 B.C.), private people began building small, pointy pyramids above their tombs, as a gesture to the "good old times" of the Old Kingdom. The most famous of these are at Deir el Medineh, not far from the Valley of the Kings. Although Nubian kings may not have visited Deir el Medineh, Egyptians also built similar pyramids in lower Nubia, at Aniba and Soleb, with which the Nubians would have been familiar. These may have been the models upon which the black pharaohs of the Sudan patterned their pyramids. And the pointiness? The answer, Hinkel found, is related to the technology used to build them.

The crucial tool is the shadouf, the crane of ancient Egypt, which farmers still use today for hoisting water out of canals and into irrigation ditches. Basically a pole with a counterweight on the end, it is ideal for lifting heavy stone blocks. Hinkel knows that shadoufs were used in the construction because he found the central pole of one still embedded near the top of a pyramid he was rebuilding. Many later Nubian pyramids are solid, but not solid stone as one might think from the exterior. The blocks are only two layers thick and encase a rubble core. The shadouf was positioned at the center of the rubble to hoist the exterior blocks in place. As the pyramid rose, the shadouf was raised till the last course of exterior blocks was in place; then its central pole was left inside the pyramid, covered by the capstone. The shadouf is the key to why these pyramids are so steep. If you lift your blocks with a central shadouf, it is extremely difficult to place blocks far from where the shadouf is anchored. With a narrow base, you get sides that slope steeply.

So why are the Nubian pyramids packed so closely together? Hinkel believes that each pyramid is aligned with a different star, so if you wanted to build in one pyramid field, drawing straight lines from stars to pyramids, things get crowded. Another factor is that there are so many of them. Queens in Nubia were almost as powerful as kings and had pyramids just as large. Over the centuries there were only four locations of choice for pyramids, and with queens' pyramids occupying the same area as kings', they

110 and Counting...

"To be sure, it is not the tomb of Tutankhamun, but it recalls the story of Howard Carter and Lord Carnarvon just the same," says Michel Valloggia of his discovery of a pyramid five miles north of Giza. The find came as archaeologists from the Swiss-French team Vallogia leads explored the precinct surrounding the pyramid of the 4th Dynasty pharaoh Djedefre.

Completed at the end of April, a two-month excavation exposed the remains of the diminutive pyramid, which measures only about 35 feet on each side. The tomb beneath held limestone sarcophagus fragments, an alabaster canopic jar that would have held one of the deceased's organs, and pieces of ceramic water vessels.

Djedefre succeeded his father Khufu (r. ca. 2589 –2566 B.C.), who built the largest pyramid at Giza, but for some reason he chose to build his own pyramid and mortuary complex at Abu Roash to the north. After Djedefre's death, the throne passed to his brother Khafre, who returned to Giza where he built his own pyramid, the second largest there, and the Sphinx.

The newly found pyramid is in the southeast corner of Djedefre's pyramid precinct, corresponding to one, already known, that is in the southwest corner. It is tempting to link them with his two known wives, Khentetenka and Hetepheres II. Hieroglyphs spelling Khufu's name on a broken alabaster plate found in the tomb confirm a link to the royal family.

For those keeping track, the discovery brings the total of known pyramids to 110 according to Zahi Hawass, director of Egypt's Supreme Council of Antiquities. —MARK ROSE

had to be placed closely together.

For centuries, out of contact with Egypt and most of the rest of the world, the kings and queens of Meroe continued constructing pyramids. But like other civilizations, theirs eventually fell. Attacks by the Romans weakened the kingdom of Meroe. Eventu-ally, Christianity reached even this remote spot and sometime around A.D. 350, a king of Meroe built the last pyramid in Africa. A small affair, it has been rebuilt mostly in concrete by Hinkel, but it marks the spot where the flame of pyramid building, begun 3,000 years earlier in Egypt, finally went out. ▲

GINESTHOI! SAYETH CLEOPATRA

by ANGELA M.H. SCHUSTER

A single Greek word, *ginesthoi,* or "make it so," written at the bottom of a Ptolemaic papyrus may have been written by the Egyptian queen Cleopatra VII herself, says Dutch papyrologist Peter van Minnen of the University of Groningen. Received in Alexandria on Mecheir 26 (February 23, 33 B.C.), the papyrus text, recycled for use in the construction of a cartonnage mummy case found by a German expedition at Abusir in 1904, appears to be a royal ordinance granting tax exemption to one Publius Canidius, an associate of Mark Antony's who would command his land army during the Battle of Actium in 31 B.C. The text reads as follows:

We have granted to Publius Canidius and his heirs the annual exportation of 10,000 artabas [300 tons] of wheat and the annual importation of 5,000 Coan amphoras [ca. 34,500 gallons] of wine without anyone exacting anything in taxes from him or any other expense whatsoever. We have also granted tax exemption on all the land he owns in Egypt on the understanding that he shall not pay any taxes, either to the state account or to the account of me and my children, in any way in perpetuity. We have also granted that all his tenants are exempt from personal liabilities and from taxes without anyone exacting anything from them, not even contributing to the occasional assessments in the nomes or paying for expenses for soldiers or officers. We have also granted that the animals used for plowing and sowing as well as the beasts of burden and the ships used for the transportation [down the Nile] of the wheat are likewise exempt from 'personal' liabilities and from taxes and cannot be commandeered [by the army]. Let it be written to those to whom it may concern, so that knowing it they can act accordingly.

Make it so!

"Written in an upright hand by a court scribe, the document was meant to be an internal note from Cleopatra to a high official charged with notifying other high officials in Alexandria," says van Minnen. "The personal nature of the communication is evident in the lack of any formal introduction of Cleopatra herself (she is not even mentioned by name) and the absence of a title after the name of the official to whom it was addressed (the name cannot be read)." The manuscript is not one of the copies received by the other officials, as there is no forwarding note attached to it and because it was executed in multiple hands. The text of the ordinance was written first, Cleopatra's written approval second, and the date of the document's receipt in Alexandria third. As for the "make it so" subscription, there are only two parallels from antiquity, says van Minnen, citing one of Ptolemy X Alexander I, who signed a document "take care" in Greek in 99 B.C. and another such closing penned in Latin by the fifth-century Roman emperor Theodosius II in a petition to Appion, the bishop of Syene.

According to Lorelei Corcoran of the University of Memphis, such documents would have been both written and signed by a court scribe; however, given the nature of this particular papyrus, Cleopatra herself would have been the only one who would have had the authority to approve such edicts. The document, known as Berlin P 25 239, is on display at the Ägyptisches Museum und Papyrussammlung in Berlin. ▲

PART V:

REDISCOVERING EGYPT

NAPOLEON IN EGYPT

The general's search for glory led to the birth of Egyptology.

by BOB BRIER

Two hundred years ago Napoleon Bonaparte was in Egypt and was not enjoying his tour. His fleet had been sunk at Aboukir Bay, he had suffered his first defeat on land at Acre, and his men were dying of the plague. Amid this disaster, one of his entourage, Geoffroy St.-Hilaire, wrote home:

> *Here I once again find men who think of nothing but science; I live at the center of a flaming core of reason.... We busy ourselves enthusiastically with all the questions that are of concern to the government and with the sciences to which we have devoted ourselves freely.*

St.-Hilaire, a 26-year-old naturalist, was unconcerned that he was in the middle of a war 2,000 miles from home. He was doing what he liked to do best—studying exotic animals. St.-Hilaire had followed Bonaparte to Egypt, which the 29-year-old general hoped to conquer for

France, striking a fatal blow to England's economy by seizing control of the land trade route to India.

Bonaparte also had plans for his own career:

> Europe presents no field for glorious exploits; no great empires or revolutions are to be found, but in the East where there are six hundred million men.... My glory is declining. This little corner of Europe is too small to supply it. We must go East. All the great men of the world have there acquired their celebrity.

Bonaparte would be a new Alexander the Great, but there was far more to the young general than military ambition. Yes, he would colonize Egypt, but he would also reveal to Europe the hidden Orient. He would study and record every aspect of Egypt. To this end, he brought with him more than 500 civilians, including about 150 biologists, mineralogists, linguists, mathematicians, chemists, and other scholars. Nothing like it had ever been done before. The results of their labors would appear in the monumental 20-volume *Description de l'Égypte*, completed in 1828, and in the course of their research Egyptology was born.

The scientists Bonaparte assembled included the best minds of France. Bonaparte himself was a member of the mathematics section of the Institut de France, the most important French scholarly organization, and early in his career he proudly signed his name "Bonaparte, membre de l'Institut." He was familiar with learning and the finer things in life. During his successful Italian campaign of 1796–1797 he had befriended the chemist Claude Louis Berthollet and the mathematician Gaspard Monge. Berthollet taught Bonaparte some chemistry, and Monge helped the young general select Italian art works, which were confiscated, brought back to Paris, and displayed in the Musée Napoleon (later the Louvre).

When Napoleon sailed for Egypt, Berthollet and Monge accompanied him, along with even greater luminaries: mathematician Jean Baptiste Joseph Fourier, mineralogist Déodat Guy Gratet de Dolomieu, and well-known botanical artist Pierre Joseph Redouté. One of the older savants was the artist Dominique Vivant Denon, who had also assisted Bonaparte in selecting art on the Italian campaign; he later became the first curator of the Louvre. Although these established men were important, most members of the commission were in their early twenties or even younger. These scholars formed the Scientific and Artistic Commission of Egypt; some of the senior members were professors at prestigious schools like the École Polytechnique in Paris, and they brought their most promising students with them on the trip of their lives.

The fleet landed at Alexandria on July 1, 1798, and almost immediately the savants were left to fend for themselves. There was a war to fight and the generals were too preoccupied with getting supplies for their troops to worry about the scholars. So Monge, Fourier, Denon, and the students had to scrounge for themselves. Conditions at Alexandria were squalid, and some of the men went to nearby Port Rashid (ancient Rosetta) looking for better accommodations. Once Cairo was secured they would be summoned and established in permanent quarters.

Engraving from Dominique Vivant Denon's Voyages in Upper and Lower Egypt *(1802) shows Napoleon's savants measuring the Sphinx at Giza.*

During their first month in Egypt, the French fought the two most important battles of the campaign. Both are misnamed: The Battle of the Pyramids was fought in a melon field at Embabba nearly ten miles from the pyramids, and the Battle of the Nile was fought not on the Nile but at Aboukir Bay.

The Battle of the Pyramids, fought three weeks after the landing at Alexandria, established Napoleon's military superiority over the Mamluks, Egypt's elite fighting class. The Mamluks were superb horsemen, skilled with sabres and pistols, but they were no match for a disciplined professional army. The French army formed squares, with rifles at the sides, artillery at the corners, and cavalry within. The Mamluks pranced in front

of them in their silk pantaloons, vests, and turbans decorated with feathers and jewels. The French could see the pyramids in the distance and, just as the battle was about to begin, Napoleon declared, "Soldiers, from these heights 40 centuries look down upon you." Given that hieroglyphs had not been deciphered and the chronology of the pharaohs was virtually unknown except from the Bible, his estimate of the age of the pyramids turned out to be remarkably accurate, only about four centuries off. The Mamluks, led by Murad Bey, charged with sabres and pistols drawn; the French waited until they were nearly upon them and then blew them away.

Napoleon had little time to enjoy his victory. Ten days later his entire fighting fleet was destroyed by England's Admiral Horatio Nelson. The fleet's 13 ships were anchored in a line close to shore at Aboukir Bay, a few miles from Alexandria. At 2:00 P.M. on August 1, Nelson sailed into Aboukir Bay and decided to fight then and there. With no soundings to guide him, he sailed between the French fleet and the shore. The French, believing this impossible, had left their landward cannons unprepared for battle, and Nelson fired broadside after broadside into their ships. Admiral Bruyes aboard the French flagship *L'Orient*, having lost both his legs to cannon fire, was seated in a chair with tourniquets on the stumps, still giving orders, when a cannonball hit him. Captain Casabianca assumed command, though himself badly wounded, and fought on in the burning ship to the end. When the fire on *L'Orient* reached her powder magazine the ship exploded with a deafening roar that could be heard 50 miles away. When the ship sank, much of the savants' scientific instrumentation, surveying equipment, and supplies went with it.

In spite of this setback, the savants settled into their tasks. The senior men, Monge, Berthollet, and a one-legged general named Louis Cafarelli, in charge of financial and administrative matters, were housed in the palace of Hassan Kashef in Cairo. The botanists set up their experiments in the garden of Qassim Bey's palace. St.-Hilaire was ecstatic about the space and was soon involved in helping set up chemistry labs and collecting mineral, botanical, and zoological specimens. The Egyptian chronicler Abd al-Rahman al-Jabarti described with wonder the library they set up in the house of Hassan Kashef:

The administrators, astronomers, and some of the physicians lived in this house in which they placed a great number of their books and with a keeper taking care of them and arranging them. And the students among them would gather two hours before noon every day in an open space opposite the shelves of books, sitting on chairs arranged in parallel rows before a wide long board. Whoever wishes to look up something in a book asks for whatever volumes he wants and the librarian brings them to him. Then he thumbs through the pages, looking through the book and writes. All the while they are quiet and no one disturbs his neighbor. When some Muslims would come to look around they would not prevent them from entering. Indeed they would bring them all kinds of printed books in which there were all sorts of illustrations and maps of the countries and regions, animals, birds, plants, histories of the ancients, campaigns of the nations, tales of the prophets including pictures of them, their miracles and wondrous deeds, the events of their respective peoples and such things which baffle the mind.

More important to the expedition than the laboratories and collections were the workshops under the direction of Nicolas-Jacques Conte. An artist and engineer, Conte had an uncanny ability to design and build almost anything that was needed. Once, when lead was in short supply and the artists needed pencils, he used graphite, thus inventing the modern pencil—the crayon Conte. He made replacements for the scientific instruments lost at Aboukir Bay and elsewhere and also made a study of the contemporary manufacturing of various products in Cairo so what was useful could be duplicated in his workshops. According to Napoleon, Conte was capable of creating "the arts of France in the deserts of Arabia." Monge said he had "all the arts in his hands and all the sciences in his head." To Berthollet he was "the pillar of the expedition."

A month after the Battle of the Pyramids, on August 22, 1798, Bonaparte formed the Institut d'Égypte, modeled after the Institut de France. Its goals were to enlighten Egypt; advise the Egyptian government; and study the country's history, industry, and natural phenomena. Bringing savants on a military expedition was certainly in the spirit of the Enlightenment, as were the goals of the institute, but Bonaparte's main concern was clearly practical. His savants had skills that would be useful to an army far from home. Many were civil engineers who could build bridges and forts; others could manufacture whatever the army might need. At the institute's first session, on August 23, Bonaparte, its vice-president, suggested six research topics:

1) How can the bread ovens be improved?
2) How can the Nile water be purified?
3) Are windmills practical for Cairo?
4) Can beer without hops be brewed in Egypt?
5) Are the raw materials for gunpowder available in Egypt?
6) What is the legal system in Egypt, and what improvements do the citizens want?

The savants were also free to investigate topics of their own, and even the dullest engineer was more eager to explore the temple of Dendera than study bread ovens.

(They did report that reeds and safflower stalks would fuel the ovens better than the wood used in France.)

Of all the memoirs published by members of the expedition, by far the most popular was Denon's *Travels in Upper and Lower Egypt*. At 55, Denon was the oldest on the expedition, but was always in the middle of things. When Napoleon instructed General Desaix to pursue the retreating Mamluks south, Denon saw it as a chance to sketch the monuments of Upper Egypt and went along. He was constantly asking Desaix for more time to draw the temples and tombs. In the Valley of the Kings, Denon was overwhelmed by the tombs and the vibrant colors of the paintings in them, but was told they had to press on:

How was it possible to leave such precious curiosities without taking a drawing of them? How to return without a sketch to show? I earnestly demanded a quarter of an hour's grace: I was allowed twenty minutes. One person highlighted me while another held a taper to every object that I pointed out to him, and I completed my task prescribed with spirit and correctness.

Denon's excitement was contagious, and soon General Desaix became his fellow archaeologist, as Barthelemy Mery's epic poem notes:

> *Desaix now far from the sky of Idumia*
> *commends the exploits of the army to*
> *the engraving tool,*
>   *and the same hand that harasses*
> *Mamluks*
>   *during a day's respite, captures monuments in*
>   *wonderful work to commemorate his*

remarkable journey.

While exploring the Valley of the Kings, Denon came upon a relief of a scribe writing on a scroll. Unaware, despite his education, that Egyptians wrote on papyrus and that travelers had already brought papyri back to Europe, Denon congratulated himself on being "the first who had made this important discovery." This reveals a great deal about both Denon and early Egyptology and explains his excitement when local guides brought him a mummy with a papyrus rolled up under its left arm:

> I turned pale...my voice failed me...so great was my fear of destroying it, that I knew not what to do with my treasure; I was afraid to touch this book, the most ancient of books at this day known; I dared confide it to no person, deposit it no where; all the cotton of the quilt that served me for a bed did not seem sufficient to embalm it with sufficient softness.

In spite of his almost pathological enthusiasm, Denon made some reasonable observations about ancient Egypt. The papyrus he so treasured was a Book of the Dead, a series of spells and prayers intended to ensure that the deceased would be resurrected in the next world. Denon noticed that a section of the text ended in the middle of a line and that the space to the left of the writing had been left blank. From this he correctly deduced that the writing was from right to left. (Right to left was the more common direction of writing, but ancient Egyptian could also be written from left to right.) Denon returned to France with Bona-

parte, a full two years before the rest of the savants, so he had a head start on publishing. His *Travels in Upper and Lower Egypt*, which appeared in 1802, was a sensation, going through more than 20 editions in various languages. It was the first relatively accurate depiction of Egypt that Europe had seen. Prior to that, Richard Pococke's *Description of the East, and Some Other Countries* (1743–45) and Fredrik Norden's *Voyages d'Égypte et de Nubie* (1755) were the primary references, and neither author was an artist.

Denon's illustrations were clearly a step up, but while generating interest they were not the beginning of Egyptology (see page 4 of color insert). It was the younger men Denon left behind who measured and drafted the monuments with the precision of engineers. This was the start of scientific archaeology. One of the youngest, René-Edouard Devilliers, an 18-year-old engineering student, brought his books with him, and in October 1798 Monge tested him and pronounced him a civil engineer. For most of the campaign he teamed up with the 21-year-old engineer Prosper Jollois; as far as one can tell from their memoirs, they forgot about bridges and roads and fell in love with antiquity. Between letters home complaining about bad food and poor accommodations, they mapped, drew, and described dozens of monuments in detail.

Denon had quickly sketched the now-famous zodiac ceiling at Dendera temple, but Jollois and Devilliers, retracing his route south, drew it carefully and accurately, which was far from easy. The ceiling on which were carved hundreds of details of the sky as the Egyptians saw it had been blackened by soot from the fires of centuries of squatters who had lived in the temple. The pair recorded

Reading the Rosetta Stone

Unearthed by the French in July 1799, the Rosetta Stone bears three inscriptions, Greek, hieroglyphic, and demotic (the Egyptian script used for mundane transactions). Napoleon's savants realized the stone was the key to deciphering the ancient Egyptian language because the last line of Greek, which they could read, said the three inscriptions contained the same text (dating to 196 B.C., it praises Ptolemy V for reducing taxes on priests). Comparison of them would unlock the Egyptian writings. But the decipherment was not as easy as scholars had expected, primarily because everyone made the same mistaken assumption that the hieroglyphic inscription was purely ideographic, with hieroglyphs standing only for concepts. Thus, scholars concentrated on the demotic text because they believed it alone was an alphabetic script and would provide a close parallel to the Greek text. The idea that a script had to be either totally alphabetic or totally ideographic was firmly entrenched by the time the stone was discovered.

The British physician and physicist Thomas Young made the first crucial breakthrough around 1814. He realized that the demotic was a mixture of phonetic and symbolic signs. Then, using the phonetic values obtained from the demotic, he figured out phonetic values for some of the hieroglyphs. He knew from the Greek and demotic texts that King Ptolemy's name appeared repeatedly and deduced that it was inside the ovals in the hieroglyphic text. The name for these ovals, cartouche, is the French word for cartridge—given by the soldiers who saw them carved on temple walls and thought they looked like ammunition.

Young's discovery was crucial, but it would be another decade before the Egyptian language was truly deciphered. Even Young, who first deciphered

the phonetics of the name in the cartouches, was a victim of the entrenched assumption that hieroglyphs were pictorial. He thought the non-Egyptian name Ptolemy was the exception to the rule. It would be Jean François Champollion in 1822 who realized that hieroglyphs were both ideographic and phonetic. With the cracking of the code, Egyptologists could now read the history of the country they had been studying for decades.

British Museum conservators have given the Rosetta Stone its most thorough cleaning since it arrived at the museum in 1802, according to an Art Newspaper report (February 1999). The familiar appearance of the three-quarter-ton monolith— black stone with white inscriptions—has changed considerably. To make the inscriptions more legible, they were filled with white chalk, perhaps in 1847. Much of the chalk had been lost by 1980, when it was replaced with a water-soluble white paint. During the recent cleaning, conservators removed this white paint and found beneath it ink dating from 1799, the year the stone was discovered by a French officer serving in Egypt. Copies of the inscriptions had been printed then directly from the stone. In some of the incisions, traces of a light red iron-earth pigment were discovered under the ink. Curator Richard Parkinson told The Art Newspaper *that it seems likely that when the stone was originally erected the inscriptions were filled with light red pigment, making them stand out from the gray surface. That the stone is, in fact, gray rather than black became apparent when layers of protective wax were removed. The wax, applied decades ago, had darkened from airborne dirt and the hands of museumgoers who couldn't resist touching the stone.*

—BOB BRIER

the temples at Philae, Esneh, Edfu, and Kom Ombo, and sketched the colossi of Memnon and Luxor temple. Jollois was not impressed with ancient construction techniques and noted that the temple walls were irregular, some slanting inward, others outward.

Their greatest adventure, however, was in the Valley of the Kings. The valley had been drawn by Pococke, but to skilled draftsmen his work seemed amateurish. Not only did Jollois and Devilliers produce the first professional map of the valley, they discovered a new tomb. When Napoleon's forces entered Egypt there were 11 open tombs in the valley; exploring the valley's remote western branch, the young engineers found the tomb of Amenhotep III. Its walls had been damaged by centuries of flooding, and much of the painted plaster lay on the ground, too fragile to be removed. Small antiquities, such as figurines of servants intended to wait on the king in the next world, littered the floor of the pharaoh's tomb, and the boys took some as royal souvenirs. Four that Devilliers brought back to France are still owned by his descendants. A small green schist head of Amenhotep III that they discovered is now in the Louvre.

While the artists and engineers measured and drew monuments, the naturalists amassed collections of minerals, insects, birds, and plants. These collections became a major point of contention when it was time to leave Egypt. Plague and an inability to replace troops had doomed the expedition from the moment Nelson sank the French fleet. In 1801 the British, under General Hutchinson, dictated terms of surrender, article 16 stipulating that all antiquities and the savants' collections become British prop-

erty. Bonaparte was in France, having left Egypt two years before when he saw that the campaign was a lost cause. Departing secretly by night, he had left a letter placing General Kleber in charge, but Kleber was assassinated a few months later by a religious fanatic. The next and last commander-in-chief was the highly eccentric general Abdullah Menou, who had converted to Islam so he could marry a bathkeeper's daughter and was little respected by either French or British. The distraught scientists pleaded with Menou to defend their collections. Menou protested vehemently, calling the English "common thieves" for wanting to take the scientists' collections. Edward Clarke, a Cambridge mineralogy professor present at the negotiations, wrote in a letter to his friend Reverend William Otter,

We found much more in their possession than was represented or imagined…Statues, Sarcophagi, Maps, MSS., Drawings, Plans, Charts, Botany, Stuffed Birds, Animals, Dried Fishes, &c. Savigny, who has been years in forming the beautiful collection of Natural History for the Republic, and which is the first thing of the kind in the world, is in despair. Therefore, we represented it to General Hutchinson, that it would be the best plan to send him to England also, as the most proper person to take care of the collection and to publish its description, if necessary. This is now agreed to by all parties.

When the other French naturalists heard that Savigny was going to England, they offered to go as well. These men had risked their lives, endured hardships, and were not easily separated from their trophies. Many realized that their academic careers would be forever established if they published their findings. In the end, the naturalists were permitted to return to France with their collections.

Letting drawings, paintings, rocks, and plants go was one thing, but the Rosetta Stone—the key to the decipherment of hieroglyphs—was quite something else. The French had unearthed the Rosetta Stone at the port of el-Rashid in July 1799 as they were strengthening the foundations of a fort. Lieutenant Bouchard, the officer in charge, realized that the stone was important, and by August it was being studied in Cairo. The 47-inch-tall, 30-inch-wide stone slab bore three inscriptions, of which one was Greek, which the savants could read (inscribed in 196 B.C., it praises King Ptolemy V for reducing taxes on priests). They immediately realized they had the key to deciphering the ancient Egyptian language, because the last line of Greek said that the inscriptions were the same text in "sacred and native and Greek characters." The top inscription is in "sacred" characters (hieroglyphs), while the middle is in the "native" script used in the late period (after about 600 B.C.) for mundane transactions (known as demotic from the Greek word for people). Thus there are only two languages on the Rosetta Stone—Egyptian (written in two forms) and Greek.

By the time of the French surrender in 1801, the existence of the Rosetta Stone was known throughout the scholarly world. When the treaty was signed, the British were not about to let it go to France. In an attempt to protect it, General Menou claimed that the stone was not the property of the French government, but his private property, and that as an officer he should be permitted to keep it. Clarke, who was party to the negotiations, was adamant that the stone should go to England:

I was in Cairo when the capitulation began. There I learned from the Imperial consul, that the famous inscription which is to explain the Hieroglyphics was still at Alexandria. I then intended to write to General Hutchinson and Lord Keith on the subject, to beg it might be obtained for the University of Cambridge, or the British Museum, as I know full well, we have better Orientalists than the French and a knowledge of eastern languages may be necessary in some degree towards the decipherment of these inscriptions.

Ultimately, the stone was taken to England and placed in the British Museum.

Although the Rosetta Stone was the key to modern Egyptology, the publications of the scientists on the expedition were almost as important. When they returned to France, Bonaparte became first consul and authorized funds for the publication of the *Description de l'Égypte*. The work was to cover everything—the ancient monuments, natural history, and modern country (ca. 1800), and was to include the first comprehensive map of Egypt. Edmé Jomard, one of the expedition's young engineers, was named editor and was soon soliciting drawings, paintings, and research papers from his colleagues. As the submissions accumulated and the years passed, it became evident that the project would be larger than anyone had

Napoleon's Lost Fleet

Aboukir, Egypt—

Six-foot waves propelled by a small weather system over the Mediterranean rock the research vessel Princess Duda, anchored at the entrance to Aboukir Bay, as divers prepare for another foray into the deep. Falling overboard one by one, they submerge, meeting at the anchor line for a group descent. Near the seabed some 40 feet below, the waters are quiet. Waterlogged timbers—the center section of Napoleon's 120-gun warship L'Orient—lie among a scatter of bronze cannon, twisted and torn; gold, silver, and copper coins minted in Malta, Venice, Spain, France, Portugal, and the Ottoman Empire; cooking pots and silverware; bits of clothing; human bones; and a heap of lead type from a shipboard printing press. The strong scent of gunpowder permeates the site; you can smell the battle. The ship's 35-foot-long rudder, emblazoned with the words Dauphin Royal, L'Orient's original name, lies on its side 200 feet from the wreckage. Anchors of Napoleon's ships Guerrier, Conquérant, Spartiate, Aquillon, Peuple Souverain, and Franklin are scattered about the site.

Here, 15 miles east of Alexandria, an international team under the direction of French marine archaeologist Franck Goddio is exploring ships sunk at one of the most decisive battles in maritime history, the Battle of the Nile, or more accurately, the Battle of Aboukir. Waged on the night of August 1–2, 1798, the engagement pitted Britain's finest, under the command of Rear Admiral Sir Horatio Nelson, against a French fleet led by Admiral François Paul Brueys d'Aigailliers; its outcome ended forever Napoleon's dream of conquering Egypt and the east.

Having pursued the French fleet for nearly four months, Nelson happened upon it late in the afternoon of August 1 during a sweep of Egypt's north coast. As he rounded what is now known as Nelson Island and entered Aboukir Bay, he saw 13 French battleships moored in a north-south line near its western shore.

Four frigates were anchored still closer to the shoals.

Against Napoleon's wishes, Brueys had selected the bay over the harbors at Alexandria, believing it afforded his cumbersome, deep-draft vessels a better anchorage and, with its wide open mouth, would be hard for the British to blockade.

Nelson noticed that the French ships were anchored at the stern only and that enough room had been left between them so they could swing on their anchors with the tide. More importantly, he surmised, enough room had been left between the ships and the shoals so that his vessels, far more agile and of shallower draft, could sail inside the French line.

Nelson and his "band of brothers," as he would later call his men, seized the opportunity to attack. In a bold move, the first in line of the British ships, Goliath, under the command of Captain Thomas Foley, sailed between Guerrier, the leading French ship, and the shore. Zealous, Orion, Theseus, and Audacious followed. As each ship passed Guerrier, then Conquérant and Spartiate, it delivered a thunderous broadside. Anticipating attack from the seaward side, the French were caught off guard. Within 20 minutes these three French ships were silenced. The remaining British ships stormed down the seaward side, bombarding the French fleet and breaking through the line.

In the hours that followed, the battle escalated as the British ships picked off the French vessels one after another. A fire broke out aboard L'Orient during the melee. At about 10:30 P.M. it ignited L'Orient's aft powder magazine and the ship exploded. The blast was so great that it was heard in Rosetta, ten miles to the east. Stunned by the explosion, both sides ceased fire for a quarter of an hour.

"Victory is not a name strong enough for such a scene," Nelson would later write as he recalled the smoldering, sinking hulks of his enemy's fleet. By daybreak all but two French battleships, Guillaume Tell and Généreux, had been sunk or captured. Some 1,700 Frenchmen had lost their lives; 800

were killed instantly in the explosion aboard L'Orient. The British had lost only two ships and 218 men. Some 3,000 French were taken prisoner, only to be released a short time later when Nelson could no longer feed them.

Discovered in 1983 by the late underwater explorer Jacques Dumas, the wreck of L'Orient is spread over a quarter mile square. "The scatter of debris, along with the remains we have found of the frigates Sérieuse and Artemise and anchors left behind by French ships attempting to flee," says Goddio, "are providing a wealth of new information on the battle. We know, for instance, that there were two nearly simultaneous explosions aboard L'Orient rather than one as previously thought. It is quite clear from the wreckage that when the aft powder magazine blew, flaming debris ignited auxiliary powder stores in the front of the ship. From the burning and scarring of the forwardmost timbers of the center section, we know that the bow as well as the stern was blown off and probably burned up, leaving only the ship's center section to founder. All that remains of the stern is its bronze and wood rudder. Its distance from the rest of the wreckage suggests that the explosion of the stern propelled the ship forward several hundred feet.

"We also know just how poorly positioned the French fleet was. According to historical sources, the French ships were both closer to shore and to each other. The anchors, which are separated by more than 400 feet, tell a different story. We have a snapshot of the position of the French forward guard at the moment the battle began and it is clear that they were in no position to close up gaps in the flotilla."

"The conventional story of how Nelson's fleet sailed behind the French line is a bit simplistic," says Royal Naval Museum deputy director and Nelson biographer Colin White, who, along with French naval historian Michèle Battesti, was in Alexandria this past June to inspect the wrecksite firsthand. "Nelson did catch the French fleet by surprise, and their landward guns were not prepared for battle," says White. "But the problems the French faced were

far greater. Brueys simply did not understand Nelson's strategy. The French were prepared for a traditional one-on-one naval engagement, a battle for which the fleets were well matched in both size and number." The British fleet comprised 13 warships carrying 74 guns each and one with 50 guns which delivered 18–32 pound shot; the French fleet, 13 warships, carrying between 74 and 120 guns each delivering 24–36 pound shot, and four frigates.

Ships delivered what are called broadsides; teams of gunners responsible for manning pairs of guns, one on each side of the ship, would all fire from one side of the vessel. Knowing that there were not enough crew to fire all port and starboard guns simultaneously, Nelson split his fleet, sending vessels down both sides of the French line.

In addition to details of the battle, Goddio notes other inconsistencies in the historical record, particularly with regard to the ship's manifest. "We were surprised at the number of coins we found minted at so many different locations. According to historical sources Napoleon looted the Maltese treasury before sailing to Alexandria, unloading the booty on his arrival. That he looted the treasury is not a question, why so much of it remained aboard L'Orient is."

"Perhaps the most important aspect of this excavation," adds White, "is that it has given a life to the story of the battle that simply cannot be conveyed in history books. To read a description of the battle and the explosion aboard L'Orient and then actually to see the damage makes for a far more compelling narrative."

The gathering between site excavators and naval historians ended with a handshake between Anna Tribe and Louis Napoleon Bonaparte-Wyse, descendants, respectively, of Nelson and Napoleon. Artifacts raised from L'Orient are being conserved by the Supreme Council for Antiquities. Human remains are to be reburied on Nelson Island where the British admiral interred the dead from both sides more than two centuries ago.

—ANGELA M.H. SCHUSTER

anticipated. In all it took 20 years to complete, and many who had participated in the campaign were dead by the time the final volume was published.

One thousand sets of the *Description* were printed, each containing nearly 1,000 large engravings. A small army of engravers transferred the savants' drawings to copper plates, but eventually they realized that if something was not done to speed the process they would never complete the work. Once again, Conte saved the day, inventing a machine to engrave the skies mechanically for the plates with views of monuments. It even had a little adjustable wheel so it could be programmed for clouds. Nearly a million large sheets of handmade paper were needed for the publication, and five paper manufacturers were kept busy on the project. Five massive volumes of engravings depicted antiquities, three natural history, and two modern Egypt. Because Bonaparte ordered that the maps should "remain under the seal of a state secret," that volume was the most problematic. Even after his exile they were considered secret, delaying their publication until 1828.

The antiquities volumes of the *Description* set the standard for Egyptological publications for nearly a century. Jollois and Devillier's rendering of the zodiac ceiling of the Dendera temple was so impressive that in 1821 a French expedition went back, dynamited it out, and brought it back to France, a worthy replacement for the Rosetta Stone they had so reluctantly relinquished. The illustrations in the volumes, drawn not by professional artists but by architects and engineers, were the first accurate depictions of Egyptian monuments Europe had ever seen. Though unable to translate the inscriptions they copied, they were aware that their work would have long-lasting effects if it led to decipherment; indeed, it would be the foundation of modern epigraphy. Often the illustrators drew themselves into their sketches, and many can be seen at work in the drawings of the *Description*. My favorite, a curly-headed artist with a monumental ego, Cecile, drew himself into a dozen of his own engravings. In France the *Description* set off a wave of Egyptomania in everything from furniture to women's fashion.

One important legacy of Napoleon's savants is their record of the city of Antinoöpolis, built by the Roman emperor Hadrian on the site where his lover, Antinous, drowned himself in the Nile. The savants realized it was the best-preserved Roman city in Egypt and returned to it four times to document every detail of its ruins. Their account and illustrations in the *Description de l'Égypte* are our only record of the city, which was dismantled in the nineteenth century to build a sugar refinery in the village of El-Sheikh 'Ibada.

Thirty-four of Napoleon's scholars died in Egypt, many of the plague, some in battle. In later decades, others would return to Egypt to complete the description begun by the savants, and the French would dominate Egyptian archaeology for a century. In 1859 a group of French scholars working in Egypt founded the Institut Égyptien, a direct descendant of Napoleon's Institut d'Égypte. Among those present was 84-year-old Gaspard Monge, president of the first institute and the last surviving savant of Bonaparte's Egyptian campaign. ▲

SAGA OF CLEOPATRA'S NEEDLES

by BOB BRIER

Scores of obelisks once stretched skyward along the Nile, standing in pairs in front of temples, their inscriptions proclaiming the glory of the pharaohs. Now less than half a dozen remain standing in Egypt. The Romans brought obelisks home as trophies of a conquered land and today there are more standing in Rome—thirteen of them—than in all of Egypt. The urge to adorn modern cities with ancient obelisks continued into the nineteenth century. The last two to depart Egypt were taken from Alexandria to London and New York in the late 1870s. Disaster struck during the British attempt: six sailors perished and the obelisk was almost lost at sea. If the Americans were more successful, it was largely because of Henry Honychurch Gorringe, a U.S. Navy Lt.-Commander of remarkable ingenuity and perseverance.

England had long planned to remove an obelisk. After defeating Napoleon's troops at the Battle of Alexandria in 1801, British soldiers voted to give up several days' pay to bring one of two 220-ton, 69-foot-tall, granite obelisks at Alexandria home to England to commemorate their fallen comrades. When they realized they had neither a ship that could transport an obelisk, nor the means of loading an obelisk onto one, their enthusiasm waned and they abandoned the project. It became reality three-quarters of a century later, when Egypt was bankrupt and its ruler, the Khedive Ismael, needed European technology and help to modernize his country. Obelisks became his ambassadors, and he offered one to England.

Both Alexandrian obelisks were originally erected in front of the temple of the Sun at Heliopolis, near modern Cairo, by the pharaoh Tuthmosis III (1504–1450 B.C.), and he is shown on them making offerings to the gods. Hieroglyphic inscriptions on the obelisks praise him and promise he will "exercise enduring kingship throughout eternity." Two centuries later, Ramesses II squeezed alongside the inscriptions hieroglyphs boasting of his own greatness. For centuries the obelisks had been called "Cleopatra's Needles," but the queen has no real connection with them. It wasn't until after her death that they were transported to Alexandria by the Romans and erected in front of the Caesarium, a temple to the deified Julius Caesar. The association with Cleopatra comes from the writings of Abd al-Latif, a twelfth-century Arab physician, who called obelisks in general misallati Firun ("pharaohs' big needles"), and the two at Alexandria "Cleopatra's big needles." When the British took their obelisk home, they quickly adopted the name "Cleopatra's Needle."

One of the Alexandrian obelisks had toppled during an earthquake in 1301, but had not broken. The British selected that one, as it did not have to be lowered from its pedestal. The obelisk was encapsulated in an iron caisson and towed out to sea by the steamship *Olga*. The caisson, christened Cleopatra, had its own crew. At home, the English were mad with excitement over their obelisk. A waltz was written to commemorate the great event and London needle sellers handed out trade cards capitalizing on the association with Cleopatra's Needle. But the obelisk almost never made it. A powerful storm in the Bay of Biscay threatened to sink Cleopatra. In the dark of night, a small boat with volunteers from *Olga* tried to save Cleopatra's crew, but in the rough sea the six rescuers were lost. The next day the crew was safely taken off Cleopatra, which, still in danger of sinking, was cut loose. Leaving the obelisk to its fate, *Olga* searched fruitlessly for the missing rescuers. Later found floating by another ship and claimed as salvage, Cleopatra had to be bought back by the English government for £2,000. On September 13, 1878, the obelisk was erected beside the Thames, a bronze plaque listing the names of those who lost their lives bringing it to England.

The possibility of New York having an obelisk was first suggested by the Khedive Ismael at the opening of the Suez Canal in 1869 to William Hurlbert, editor of the New York World. Hurlbert became the motivating force to bring an obelisk home, and by 1877 had almost everything in place. William Vanderbilt, son of railroad baron Cornelius Vanderbilt, agreed to pay the bill and Hurlbert put the job of removing and transporting the obelisk out for bids. Gorringe's plan won and New York eagerly awaited its obelisk.

On August 24, 1878, the 38-year-old Gorringe sailed for Egypt. Unlike the British, he had to lower his obelisk first, a real engineering challenge, but even before that he had to negotiate with the Italian consul who owned the land it stood on and who demanded payment for letting him set foot on his property. Gorringe's solution, recorded in his book Egyptian Obelisks, was to drop the problem in the Egyptian government's lap: "I shall be compelled to telegraph my government," he told them, "that I have been forcibly ejected, and the Egyptian authority has failed to protect me." The matter was quickly resolved.

Removing centuries of debris that had accumulated at the foot of the obelisk, Gorringe exposed the 50-ton pedestal on which it stood and crab-shaped bronze wedges placed under the obelisk's corners by the Romans to secure it to the pedestal after they moved it to Alexandria. Latin and Greek inscriptions on the crabs proclaimed that in the eighteenth year of Augustus Caesar, Rubrius Barbarus, Prefect of Egypt, had the architect Pontius erect the obelisk. Donated by Gorringe, these crabs are in the Metropolitan Museum of Art today, passed by unnoticed by almost all visitors to the Egyptian galleries.

To lower the obelisk, Gorringe used an immense turning mechanism built by the Trenton, New Jersey, firm of John A. Roebling's Sons, which was also working on the Brooklyn Bridge, and shipped to Egypt for that purpose. The mechanism was essentially two huge, iron sawhorses with a pivot suspended between them that clamped onto the obelisk near its center of gravity. The obelisk could be swung to a horizontal position, suspended 50 feet in the air, then gently lowered to the ground. As Gorringe began pivoting the obelisk, it stuck on one of the bronze crabs. Once the crabs were removed, the obelisk moved freely. Then, as the obelisk came down, a cable snapped and it started to fall, but was stopped by a pile of timbers stacked up to catch it in case of such a mishap. With the obelisk now stationary and horizontal, it was lowered on a pair of hydraulic jacks at the rate of three feet a day. Finally, after two weeks, it was safely on the ground.

Gorringe's plan was to slide the obelisk on cannonballs resting in special constructed rails to Alexandria's harbor, less than a mile away, but he hit another snag. The bankrupt Egyptian government had given control of the streets to the foreign merchants who cleaned and repaired them. The merchants, fearing the obelisk would damage the sewers, refused Gorringe permission to move it through the streets. Undaunted, he built a caisson for the obelisk, hauled it down to the riverbank and had a tug tow it to the harbor. This added considerable expense to the project, as Gorringe had to hire divers to clear submerged debris that had fallen into the waters more than 2,000 years before.

Gorringe had overcome the major obstacles—lowering the obelisk and towing it to Alexandria harbor—but he was still far from getting it home safely. Without the luxury of having a ship specially built to transport the obelisk, he had to buy one in Alexandria. Once again, Gorringe's skills would be put to the test. In September, he found a decommissioned Egyptian postal steamer, *Dessoug*, that was in terrible condition, but could be repaired. When he began negotiations with the Egyptian authorities to purchase it, a

Thousands of spectators watched the official ceremony for raising the obelisk on its hilltop site in Central Park on January 22, 1881.

group of ship brokers immediately entered into the negotiations, intending to use their inside connections to get the vessel at a bargain price and then sell it to Gorringe, or, as bidding for the ship went higher and higher, force him to pay them to drop out. Gorringe offered £5,000; the brokers bid £6,500. Gorringe told them he would not buy *Dessoug* from them at any price, and informed the Egyptian government that he would withdraw his offer at noon on December 3. The government accepted the brokers' higher offer, but since they no longer had a customer, the brokers withdrew it. An hour before the deadline, the ship was sold to Gorringe for £5,100 (the extra £100 allowed the Egyptian government to say it had reached a compromise).

All the trials and tribulations seem to have had no effect on Gorringe's spirit. He decided not only to take the obelisk, but also the 50-ton pedestal and the steps on which it rested. There was no crane large enough in Egypt to raise the pedestal, so Gorringe used two in tandem to lift it into *Dessoug's* hold. Once it was below, he loaded the blocks of the steps, some weighing several tons, distributing them in the hold to balance the ship. The hull of *Dessoug* was now opened so the obelisk, sliding on cannonballs, could be placed in the hold. Once everything was secured, the plates removed from the hull were replaced and the ship readied for the ocean voyage.

Gorringe's next hurdle was insuring *Dessoug* for its trip to New York. At first the underwriters asked a ridiculous 25 percent of the ship's value, but when they realized that Gorringe knew what he was doing, they quickly dropped the rate to five percent—still too high. Gorringe's own words, recorded in his book *Egyptian Obelisks,* show just what a cool customer he was:

> *I gave notice to my London agent that I would pay no more than two per cent., and make the voyage without insurance if this rate was not conceded. After holding out for five per cent. until the day before our departure, the agents telegraphed to Europe that the steamer would certainly proceed to sea without insurance on the next day. This brought me a great many acceptances of the two per cent... .*

All indications are that Gorringe wasn't bluffing and would have sailed without insurance, but when it came time to register *Dessoug* he had a problem he could not solve. Under U.S. law, it couldn't be registered as an American vessel and he couldn't sail under the Egyptian flag because of "serious risk and embarrassment" should the ship be confiscated by the government's creditors. His solution, described in Egyptian Obelisks, was rather bold:

> *There was no other course than open defiance of law, which the circumstances fully justified; and I determined to make the voyage from Alexandria to New York without registering the nationality, thereby taking the risk of having my steamer seized by any vessel of war at sea, or by the authorities of any port I might be obliged to touch at.*

Indeed, when Gorringe left Alexandria for New York, he had nothing more than a bill of sale as ship's papers.

The trip was uneventful by Gorringe's standards. An engine broke a crankshaft and they drifted off the Azores for a week till the repair was completed, but finally, on July 20, 1880, *Dessoug* anchored off Staten Island for quarantine. Eventually, the obelisk was placed on pontoons and floated up the Hudson River to 96th Street—the only spot in the riverbank that wasn't too high for landing it.

The pedestal and steps were unloaded at the 51st Street dock, placed on a specially reinforced truck, and pulled by 16 pairs of horses across 51st Street, up Fifth Avenue, and then into Central Park to Graywacke Knoll, the spot selected by the park commissioners for the obelisk. On October 9, the steps and pedestal were officially put in place. When Gorringe first moved the pedestal in Alexandria, he had discovered within the steps below it a mason's trowel and other tools of that trade. Like most important men of his time, Gorringe was a Freemason, and he associated the monument with the Mason's supposed ties to ancient Egypt. Thus the laying of the cornerstone was presided over by the Grand Mason and attended by 9,000 uniformed masons.

There were empty spaces between the steps beneath the pedestal into which various boxes were inserted, creating a time cap-sule. The Treasury Department provided a set of proof 1880 coins; the War Department gave weather maps; Anglo-Saxon Masonic Lodge No. 137 contributed silver Masonic emblems; photographs of the obelisk's removal from Alexandria were included; and "Mr. William Henry Hurlbert contributed a small box, the contents of which is known only to himself."

As the cornerstone of the steps was being laid, the obelisk was already well on its way to Central Park. A small railroad was con-structed along the route and, using the anchor chain of Dessoug, a steam engine winched the obelisk forward at the rate of approximately 100 feet a day. From 96th Street it went across to West Boulevard (Broadway), where it turned its first corner, a process that took six days! Slowly but surely it made its way south, then crossed to the East Side on 86th Street. When the obelisk made some progress, the workmen picked up the tracks from behind and laid them in front of it. Huge crowds of New Yorkers turned out to see it move down Fifth Avenue and make its turn at 82nd Street into the park. Merchants fed the obelisk mania by creating souvenir cards for their customers. By the time it finally entered Central Park, it was the dead of winter and the men, who had been working in shifts around the clock, were hav-ing a hard time of it in the bitter cold. On December 28, a blizzard hit. A trestle had been built to get the obelisk up the grade to Graywacke Knoll, but the snow delayed its progress and it wasn't until January 5 of the new year that it was lying on the trestle, 42 feet above its intended home.

The Roeblings' turning mechanism used

in Alexandria was reassembled in the park, fixed to the obelisk, and the trestle disman-tled, leaving the 220-ton monument sus-pended horizontally. The official ceremony for erecting it was January 22, 1881. Shortly after midnight the night before, Gorringe and a half dozen carefully selected workmen quietly entered the park and tested the turn-ing mechanism. It worked perfectly. Gor-ringe knew his work was nearly over. The next day, thousands of spectators crowded around to see Gorringe give the signal and the obelisk moved effortlessly to about a 45-degree angle. Then he ordered the move-ment stopped so photographer Edward Bierstadt could document it and then gave the sign to bring the obelisk to its final posi-tion. Gorringe recalled the final moments in *Egyptian Obelisks:*

> *This seemed to break the spell that bound the spectators in silence, and when the signal was given to continue the turning there arose a loud cheer that was prolonged until the shaft stood erect....It was to me an inexpressible relief to feel that my work was complete. And that no accident or incident had happened that would make my countrymen regret that I had been intrusted with the work of removing and re-erecting in their metrop-olis one of the most famous monuments of the Old World.*

New York finally had its obelisk.

Gorringe enjoyed his accomplishment only briefly. In 1885, he was killed at the age of 44 when he tried to board a moving train and slipped. A handsome 25-foot-high stone obelisk surmounts his grave in Rockland

Cemetery in Nyack, New York. On its base is the inscription:

> *His crowning work was the removal of Cleopatra's needle from Egypt to the United States, a feat of engineering without parallel.*
>
> *Brave, tender, and true, he passed away lamented by those who knew his worth. Whose loving hands have raised this obelisk to his memory.* ▲

SAILING INTO EGYPT'S PAST

Does a celebration of Luxor's patron saint echo ancient pharaonic traditions?

by SHELLEY WACHSMANN

Each year, on the fourteenth day of the Islamic month of Shaaban, two weeks prior to the beginning of Ramadan, Egypt's ancient city of Luxor shakes itself awake to celebrate the moulid, the birthday celebration of Sheikh Yusuf Abu el Haggag el Uqsuri, the city's medieval Islamic patron saint. The culmination of the weeklong event is a carnival-like procession in which boats, mounted on wagons, are towed through the streets. Egyptologists believe that this unusual custom is a faint memory of celebrations that date back to pharaonic times.

Watercraft have always been a practical way to travel in Egypt; it comes as little surprise then, that in antiquity when the cult statues of Egyptian deities traveled—which they did frequently, either in festivals, or to visit their domains—they generally did so in cult boats, which were transported on the shoulders of priests. When not in use, these boats were stored either inside the temple's inner sanctum, or within boat shrines.

Beginning in the 18th Dynasty (1550–1298 B.C.), the Opet Festival became one of the preeminent events of the Egyptian cultic calendar. It celebrated the Theban triad of the sun- and creator-god Amun, his consort Mut, and their son Khonsu. During the Opet, statues of deities were transported in their boat-shrines between Karnak and Luxor temples. In some periods, they followed a land route, while at other times the vessels were loaded onboard special Nile craft, which were then towed between the temples.

In ancient Egypt, commoners had few opportunities to interact with the images of their gods. Temples did have public functions, but their inner sanctums, where the cult statues normally resided, were off-limits to the general population. When the statues journeyed out from their temples in their cult boats, they were quickly surrounded by throngs of joyous worshipers.

The temple at Luxor was the epicenter of the Opet Festival. Today the mosque of Abu el Haggag, the focal point of the moulid, sits in the northeastern corner of Ramesses II's court inside the temple. Relatively little is known of the saint himself. He came from a noble family of Mecca that traced its lineage to Mohammed. A branch of the family eventually reached Tunisia, where Abu el Haggag was born in the twelfth century. After studying under a leading Sufi, or Islamic mystic, he eventually moved to Egypt where, atop the ruins of the Luxor temple, he founded a Sufi mosque that

attracted numerous students. He died in 1244 and is buried in the mosque.

The most striking aspect of the Luxor moulid—one of 126 moulids of saints recorded in Egypt, but the only one today that involves a boat procession—is its extremely devout Islamic character. The festivities begin with a convocation before an assembled audience inside the mosque led by Mohammed el Hussein el Haggagi, the current family patriarch, and other family leaders.

While the procession is the high point of the festival, the week preceding it is filled with a variety of activities. Sufi dances take place in great carpet-walled tents, equestrian skills are showcased in fields on the outskirts of the city, and on the evening before the procession, the Haggagi family hosts an enormous all-male tent meeting featuring leading Egyptian scholars and muezzins, and provides meals to all who wish to partake of them. On the streets around the mosque, vendors who travel from one moulid to another hawk gaudy tinfoil baubles and sweetmeats from booths and carts.

The moulid's procession, its main event, is called the dura. The term means "circuit," which refers to the path that the parade follows. According to legend, upon his arrival in Egypt, Abu el Haggag found Luxor still primarily Christian. He had an audience with Tharzah, a devout Christian woman who ruled the city: stories identify her as the daughter of the "Caesar" or the "pharaoh." Abu el Haggag asked Tharzah only for the amount of land that he could cover with a camel's hide. When she granted this request, Abu el Haggag set about slitting the hide into narrow strips with which he encompassed all of Luxor. The route of the dura is said to follow the path defined by the saint's camel-hide encirclement of the medieval city. After she agreed to convert to Islam, Tharzah married Abu el Haggag, and she is buried in his mosque.

The earliest modern reference to the use of boats in Abu el Haggag's moulid dates to the mid-nineteenth century. Lady Lucie Duff Gordon, a frail Englishwoman who had moved to Egypt for health reasons, lived near the mosque of Abu el Haggag and mentions the moulid several times in her memoirs. In her description of the 1864 festivities she wrote:

> The moolid of the Shaikh terminated last Saturday with a procession, in which the new cover of his tomb, and the ancient sacred boat, were carried on men's shoulders. It all seemed to have walked out of the royal tombs, only dusty and shabby instead of gorgeous….

Since Duff Gordon's time there have been two notable changes. First, there are now six boats taking part in the dura. Second, and perhaps more important, the boats are no longer carried on men's shoulders; instead, they are placed on wagons that are towed by means of two long, thick cables.

All but one of the vessels are wooden planked boats—decorated with green and white inscriptions—that vary in length between 12 and 18 feet. They have rather unusual sharp bows, and are quite unlike modern boats on the Nile.

The vessels, none of which serve any use other than the part they play in the dura, are named after their owners. The Abdul Fatah

boat is purportedly the oldest boat presently taking part in the festivities, although no one knows exactly how old it is. Perhaps the most unusual of all is the "boat of the felucca men." This iron hull, which was built specifically for the moulid and is never used on the Nile, bears no resemblance whatsoever to a felucca, a narrow, swift sailing vessel. It is reportedly about 20 years old and is the first of the fleet of boats in the dura. Except for the "felucca," all the others carry masts bearing brightly colored lateen sails.

The procession follows a strict order. First come the heads of the Haggagi family— Mohammed el Husein el Haggagi and his brother Nagdi el Husein el Haggagi. Although formerly they rode horses, they now drive in an open carriage in consideration of Mohammed's advanced age. Their sons follow on horseback. Next come a line of camels in single file, each bearing a wood-and-cloth mockup of one of the sheikhs' tombs from inside the mosque. Following the camels is the small fleet of boats led by that of the felucca men.

Watching the dura as it went by, I was reminded of the celebrants depicted in the most detailed relief of the Opet Festival, which was carved during Tutankhamun's reign in the colonnade hall of the Luxor temple. On the felucca men's boat, youths hold aloft models of feluccas in a scene eerily reminiscent of a 3,000-year-old Egyptian graffito in which figures, presumably taking part in a cultic activity, hold aloft model ships similar to the one on which they stand.

The Haggag family is not certain why boats are used in the moulid. Family members I interviewed told me they believed the tradition to be relatively new, probably not predating the early twentieth century. That such is not the case is clear from Lady Duff Gordon's reference to a boat that she described as already "ancient" in her day.

I heard a variety of possible explanations from participants for the traditional use of boats in the dura that included the following: once the dura occurred during a flooding of the Nile, so a boat was used to continue the procession; Abu el Haggag arrived at Luxor by boat, and of course used vessels in his travels; boats and camels symbolize methods of transportation used in accomplishing the pilgrimage to Mecca (hajj); or the boats signify a miracle performed by Abu el Haggag in which he is reported to have saved his seagoing ship from sinking during a violent storm during a hajj.

Do the boats that are such an integral part of the moulid of Abu el Haggag actually hearken back in time to pharaonic rituals? The latest depictions from antiquity displaying the continued use of cultic boat litters seem to date to the fourth century B.C. Lady Duff Gordon's 1864 reference to the moulid custom lies on the other side of a great time divide.

The parallels between the ancient and modern practice—the fact that both the Opet Festival and the dura center around Luxor Temple, which appears to have served as a center of worship for most, if not all, of that stretch of time—are striking. "It would be unrealistic to imagine that the transport of boats within the context of the Abu Haggag festival was a development independent of pharaonic tradition," says Lanny Bell, an Egyptologist who has written extensively on the archaeology and ancient customs of the Luxor region. The boats used today in the moulid of Abu el Haggag do indeed represent a brightly shining ancient thread in the wonderful weave of a distinctly Islamic, modern folk festival. ▲

THE FREDERICK SCHULTZ CASE

Selling the Past

by ALEXI BAKER

On February 12, jurors in federal district court in Lower Manhattan convicted Schultz, 47, of conspiring to smuggle and possess looted ancient Egyptian artifacts. His conviction highlighted the differences between advocates for the antiquities trade and supporters of cultural protection. If upheld, it will likely bolster the application of foreign antiquities laws on American soil in favor of protection. "This sends the message to those who will deal in the international traffic of cultural property stolen from Egypt and other countries that they will be prosecuted under the law of the United States," says Lawrence Kaye, who represented the Egyptian officials testifying at trial.

The Egyptian government, encouraged by this and other successful efforts to repatriate looted and smuggled objects, is taking even more steps to police antiquities dealing and collecting. Zahi Hawass, head of the Supreme Council of Antiquities in Egypt, reports that the Council is forming a

Department of Returning Stolen Artifacts to investigate the antiquities in catalogues, museums, and private collections.

"If the investigation reveals that any museum or institution purchased stolen artifacts, we will completely sever all ties with the institution," he says. "At the same time, we are hopeful that people will give us their full cooperation and support to preserve the Egyptian heritage."

Schultz's trial was the last of five related to a prolific British smuggler of Egyptian goods named Jonathan Foreman. A former cavalryman with a Cambridge degree in moral sciences, Foreman envisioned himself as James Bond. He changed his name to the less pedestrian "Jonathan Tokeley-Parry" and sometimes signed his correspondences with a "003" or "006 1/2."

Tokeley-Parry retrieved more than 2,000 ancient artifacts from Egypt during the 1990s through subterfuge, intimidation, and a web of international conspirators. According to testimony, Schultz sent large payments for antiquities to Tokeley-Parry, who smuggled them into Switzerland disguised as cheap souvenirs.

Yet it was also the smuggler who testified extensively against Schultz in New York, asserting that the American dealer was even involved in faking old labels for the looted antiquities out of paper daubed with tea and baked in an oven. Schultz now faces five years in prison and fines of $250,000, or twice his ill-gotten gains, at a sentencing on June 11. His lawyers, who have appealed the conviction, could not be reached for comment. If the conviction is upheld, then Tokeley-Parry and his accomplices will have received a total of 12 convictions and sen-

tenced to over 100 years of jail time across three continents.

In the New York trial, presiding Judge Jed Rakoff accepted the position of the prosecution, headed by Assistant U.S. Attorney Marcia R. Isaacson, that the National Stolen Property Act was applicable to Schultz's case. He defined the dealer's acquisitions, including a $1.2 million statue of the pharaoh Amenhotep III, as stolen because they had been removed from Egypt in violation of a 1983 law that declared all newly discovered artifacts national property. Witnesses testified that Tokeley-Parry had bought the sculpture of Amenhotep from looters while it still trailed dirt from where it was dug up. "Every pharaoh it seems has a price on his head, at least if that head is cast in stone," quipped Judge Rakoff.

If maintained, Judge Rakoff's decision to uphold foreign antiquities laws within the United States may help to eliminate the economic niche occupied by less ethical collectors and dealers. Lord Renfrew of the Illicit Antiquities Research Centre at Cambridge University says that he feels the conviction may also demand a sea change in the practices of many well-known museums. "It should serve as a warning not only to dealers but also to museum trustees that they risk bringing their institutions into disrepute worldwide if they fail to develop and apply ethical acquisitions policies," he says.

Most importantly, the conviction should lay the legal groundwork for previously exploited nations to have greater control over their own past, while preserving vital details of the archaeological record that looters have so often swept away.

"If affirmed on appeal it will establish the

McClain doctrine for the New York area, the center of the antiquities trade in the United States," says Gerstenblith. "The McClain doctrine is very important for assisting in the preservation of archaeological sites throughout the world and ensuring that the U.S. does not become a haven for looted objects."

According to Egyptian newspaper reports, almost all of the antiquities involved in the case have been recovered and are on display in the Cairo Museum except for the head of Amenhotep III, which was used as collateral for a Citibank loan. ▲

Last Shot for Schultz?

by MARISA MACARI

Found guilty of conspiring to receive, conceal, and sell stolen antiquities in violation of the National Stolen Property Act (NSPA) on February 12, 2002, Frederick Schultz was fined $50,000 and sentenced to 33 months in jail. His attorneys appealed the court's decision. Oral arguments on the appeal were presented at the Second Circuit Court in Lower Manhattan on March 10, 2003. Schultz's lawyers disputed the legitimacy of the McClain doctrine, which is based on the use of the NSPA in a 1970s prosecution of art dealers trafficking Mexican antiquities. Schultz's lawyers feel the U.S. is using Egyptian law to convict him, though the government maintains that he is being charged with violating the NSPA. Schultz's attorneys say that the Cultural Property Implementation Act should be applied in this case. Ironically, many art dealers have lobbied against this act in the past. The Government says that the application of the NSPA is legitimate. On April 14, 2003, Secretary of State Colin Powell publicly sanctioned its application following the looting of museums and libraries in Iraq, stating that "objects and documents taken from museums and sites are the property of the Iraqi nation under Iraqi and international law. Anyone knowingly possessing or dealing in such objects is committing a crime. Such individuals may be prosecuted under Iraqi law and under the United States National Stolen Property Act." Although attorney Lawrence M. Kaye of Herrick, Feinstein, the firm representing Egypt at the trial, believes the Schultz case reiterates what was established in United States v. McClain, many feel the decision in the Schultz appeal will be crucial in determining the adequacy of U.S. laws in deterring the illegal trade of antiquities.

On June 25, 2003, the United States Court of Appeals for the Second Circuit upheld Frederick Schultz's conviction, affirming the lower court's decision that cultural objects subject to national ownership laws are considered to be stolen property when removed from their country of origin without the consent of that government. In January 2004, the U.S. Supreme Court denied Schultz's writ of certiorari (appeal). The Archaeological Institute of America and other scholarly organizations applauded this outcome as a significant step forward in the effort to preserve the world's cultural and archaeological heritage. For more on this case, see www.archaeology.org/magazine.php?page=online/features/schultz/index. ▲

SHAKING UP THE LAND OF THE PHARAOHS

Egypt's new archaeology czar, Zahi Hawass, describes major changes and improvements he hopes to push through in an ambitious ten-year program.

by MARK ROSE

Zahi Hawass does not have an easy job. Recently named Director-General of Egypt's Supreme Council of Antiquities (SCA), he wants to revamp how archaeology is done in his country. Hawass is more familiar to Americans from his television appearances from "The Today Show," to live broadcasts from Giza carried by FOX, to BBC, Discovery Channel, and The Learning Channel documentaries. On the scholarly side, he received his doctorate in Egyptology from the University of Pennsylvania in 1987 and his books include *Silent Images: Women in*

Pharaonic Egypt, Secrets of the Sphinx, and *The Valley of the Golden Mummies.*

The future according to Hawass includes implementing site management policies throughout the country, redirecting new excavations by foreign institutions to areas that need the most work, an agressive museum-building program, improved training of guards and archaeologists, educating the public about the importance of their ancient heritage, and tracking down stolen Egyptian antiquities worldwide and bringing them back home.

This means dealing with entrenched attitudes and institutions, at home and abroad, at a time when resources are diminished through a drop off in the number of tourists—mostly big-spending Americans—in the wake of September 11 and given the unsettled state of affairs in Palestine and Israel. No matter how good your plan, carrying it out under such circumstances would be a challenge.

Will Hawass succeed? Nobody doubts his energy and commitment, but consider the enormous undertaking represented by even one aspect of his plan: "We are working now on documenting all the tombs and temples in Egypt on computers. There are many tombs that have been published but we need to have every tomb documented. If we do this we, would be able to quickly detect the stolen artifacts and ensure their speedy return. Each tomb should be opened periodically for inspection. It is not good to leave tombs closed for long periods of time. They need constant care to protect them from all the dangers that they face." That this one part of the overall plan is monumental itself is not to say that Hawass's plan is a

dream that can never be realized. Indeed, it must be attempted if the heritage of ancient Egypt is to be preserved for the future.

Herewith are Zahi Hawass's descriptions of what is being done, and what will be done, to bring archaeology in Egypt into the twenty-first century:

SITE MANAGEMENT: One of the things I am most proud of in my career is the site management project at Giza. It has many aspects and I plan to implement them at all the historical sites in Egypt. Site management programs are now in progress at the biggest tourist attractions, such as Luxor Temple, Karnak Temple, the Obelisk in Aswan and others. One aspect of the site management program is the rotation system. The rotation system is designed to control the flow of tourists, helping with the maintenance and preservation of the monuments. For example, at Giza we have one pyramid closed for cleaning and restoration and two pyramids open to the public. Each year a different pyramid is closed to do conservation and preservation work. The tombs are also on a rotation schedule.

When people come to the Giza plateau they often just visit the Great pyramid, the Valley Temple of Khafre and the Sphinx. They only spend about two hours at the site. They are missing so much, there are beautiful and historic tombs that have recently been opened to the public. With more tombs open it should take some of the stress off of the high traffic areas. The Giza plateau looks better than it has in years, 12 years ago, when we started the site management project, trash littered the area and venders were everywhere but with the new regulations and programs, the area is clean once again and we have succeeded at keeping most of the venders at bay. The number of people that can enter the Great Pyramid has been restricted to 150 a day. This will help keep the moisture and other eroding factors under control. The number of visitors has also been limited at the beautiful colored tomb of Queen Nefertari in Luxor. Also, in Giza a new entrance to the pyramid area has been completed and soon all vehicle traffic will be prohibited near the pyramids. At the Giza plateau, there will be an information center and electric cars that transport the tourists. A picnic ground was built for the tourists. After all, many tourists come to the pyramids, especially on holidays just to have a picnic under the shadow of the pyramids, by creating a place for them we are controlling the congestion near the monuments

New sites have been opened all over Egypt to encourage tourism. Such as Gerf Hussein and Beit el-Wali. And we have opened more tombs at the most popular sites, presently we have more tombs open at Giza and Saqqara than ever before. The SCA has also closed some sites completely to ensure their protection like the pyramid of Unas, the first king of the 5th Dynasty. The hours the Egyptian Museum in Cairo have been extended. Until recently, the museum closed at 4:30 and now it is open until 7:00 pm. This will stop the rush and keep the crowds under control.

CHANGING THE ROLE OF FOREIGN MISSIONS: I have decided that no mission will be granted permission for new excavation projects from Giza to Abu Simbel. Teams will only be granted permission to do survey,

restoration, GIS, and site management work. However, I will give permission for new excavation in the Delta, where sites are threatened by water table and agriculture, and the desert, where they are little known.

BUILDING MUSEUMS: In addition to renovating older museums, we plan to build seven new museums all over Egypt, including the world's largest—and maybe the best for education and display—at Giza. The locations have been selected for different reasons, for example, because there are important sites nearby, or, as with Sharm el-Sheikh, because many tourists go there. Also, this December 9 is the 100th anniversary of the Egyptian Museum in Cairo. For this, there will be a new exhibit, Hidden Treasures, which will display antiquities long kept in storage at the museum as well as new discoveries.

TRAINING GUARDS AND ARCHAEOLOGISTS: One challenge is the guards protecting our monuments. Can you imagine that the guards only make LE£100 a month (about $20). I think that we should no longer have tough guards with big sticks protecting our monuments using their strong personalities and family connections. We need to change the people who are guarding our sacred treasures and open a Guard Institute to train qualified people to protect and act as the guardians of the monuments. The Institute should only accept applicants with high school diplomas, and it should teach archaeology and discipline. The guards, salaries should be higher. These underpaid men are in charge of guarding the world's greatest monuments. This is ridiculous! How can we expect the average guard to care about the monuments when they don't even know the history of what they are protecting, and they make such a small salary. The archaeologists or, as we call them, Inspectors of Antiquities are our the future protectors of the monuments therefore, it is important that we promote and establish the best training program in the world to ensure that Egypt's treasures, our world's shared heritage is left in safe and competent hand.

EDUCATION IN EGYPT: Thirty years ago, when I first started my career with the SCA, most Egyptians were not interested in the history of ancient Egypt. However, over the years I have had the privilege to witness the ever-growing interest in our extraordinary past. Now, Egyptians are interested in our antiquities, they come to listen to my public lectures. They ask me about my adventures and are intrigued with our new discoveries. I plan to increase the interest in Egypt's children. We are currently copying 20 of the artifacts from the Egyptian Museum and these copies will be on exhibit permanently at every primary school in Egypt. We are currently developing a program to teach children Archeology. The Egyptian Museum will host birthday parties for children and I am writing a series of children's books.

TRACKING DOWN STOLEN ANTIQUITIES: I believe that the United States ruling in the Schultz case shows an important and honest collaboration to preserve the Egyptian heritage. The Egyptian heritage not only belongs to Egypt but to everyone. The sincere concern of the District Attorney of New York and her study of the Egyptian law should be an example for other countries to follow. When I was in New York, I visited the FBI building to examine and describe the four artifacts they had in custody, I wondered how these crimes continued to go unnoticed. Two of the artifacts were wall reliefs form the Old Kingdom, 6th Dynasty. These reliefs were cut from the tombs. You can imagine the horrible appearance of the tombs after they were brutally desecrated. The tomb robbers are not only destroying the tomb but it's spiritual value. A new department created by the Supreme Council of Antiquities, The Department of Returning Stolen Artifacts, will investigate the catalogues, museums, and private collections for stolen artifacts. Their goal is to secure the safe return of Egypt's stolen antiquities. If the investigation reveals that any museum or institution purchased stolen artifacts we will completely sever all ties with the institution. At the same time, we are hopeful people will give us their full cooperation and support to preserve the Egyptian heritage. ▲

ABOUT THE AUTHORS

MATTHEW ADAMS is a research scholar with the Institute of Fine Arts and the University of Pennsylvania Museum.

ALEXI SHANNON BAKER received a master's degree in science and environmental reporting from New York University in 2002 and is currently in the "Instruments, Museums, Science, Technology" graduate degree program at the University of Oxford's Museum of the History of Science.

BRENDA J. BAKER is assistant professor of anthropology at Arizona State University.

ROBERT S. BIANCHI, formerly a contributing editor to ARCHAEOLOGY, is currently affiliated with The Arts & Science Center for Southeast Arkansas in Pinebluff, Arkansas.

BOB BRIER is a professor of philosophy at the C. W. Post Campus of Long Island University, Brookville, New York. His most recent book, *The Murder of Tutankhamun: A True Story*, was published in 1999.

JOYCE M. FILER is a curator in the department of Egyptian antiquities at the British Museum, London.

BRANDON C. FOSTER is an art history graduate student at Emory University.

RENÉE FRIEDMAN directs excavations at Hierakonpolis, made possible by permission of Egypt's Supreme Council of Antiquities and its General Secretary Zahi Hawass with funds from the National Science Foundation, University of Arkansas, Tom and Linda Heagy, and the Friends of Nekhen.

W.B. HAFFORD is the Robert H. Dyson, Jr., Postdoctoral Fellow at the University of Pennsylvania Museum and assistant director of the Howard University Giza Cemetery Project. The project acknowledges the generous support of the National Endowment for the Humanities and supervision of Zahi Hawass, General Secretary of the Supreme Council of Antiquities.

STEPHEN P. HARVEY is assistant director of the Institute of Egyptian Art & Archaeology, The University of Memphis. He received his Ph.D. in 1998 in Egyptian archaeology from the University of Pennsylvania. Since 1993 he has been field director of the Ahmose and Tetisheri Project at Abydos. The investigations of Abydos by

the joint expedition from the University of Pennsylvania, Yale University, and New York University's Institute of Fine Arts are directed by William Kelly Simpson and David O'Connor and are conducted in cooperation with Egypt's Supreme Council for Antiquities.

ZAHI HAWASS is General Secretary of Egypt's Supreme Council for Antiquities.

FRANK L. HOLT is professor of history at the University of Houston and author of *Alexander the Great and the Elephant Medallions* (2003).

THE DAVID H. KOCH PYRAMIDS RADIOCARBON PROJECT is a collaborative effort of Shawki Nakhla and Zahi Hawass, The Egyptian Supreme Council of Antiquities; Georges Bonani and Willy Wölfli, Institüt für Mittelenergiephysik, Eidgenossische Technische Hochschule; Herbert Haas, Desert Research Institute; Mark Lehner, The Oriental Institute and the Harvard Semitic Museum; Robert Wenke, University of Washington; John Nolan, University of Chicago; and Wilma Wetterstrom, Harvard Botanical Museum. The project is administered by Ancient Egypt Research Associates, Inc.

MARK LEHNER was Field Director for the American Research Center in Egypt (ARCE) Sphinx Project from 1979 until 1983. With assistance from the German Archaeological Institute in Cairo, this project produced the first and only scale elevation drawings and detailed maps of the Sphinx now being used in restoration work.

Lehner directs the Koch-Ludwig Giza Plateau Project. He is an assistant professor of Egyptology at the Oriental Institute, University of Chicago.

MARISA MACARI is a recent graduate of New York University with degrees in anthropology and comparative literature.

VEERLE LINSEELE is a Ph.D. student in archaeozoology at the Royal Museum of Central Africa in Tervuren, Belgium.

WIM VAN NEER is curator at the Royal Museum of Central Africa in Tervuren Belgium, where he studies the faunal remains from Africa, the Near East, and Belgium. He has been working in Egypt since 1984 on sites dating from the Palaeolithic to the Coptic period.

JANET RICHARDS is assistant professor at the University of Michigan, and directs the Abydos Middle Cemetery Project.

JEAN-LOUIS RIVARD is a Toronto-based architect and a visiting lecturer at the University of Waterloo.

MARK ROSE is the executive editor of ARCHAEOLOGY.

DONALD P. RYAN is a member of the Division of Humanities at Pacific Lutheran University, in Tacoma, Washington.

ANGELA M.H. SCHUSTER, formerly a senior editor of ARCHAEOLOGY, is now with the World Monuments Fund.

STEVEN E. SIDEBOTHAM is a professor of history at the University of Delaware and director of the Sikait Project.

ANDREW L. SLAYMAN, a professional photographer (www.slayman.com), is a former senior editor of ARCHAEOLOGY.

SHELLEY WACHSMANN is Meadows Associate Professor of Biblical Archaeology at Texas A&M.

JOSEF WEGNER is assistant professor of Egyptology in the Department of Asian and Middle Eastern Studies, University of Pennsylvania, and assistant curator of the Egyptian Section, University of Pennsylvania Museum of Archaeology and Anthropology.

Further Reading

PART I: MUMMIES

General. B. Brier, *Egyptian Mummies: Unraveling the Secrets of an Ancient Art* (New York, 1994) and *Encyclopedia of Mummies* (New York, 1998), S. Ikram and A. Dodson, *The Mummy in Ancient Egypt: Equipping the Dead for Eternity* (London, 1998), and R. David and R. Archbold, *Conversations with Mummies: New Light on the Lives of the Ancient Egyptians* (New York, 2000). On Egyptian funerary art and custom, see: S. D'Auria, P. Lacovara, and C. Roehrig, eds., *Mummies and Magic* (Boston, 1988, and repr. 1992) and J.H. Taylor, *Death and the Afterlife in Ancient Egypt* (Chicago, 2001).

The Royal Mummy. The antiquities trade in Luxor was noted by many mid-nineteenth-century travel writers and expatriates, for example, L. Duff Gordon, *Letters from Egypt* (London, 1983), C.D. Warner, *Mummies and Moslems* (Hartford, 1876), and A. Edwards, *A Thousand Miles up the Nile* (London, 1877). Accounts dealing more directly with the royal mummies cache are J. Capart, ed., *Travels in Egypt (December 1880 to May 1891). Letters of Charles Edwin Wilbour* (Brooklyn, 1936), A. Edwards, "Lying in State in Cairo," *Harper's New Monthly Magazine* 65 (July 1882), pp. 185–204, and E.L. Wilson, "Finding Pharaoh," *The Century Magazine* 34:1 (May 1887), pp. 3–10. See also D. Bickerstaffe, "The Mummy in the Nile," *KMT* 13:2 (2002), pp. 74–79, for the fate of a mummy thought by some to be from the cache. The story of the royal mummies cache is presented in N. Reeves and R. Wilkinson, *The Complete Valley of the Kings* (New York, 1996), N. Reeves, *Ancient Egypt, The Great Discoveries* (above), and D. Forbes, *Tombs, Treasures, Mummies* (above). A good brief introduction to the royal mummies is

A. Dodson and S. Ikram, *Royal Mummies in the Egyptian Museum* (Cairo, 1997). If you want more, there is a reprint of an early examination of them, G. Elliot Smith's *The Royal Mummies* (London: Duckworth, 2000), and J.E. Harris and E.F. Wente's *An X-Ray Atlas of the Royal Mummies* (Chicago, 1980) (their identifications of some of the mummies are debated). For the Niagara Falls Museum and its Egyptian collection, see P. Lacovara, et al., "New Life for the Dead," ARCHAEOLOGY 54:5 (September/October 2001), pp. 22–27.

PART II: EGYPTIAN ORIGINS

Hierakonpolis. See www.archaeology.org/interactive/hierakonpolis/index/index.html for the ongoing excavations at the site. For more information about Hierakonpolis, publications of earlier finds, and information on how to join the Friends of Nekhen and receive *Nekhen News,* the annual bulletin of developments at the site, log on to www.hierakonpolis.org.

Abydos. The original reports on Abydos are W.F. Petrie, *Abydos I and II* (London, 1902 and 1903) and E.R. Ayrton, C.T. Currelly, and A.E.P. Weigall, *Abydos III* (London, 1903), which details the discovery of Ahmose's terrace temple, underground tomb, Tetisheri shrine, town, and private cemetery. S.P. Harvey, "Monuments of Ahmose at Abydos," *Egyptian Archaeology* 4 (1994), pp. 3–5, describes the 1993 discoveries. Matthew Douglas Adams, "The Abydos Settlement Site Project. Investigation of a Major Provincial Town in the Old Kingdom and First Intermediate Period," in C.J. Eyre, ed., *Proceedings of the 7th International Congress of Egyptologists* (in press) is an overview of the results of the excavations of the Pennsylvania-Yale-Institute of Fine Arts Expedition. For the the excavation of the mortuary temple of Senwosret III and associated town, see J. Wegner, "A Hundred Years at South Abydos: Reconstructing the Temple of Pharaoh Senwosret III," *Expedition* 42:2 (2000), pp. 9–18; "A Middle Kingdom Town at South Abydos," *Egyptian Archaeology* 17 (2000), pp. 8–11; and "Excavations at the Town of Enduring-are-the-Places-of-Khakaure-Maa-Kheru-in-Abydos; A Preliminary Report on the 1994 and 1997 Seasons," *Journal of the American Research Center in Egypt* 35 (1998), pp. 1–44.

PART III: MARVELS OF GIZA

General. George Reisner's works include *A History of the Giza Necropolis* I (Cambridge, Mass., 1942) and *The Development of the Egyptian Tomb Down to the Accession of Cheops* (Cambridge, Mass., 1936). The memoirs of Reisner's student Dows Dunham, *Recollections of an Egyptologist* (Boston, 1972) have much about working in the field with the esteemed professor. An engaging account of the experiences of an artist who worked with and was confidant to Reisner can be found in J. Smith's *Tombs, Temples & Ancient Art* (Norman, 1956). G. Steindorff, "George Andrew Reisner," *Bulletin of the Museum of Fine Arts, Boston* 40, (1942), pp. 92–93, is an informative and poignant tribute to Reisner from a longtime friend. See also the Boston museum Web site on Reisner's life and work at: www.mfa.org/giza/pages/reis-ner.html.

Pyramids. M. Lehner, *The Complete Pyramids* (New York, 1997). Z. Hawass, *The Pyramids of Ancient Egypt* (Pittsburgh, 1990) is a short account of the pyramids. Barry J. Kemp, "Old Kingdom, Middle Kingdom, and Second Intermediate Period, c. 2686–1552 B.C.," pp. 71–182 in *Ancient Egypt, A Social History* (Cambridge, Mass., 1983), deals with the pyramid age from the perspective of social history. W.F. Petrie, *The Pyramids and Temples of Gizeh* (London, 1883) is the classic study of the Giza Pyramids.

The Sphinx. S. Hassan, *The Sphinx: Its History in Light of Recent Excavations* (Cairo, 1949) and M. Lehner, "Computer Rebuilds the Ancient Sphinx," *National Geographic* 179:4 (April 1991), pp. 32–39, and "Reconstructing the Sphinx," *Cambridge Archaeological Journal* 2:1 (April 1992), pp. 3–26.

PART IV: FARTHER AFIELD—OTHER SITES AND FINDS

Valley of the Kings. N. Reeves and R. Wilkinson's *The Complete Valley of the Kings* (New York, 1996), along with E. Hornung's *The Valley of the Kings* (New York, 1990) and N. Reeves, ed., *After Tutankhamun: Research and Excavation in the Royal Necropolis of Thebes* (London, 1992). The Theban Mapping Project's website (www.thebanmappingproject.com) includes descriptions of each tomb and combines features geared to the general public with an adaptation of a scholarly work, the *Atlas of the Valley of the Kings*. For the remarkable KV5, see Kent Weeks' *The Lost Tomb* (New York 1998), but also B. Fagan and M. Rose, "Ethics and the Media," pp. 163–176 in L. Zimmerman et al., eds, *Ethical Issues in Archaeology* (Walnut Creek, California, 2003), and K. Weeks, ed., *KV5: A Preliminary Report* (Cairo, 2000) and the review of it by Daniel Polz in the *American Journal of Archaeology* 107:1 (2003), pp. 118–119.

Tomb 55. T. Davis, et al., *The Tomb of Queen Tiyi* (Sebastopol, California, 1990; repr. with introduction by N. Reeves); D. Forbes, *Tombs, Treasures, Mummies* (above). For the late 18th Dynasty, see J.P. Allen, "Two altered inscriptions of the late Amarna period, II. 'Son of Akhenaten'," *Journal of the American Research Center in Egypt* 25 (1988), pp. 121–126, and "Akhenaten's 'Mystery' Coregent and Successor," *Amarna Letters 1* (1991), pp. 74–85; A. Dodson, "King's Valley Tomb 55 and the Fates of the Amarna Kings," *Amarna Letters 3* (1994), pp. 92–103, and *Monarchs of the Nile* (Cairo, 2000); L. Green, "Who was Who," pp. 6–15 in D. Arnold, *The Royal Women of Amarna* (New York, 1996); and N. Reeves, "The Royal Family," pp. 81–96 in R. Freed et al., eds., *Pharaohs of the Sun* (Boston, 1999). On Tut's tomb, see N. Reeves, *The Complete Tutankhamun* (New York, 1990) and T.G.H. James, *Tutankhamun* (New York, 2000).

Emerald City. F. Cailliaud, *Voyage à l'Oasis de Thèbes et dans les déserts situés à l'Orient et à l'Occident de la Thébaïde* (Paris, 1821) has the earliest modern drawings of the Sikait temples and inscriptions. I. Shaw, "Sikait-Zubara," pp. 731–733 in K.A. Bard, ed., *Encyclopedia of the Archaeology of Ancient Egypt* (New York, 1999) is a succinct account of the mines' history. I. Shaw et al., "Emerald Mining in Roman and Byzantine Egypt," *Journal of Roman Archaeology* 12 (1999), pp. 203–215 is the most recent publication about the geology of the Mons Smaragdus area. G. Giuliani, et al., "Oxygen Isotopes and Emerald Trade Routes Since Antiquity," *Science* (January 28, 2000), pp. 631–633, identifies emerald sources from antiquity in the Old World.

Alexandria. J.-Y. Empereur, *Alexandria Rediscovered* (New York, 1998) presents recent excavations, incuding those underwater near the location of the Pharos lighthouse and at the Gabbari necropolis.

Bahariyah. Z. Hawass, *Valley of the Golden Mummies* (New York, 2000) recounts the discovery and excavation of the Roman period mummies at the Bahariya Oasis and investigations of other sites nearby. See S. Walker and M. Bierbrier, *Ancient Faces: Mummy Portraits from Roman Egypt* (London, 1997) for mummification and funerary iconography in Roman Egypt.

The Other Pyramids. *Sudan, Ancient Kingdoms of the Nile* (New York, 1997), edited by D. Wildung, covers most aspects of the ancient civilization. D. Welsby outlines Nubian archaeology in *The Kingdom of Kush* (London, 1996). R. Morkot's *The Black Pharaohs, Egypt's Nubian Rulers* (London, 2000) is a tightly written history of the Nubian kings. Ferlini's story is in K.-H. Priese's *The Gold of Meroe* (New York, 1992). For Timothy Kendall's work at Gebel Barkal, see *National Geographic* 178:11 (November 1990).

PART V: REDISCOVERING EGYPT

Napoleon in Egypt. J.C. Herold, *Bonaparte in Egypt* (New York, 1962) for a general history of Napoleon's Egyptian campaign. An abridged version of the archaeological section of the *Description de l'Égypte* appears in C. Gillispie's Monuments of *Egypt: The Napoleonic Edition* (Princeton, 1987). See also V. Denon, *Travels in Upper and Lower Egypt* (London, 1802). Three centuries of exploration of Egypt are covered in A. Siliotti's *Egypt Lost and Found: Explorers and Travelers on the Nile* (New York, 1999). B. Brier's *Napoleon in Egypt* (Brookville, New York, 1990) is a catalog of an exhibition relating to Napoleon's Egyptian campaign.

Cleopatra's Needles. M. Dalton's *The New York Obelisk or How Cleopatra's Needle Came to New York and What Happened When It Got Here* is a delightful account with excellent illustrations (New York, 1993). H. Gorringe's *Egyptian Obelisks* (New York, 1882), which he published privately, is both a wonderful read and the best on the subject of moving the New York obelisk. L. Habachi's *The Obelisks of Egypt* (New York, 1977) is perhaps the finest overall popular book on obelisks.

Sailing into Egypt's Past. For more on Egypt's moulids, see T. Atia's *Mulid! Carnival of Faith* (Cairo, 1999) and J. McPherson's *The Moulids of Egypt* (Cairo, 1941). Lady Duff Gordon's account of the moulid of Abu el Haggag can be found in her book *Letters from Egypt (1862–1869)* (New York: Praeger, 1969). The new revised edition of J. Kamil's *Luxor: Ancient Thebes and the Necropolis* (Cairo, 1996) provides excellent background information about this historic city.

Schultz Trial. For details on the case, legal issues, and antiquities legislation, see "Selling the Past: United States v. Frederick Schultz" at www.archaeology.org/magazine.php?page =online/features/schultz/index.

GENERAL INTEREST

V. Davies and R. Friedman, *Egypt Uncovered* (New York, 1998) is a good overview of archaeology in Egypt and current issues. For earlier finds, see N. Reeves, *Ancient Egypt, The Great Discoveries: A Year by Year Chronicle* (New York, 2000) and D. Forbes, *Tombs, Treasures, Mummies* (Sebastopol, California, 1998). For the lives and chronology of the pharaoh's see A. Dodson, *Monarchs of the Nile* (Cairo, rev. ed., 2000) and P. Clayton, *Chronicle of the Pharaohs* (New York, 1994). D. Reid, *Whose Pharaohs? Archaeology, Museums, and Egyptian National Identity from Napoleon to World War I* (Berkeley, 2002) charts the development of Egyptology with a focus on overlooked Egyptian pioneers such as Rifaa al-Tahtawi and Ahmad Kamal.

INDEX

Free Catalog!

BUSINESS REPLY MAIL
FIRST-CLASS MAIL PERMIT NO.409 LONG ISLAND CITY, NY

POSTAGE WILL BE PAID BY ADDRESSEE

HATHERLEIGH PRESS
**5-22 46TH AVE. STE 200
LONG ISLAND CITY, NY 11101-9825**

BUSINESS REPLY MAIL
FIRST-CLASS MAIL PERMIT NO.38 MT MORRIS, IL

POSTAGE WILL BE PAID BY ADDRESSEE

ARCHAEOLOGY
**P.O. BOX 549
MT MORRIS, IL 61054-7559**